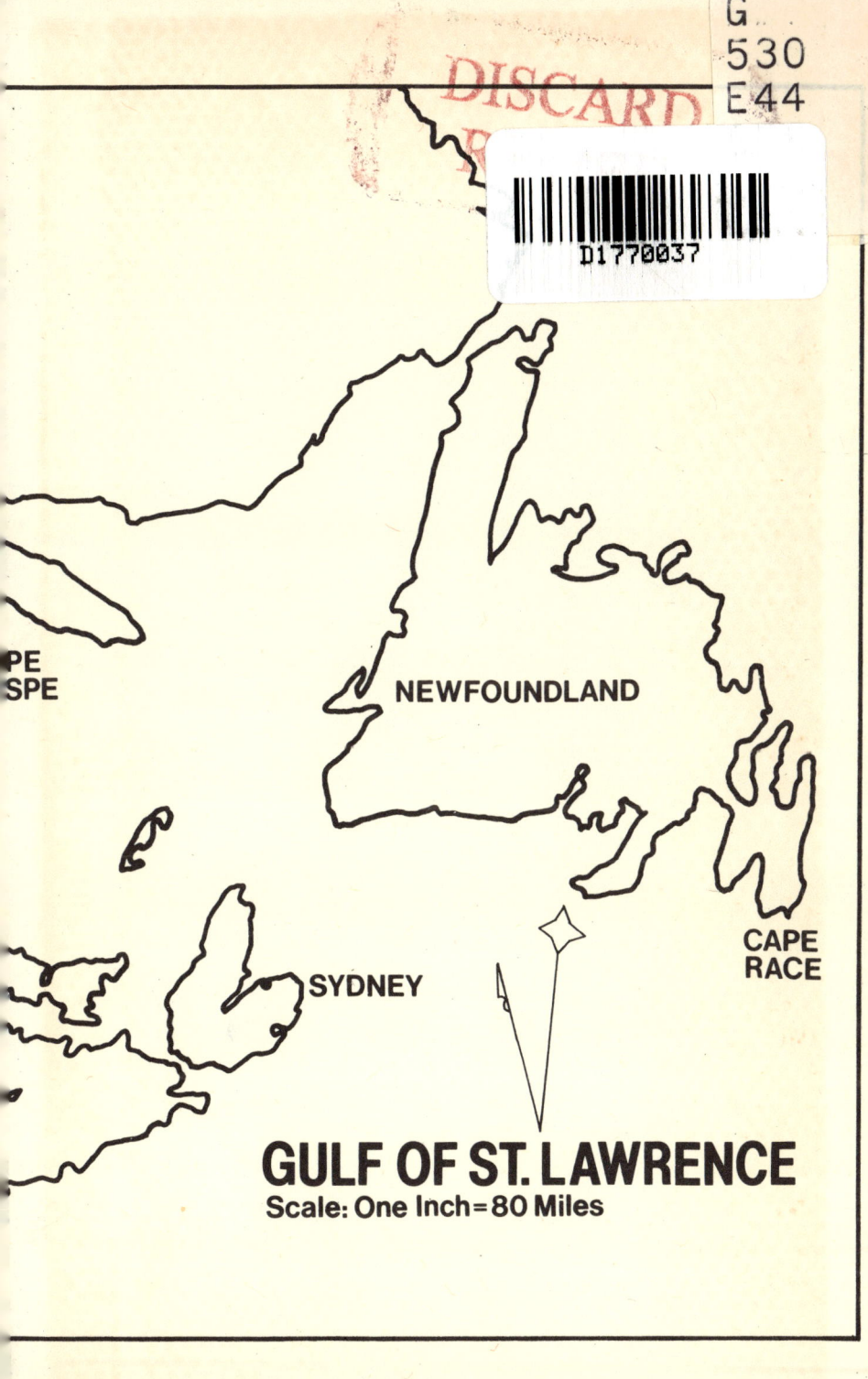

Fourteen Minutes

James Croall

FOURTEEN MINUTES

The Last Voyage of the
Empress of Ireland

MICHAEL JOSEPH
LONDON

First published in Great Britain by Michael Joseph Limited
52 Bedford Square, London WC1B 3EF
1978

© 1978 by James Croall

All Rights Reserved. No part of this publication
may be reproduced, stored in a retrieval system,
or transmitted in any form or by any means,
electronic, mechanical, photocopying, recording
or otherwise, without the prior permission
of the Copyright owner.

ISBN: 0 7181 1736 0

Photoset in Baskerville eleven on 12 point
by Saildean Limited
Printed in Great Britain by
Billing & Sons Limited,
Guildford, London and Worcester

Contents

1	The *Empress of Ireland*	9
2	Captain Kendall	22
3	The Passengers	30
4	The Gulf of St Lawrence	40
5	First Evening at Sea	47
6	Fog	54
7	The *Storstad*	59
8	Collision	70
9	Last Message from the *Empress*	80
10	The *Storstad* to the Rescue	87
11	The Crew in Action	93
12	Struggle for Survival	109
13	Rescue	137
14	The Mathematics of Disaster	147
15	Homecoming	158
16	Attempt at Salvage	166
17	Inquest	172
18	Public Inquiry	186
19	Closing Addresses	213
20	The Findings	221
21	The End of the Story	229
	Conclusion	233

Illustrations

Appearing between pages 112 and 113:

1 The *Empress* leaving the Mersey
2 The *Storstad* in 1910
3 The First Class entrance lobby of the *Empress*
4 Mr Laurence Irving and his wife
5 Captain H.G. Kendall
6 Thomas Andersen
7 Doctor James Grant
8A & 8B The *Empress* as her builders envisaged her
9 The *Storstad* approaching the wharf at Montreal
10 The vigil: crowds wait for bulletins in Cockspur Street, London
11 The aftermath

The author wishes to express thanks to the National Maritime Museum, the *Radio Times* Hulton Picture Library, *The Illustrated London News* and the Keeper of the Scottish Records, Edinburgh, for their kind permission to allow photographs and plans to be reproduced in this book.

CHAPTER 1

The *Empress of Ireland*

The ice broke on 25 April. Day by day, threads of black water lengthened and widened across the frozen expanse that for months had held the St Lawrence river in a grip like concrete. One by one, the great floes broke away from the softening mass, swinging slowly down river to melt and vanish on their way to the distant sea.

For the great passenger steamers that linked Canada with the Old World in the opening decades of this century, the official opening of the St Lawrence to navigation meant the resumption of their traditional summer pattern of operation. During the winter months, when the river was icebound for hundreds of miles, they had perforce to lay course for the icefree ports of Halifax, Nova Scotia, or St John, New Brunswick. Both were excellent harbours, but both shared the disadvantage that passengers had a train journey of several hundred miles to the great cities to which most of them were bound, such as Montreal or Quebec.

With the coming of summer, the big ships of the crack Atlantic shipping lines could steam far up the St Lawrence to the river ports of Quebec or Montreal. The opening of the river always aroused keen interest among Canadians. There was a certain cachet in being the first ship up river, and a friendly rivalry developed as anything up to half a dozen liners competed for the honour, their movements eagerly reported by the metropolitan newspapers as they nosed through the last of the ice floes towards their goal. The captain of the first ship to dock at either Quebec or Montreal was formally presented with the traditional rewards, a silver-topped walking cane and a new silk top hat.

On a fine afternoon at the end of May 1914, one of the greatest of these ships lay along the quay at Quebec, twin wisps of smoke curling faintly from her funnels. The bustle of passengers and porters around her gangways proclaimed departure, while the Blue Peter, traditionally the signal that the ship was under sailing orders, fluttered at the forepeak beside the red and white chequered house flag of the Canadian Pacific Railway. The liner *Empress of Ireland* was about to sail for Liverpool at the beginning of her first round trip of the summer from Quebec.

The Canadian Pacific Railway Company claimed, with fair justification, to be the greatest transportation system in the world. Its railroad system spanned the Dominion from coast to coast. Its fleets of ships sailed the oceans from Liverpool to Hong Kong. A passenger bound for the Far East could take ship on the banks of the Mersey and disembark in Yokohama or the China Coast ports without ever leaving the sheltering arms of the CPR. Not only would it carry him swiftly across two oceans in its great ships and across a continent in its famous trains, but if the traveller chose to break his journey in the great cities of Canada or amid the scenic beauties of the Rockies, he could stay in the company's elegant hotels. The CPR advertised fairly lavishly in Britain, extolling, in full-page colour advertisements in the best magazines, the wonders of its fleet of *Empress* liners and of the Empire's greatest railway system. It offered through fares at moderate rates from anywhere in the United Kingdom to the farthest points in its system.

The CPR had hesitated long before turning itself into a transatlantic shipping company, but the market was booming, largely under the impetus of massive immigration from Europe to Canada. The great Allan and Elder Dempster lines were firmly established, the rival Cunard and White Star companies were planning to assault the Canadian market in force with fine new vessels, and the CPR's railroading rival, the Canadian Northern, was threatening to enter the fray. The CPR could no longer stay aloof, and in 1903 it bought the Elder Dempster group's Beaver Line. In doing so it acquired not only a fleet of modern vessels, but a strong team of competent seamen, experienced in the North Atlantic trade.

In 1904 the CPR decided to tackle the competition head on, and placed orders in Scotland for two passenger-liners designed to be the largest and fastest on the Canadian run. In the summer of 1906 the two sisters, the *Empress of Britain* and the *Empress of Ireland*, made their maiden voyages within weeks of each other, and overnight established new standards of speed and comfort on the route.

The *Empress of Ireland*, like her sister, was built in the Clyde yard of the Fairfield Shipbuilding Company, one of the greatest names in British shipbuilding. The *Empresses* were the biggest ships that the Fairfield yard had built up to that time, and they were designed and constructed to class Star 100A1 at Lloyd's. Specifically, that meant that the ships had not simply been approved after completion, but that they had been scrutinised and endorsed by Lloyd's surveyors at every stage from drawing-board to sea trials. It was the highest seal of approval that the world's most prestigious marine surveyors could bestow.

The *Empress* was a twin-screw steamer of 14,000 tons, 550 feet long, 65 feet in the beam, drawing about 27 feet of water loaded. Her quadruple expansion coal-burning engines gave her a designed speed of 20 knots, and this she achieved in her voyages. The two sisters consistently made the 2,800 mile crossing between Liverpool and Quebec in about six days. Only about four days of this was in the open waters of the North Atlantic, a feature that the CPR stressed in its advertising. The other two were passed in the sheltered waters of the St Lawrence, 'North America's greatest scenic waterway'. The North Atlantic had a formidable reputation, even in summer, and few passengers embarked upon its boisterous waters solely for the unalloyed pleasures of an ocean voyage. The assurance that a third of the voyage would be passed in the relative tranquillity of a great inland sea was calculated to appeal alike to mind and stomach.

The *Empresses* were handsome ships after the classic pattern of their age; straight stem, sweeping counter stern, two high, raking buff funnels with black tops, and tall, raking masts to match. They swiftly established a reputation not only for speed, but for their steady behaviour in the worst Atlantic weather. The *Empress of Ireland* could carry around 1550 passengers; 300 or so First Class, 450 Second Class, and over 800 in Third Class. Her capacity was limited in practice not by the number of berths available, which was rather higher, but by the capacity of her lifeboats to carry the number of people aboard. The First Class passengers were housed amidships on the upper and promenade decks, where they were closest to the fresh air and sunlight; fresh air was always available in large quantities in the North Atlantic, but sunlight could be in short supply. Second Class passengers were berthed aft, on the main and upper decks; the Third Class lived low down in the ship between the bridge and the fo'c's'le, surrounded by and almost intermingled with the seamen's quarters. The rest of the crew, stewards and engine-room staff, had their living-quarters equally deep in the bowels of the ship, but mostly further aft. Her deck officers, by contrast, enjoyed the breeziest accommodation of all. In accordance with tradition, they lived in a deck-house on the boat-deck, adjacent to the bridge where they passed most of their working hours. The captain's accommodation opened directly into the bridge itself, so that he was always within a few steps of his command-post at any hour of day or night.

The *Empress* never aspired to the standards of ostentatious luxury that were the mark of the gigantic superships competing for the rich New York market, but they did establish an unchallenged reputation for something that early twentieth-century travellers understood and appreciated, namely solid comfort. A shipping correspondent of *The Times*, who had made the crossing in her, praised her fine First Class dining-saloon, her café, 'much frequented for afternoon tea', and her delightful music-room. (He was talking about First Class facilities, of course.) Altogether, he concluded, it would be difficult to find a more cheerful or popular ship.

Contemporary photographs of her interior leave a strong impression of spaciousness and florid elegance, appropriate to an age that dearly loved its palm courts and string orchestras. The *Empress* had a five-piece string orchestra which played daily for both First and Second Class passengers, and a profusion of potted palms. The First Class passengers dined seated either in ornately-carved chairs at long tables or on overstuffed banquettes in richly decorated alcoves; the CPR had not yet adopted the recent daring German innovation of separate tables. The whole scene was redolent of heavy napery and of heavier silver and crystal, appropriate to an age when First Class gentlemen dined in boiled shirts and their ladies in evening gowns. For the gentlemen there was a smoking-room, a male sanctum to which no lady would have dreamed of seeking admittance. For her, there were the pleasures of the library and the writing-room. Their children enjoyed, or failed to enjoy, the privilege of a separate dining-room, and there was even a sandpit.

It was all rather different, of course, in Third Class. There was no music-room or café. Confined in modest quarters far below decks, the Third Class passengers neither expected nor got more than adequate board and berthing, appropriate to their slender resources and unassuming status. Not that there was anything unimportant about the Third Class passenger. It was he and his like – or her like, for immigration was often a family affair – pouring in millions into the empty spaces of the New World who had been principally responsible for turning transatlantic shipping into very big business indeed. As a direct result, the Third Class passenger had seen as sharp an improvement in travel standards as any passenger in the world. Not only had governments laid down minimum standards of accommodation before a vessel such as the *Empress* could be licensed as an emigrant ship, but enlightened shipping companies had realised that the migrant who was decently looked after on his lonely and often penniless pilgrimage in search of a better life was likely to be a repeat purchaser in Second or even First Class when one day he returned home to show the old folks how well he had done.

Accordingly, from being a kind of floating hell's kitchen in which the wretched steerage passenger starved his way across the ocean in squalor, the immigrant quarters of Atlantic liners had advanced to standards closer perhaps to those of a good-class workman's lodgings – spartan but clean, with good plain food to sustain the customers and even stewards to serve them. One Canadian writer went so far as to say that the Third Class quarters on the *Empresses*, austere though they undoubtedly were by 1914 standards, were as good as the First Class accommodation on some of the older and smaller passenger ships still serving on the Canadian route. He may well have been right.

Even though the flow of immigrants to Canada never approached the level of that to the United States, it was still an enormous traffic. In 1913 alone, a little under half a million settlers had arrived in the Dominion. It was largely the vital migrant traffic that had forced steamship fares down to the remarkable levels of 1914. For about £6.50, the settler could make the Third Class crossing from Britain to Canada or the United States. This was just about the same as he would have paid fifty years earlier, despite the vast improvements both in the speed of the crossing, and the comfort in which it was made. For £10 or so, he could travel Second Class. The splendours of First Class would have cost him about £14. If he fancied a future further afield, he could reach South Africa, Third Class, for about £12, or Australia for £18.

Emigration was not universally popular with the countries from which the settlers were drawn. The CPR had been embroiled for months in a curious feud with the Archduke Franz Ferdinand, heir-apparent to the throne of Austria-Hungary, who had apparently accused the company's agent of enticing the extraordinary total of 400,000 young males of military age to emigrate, thus weakening the Dual Monarchy's military potential. His Royal and Imperial Highness was said to have believed that it was a plot backed by

British and Russian gold. The CPR replied mildly that in the previous eighteen months they had carried only 16,000 Austro-Hungarian migrants, and that included women and children. It all blew over, but even the CPR's modest figure is an interesting indication of the scale of European migration to North America in the early twentieth century. It was taken for granted in British ships that the great bulk of the Third Class passengers would be foreigners. Even in Canada, with its strong British heritage, the influx of Continental European migrants was so great that when the *Daily Mail* sent a reporter there in 1914 with instructions to seek his fortune as a migrant, the young man swiftly found himself heading a work gang on the reasonable ground that he was the only member of it who could understand what the Scottish foreman was talking about.

The Times correspondent had been accorded special facilities for inspecting the immigrants' accommodation on the *Empress*. He could not speak too highly, he wrote, of the great care taken by the company to make every proper provision for the poorest as well as the most wealthy passengers, and he found that the two *Empresses* marked 'a new and better era in the treatment of persons belonging to the emigrant class'. Then, as was proper in a *Times* correspondent, he hurried on to speak of the popularity of the *Empress* among those who could afford more luxurious accommodation. This, he explained, was due largely to the great comfort of the vessel, which compared favourably with that of 'the colossal ships now constructed'.

Despite the mythical nature of the sovereign after whom she was named, or perhaps because of it, the *Empress of Ireland* had always been a firm favourite with Irish passengers, especially the great tide of Irish migrants to the New World. On special occasions she flew the green flag of Erin as a particular tribute, and the highlight of her social year was the gala concert that was always held on St Patrick's Day, when passengers and crew alike traditionally joined in saluting the ship to the tune of 'The Dear Little Shamrock of Ireland', with suitably amended lyrics.

Comfort was not the liner's only virtue. The *Empress*'s owners were at pains to stress that she had ample lifeboat accommodation for all on board. In 1914, the sea was still very dangerous. In the previous twenty years, some 4,700 vessels of British registry had been lost, and even though the great majority had been fishing vessels, coasters and the like, they had still taken over 18,000 passengers and crew to their deaths. The interest taken in safety at sea in 1914 sometimes bordered upon the obsessive, and for this there was a simple reason; over any discussion upon the subject there loomed the long shadow of the *Titanic*. When the world's largest liner sank in the Atlantic on her maiden voyage in April 1912, the world had been shocked and horrified by the disclosure that she had gone to sea, quite legally and with full official sanction, with life-boat capacity for 1,178 passengers and crew, or about one-third of her maximum capacity. As a result, legislation had belatedly been enacted to rectify this alarming state of affairs.

The CPR's Assistant Marine Superintendent, Mr Curtis, claimed that there were so many lifeboats aboard the *Empress* that they were piled up on the decks. It was perhaps not the happiest way of conveying an impression of good order and seamanlike prudence, but he was quite right, after a fashion. In fact the *Empress* had lifeboats of a kind for about 1,860 people, or considerably more than her actual complement. She carried sixteen steel lifeboats, seven on each side of the main boat-deck, and a further pair aft. Between them they could hold 764 people, a normal capacity for a ship of her size and type under the outdated and illogical Board of Trade regulations prevailing when she was built. To meet the requirements enacted after the *Titanic* disclosures, the CPR had increased her capacity in the best way they could, by increasing the height of the davits carrying the steel boats, and placing under each regular boat a collapsible craft, folded on the deck. Altogether, there were twenty of these Englehardt collapsibles, capable between them of holding 920 souls. In addition there were at least four collapsible Berthon boats for a further 176. The collapsibles may have sounded like a frail substitute for the real thing, but they were regarded highly by those who had actually used them. They were really broad, shallow boat-shaped rafts with high canvas sides or gunwales that folded down like an opera hat when not in use. They were said to be capacious, very stable and easy to board, virtues that by no means every seaman would have accorded to the orthodox lifeboat.

The *Empress* also carried more than 2,200 life-jackets of regulation Board of Trade pattern, including 150 for children. There were twenty-four lifebuoys, though these were intended more for succouring anybody unfortunate enough to fall overboard than for saving lives in a general emergency.

In theory, then, the *Empress* was more than adequately provided with life-saving equipment. But, as every seaman knew, what mattered was not how many lifeboats a ship carried but whether they could be lowered, manned with trained crews, and filled with clumsy, frightened passengers aboard a heavily-listing ship, possibly at night, possibly in bad weather. The odds in any normal circumstances were disturbingly high that they would jam in their davits, drop bow or stern first when the falls became tangled, or capsize when they hit the water. In one celebrated disaster, the boats had frozen in their chocks. Collapsible boats might float free, but would be of little use unless there were trained crews to erect and man them. A writer to *The Times* was on the right lines when he argued that more lives might be saved if ships were equipped with life-rafts on the upper deck that would float free of their own accord when the ship went down.

The CPR was nonetheless confident that the training of its crews in safety measures left nothing to chance. As recently as 15 May, 1914, Major Maitland Kersey, head of the company's ocean services, had attended a Board of Trade inspection of the *Empress* before she sailed from Liverpool. All her boats, he claimed, had been swung out 'very smartly' in less than a minute. Equally satisfactory fire and bulkhead drills had followed. Nor did the precautions end with formal Board of Trade inspections. The men were regularly drilled at sea, while on 27 May, only the day before the *Empress* sailed from Quebec, all three drills had been carried out once again. On that occasion the lifeboats had not only been swung out, but manned, lowered and rowed about in the St Lawrence. To ensure that safety standards were not relaxed, the CPR had engaged the services of Captain Hugh Staunton, late of the Orient Line, as inspector of boats and livesaving appliances, a position in which he was required to travel constantly to and fro inspecting and drilling CPR crews. Nonetheless, many designers held to the view that the best lifeboat of all was the ship herself. So long as she stayed afloat, the efficiency of the boats would not be tested.

The *Empress* was designed to what was known as the 'two compartment' rule; that is to say she was designed to float with any two compartments flooded. The watertight subdivision of large passenger ships was a notoriously difficult problem. A warship, inherently liable to damage by virtue of her role, could be so honeycombed with transverse and lateral bulkheads that damage by shell or torpedo would be confined to a relatively small area. The price for this relative security was paid by the crew, confined for months on end in a collection of steel cells, as nearly as possibly isolated from each other, into and out of which they must climb like spiders. The temptation to short-circuit the whole process by riddling the bulkheads with supposedly watertight doors was hard to resist, and even after the British battleship *Victoria* had gone to the bottom in 1893 after a notorious collision, her successors contained over 200 watertight doors.

Passenger-liners presented a further problem. Within a liner's hull, hundreds of passengers and crew must live for days and weeks at a time. Passengers must be able to move to and fro, and equally important, up and down between deck and cabin, stateroom and saloon. Rows of cabins, strung along the length of the ship, meant long passageways, while access from deck to deck meant broad companionways, staircases varying in width and grandeur according to class and function, but each a potential hazard. However alert designers and seamen might be to the dangers, the passengers expected to be free to move about their allotted portions of the vessel. Elderly ladies and gentlemen constrained to struggle with heavy watertight doors and scramble over knee-high coamings might incline to the view that this was not what they had paid their passage money for. It was simply not possible to run such a ship on the constant assumption that disaster was a moment away.

The *Empress* had a complex system of watertight bulkheads and doors. Altogether there were ten bulkheads dividing the ship into eleven more or less watertight comparments – more or less because they were pierced at one level or another by no fewer than twenty-four watertight doors, giving working access from one compartment to another. The CPR, like most companies, laid down rules governing the circumstances in which the doors must be closed, but in practice many of the doors were open at any given time to permit the crew to move about their duties. Two of the doors were situated at stokehold level, at the very bottom of the ship. One of these closed off the doorway in Number Five bulkhead that linked the two boiler-rooms. The other door closed a similar opening between the after-boiler room and the engine-room immediately astern of it. These two doors worked vertically, sliding down like giant guillotine blades, and were operated by the engineers from their control platforms in the engine-room. The other twenty-two doors worked horizontally and could be cranked across the door openings by a ponderous rack and pinion gear system. To close each of them, a steward had to hurry to the deck above the door, take a metal key from its clips on the bulkhead, fit it over the square head of the winding shaft, and patiently crank the door shut. Under favourable conditions, a well-drilled crew could seal off every watertight compartment in the ship in about three minutes.

It was an old-fashioned arrangement. More modern ships had automatic electric or hydraulic systems worked from the bridge, so that at the touch of a button one man could close all the watertight doors in the ship. Nevertheless the *Empress*'s system was perfectly sound mechanically and the crew were painstakingly trained in operating it. What they had not been trained to do was work the system in darkness, with the ship listing crazily and the water rising round their feet while they worked. Moreover, the system contained the inherent weakness that if one man out of twenty-two failed to reach his post, or having reached it, failed to wind the door closed, then that doorway stayed open to the inrushing sea. In any event, the ability of watertight doors to contain the area of damage was strictly limited. The most vulnerable area of the ship, simply because by its nature it could not be adequately subdivided, lay amidships. The *Empress* had machinery spaces the size of a parish church, two massive boiler-rooms 175 feet long overall to house the rows of cylindrical boilers, and astern of them a huge engine-room to provide working space for the great quadruple expansion reciprocating engines.

Even though, in theory at least, the *Empress* could float even if both boiler-rooms were flooded, her remaining margin of buoyancy would be perilously small. Moreover, a flooded boiler-room involved further hazards. Once the water rose past the stokehold deck-plates, the furnaces would flood and the fires would die. Even if the boilers did not burst, they would no longer generate steam, and without steam the ship would die as surely as an animal pierced through the heart. Without steam the pumps would not run and the dynamos would not turn. The ship would have no power, no light, no strength to staunch her wounds. It was that knowledge that had kept the engineers of the *Titanic* at their posts, striving to save the lives of their fellow men and women until it was too late to save their own.

The letter of instruction he received on assuming command could have left a CPR captain in no doubt as to how his employers regarded the safety of the vessel and her passengers and crew.

> I desire to particularly call your attention to the importance of your command and to the value of the ship and to emphasise to you the instructions of the company relative to the care of your vessel and the lives of your passengers. It is to be distinctly understood that the safe navigation of the ship is to be in all instances your first consideration. You must run no risk that by any possibility might result in accident. You must

bear in mind that the safety of lives and property entrusted to your care is the ruling principle by which you must be governed in the navigation of your ship and that no saving of time on the voyage is to be purchased at the risk of accident. I cannot sufficiently emphasise my desire that these instructions shall be carried out to the letter. It is expected that all the officers of your ship will bear this in mind, and will be specially cautioned by you.

The letter ended with the hope that everybody on board would do their utmost 'to please and gratify the Company's patrons'. It was the sort of letter that cynics claimed, no doubt with some justification, was sometimes written only to protect the company in the event of accident, and that captains were still expected to make fast passages, regardless of hazards. In fairness, while there may well have been companies of which this was true, there is no evidence that the CPR meant anything other than exactly what it said. Certainly, the CPR liked to have things done properly. At 10 a.m. precisely each morning, the captain was required to set off upon his daily inspection of the ship. With chief engineer, doctor, purser and chief steward in his train, he made his way from stem to stern, from deck to deck, turning a critical eye on every detail. The inspection of the passengers' cabins was no less thorough. The chief steward was required personally to visit every cabin, occupied or otherwise, every day.

CHAPTER 2

Captain Kendall

The man who paced the bridge wing of the big liner that afternoon, gazing with a keen eye at the last minute preparations for departure was a veteran of the North Atlantic seaway, with a quarter century of ocean-going experience behind him. Yet paradoxically, he was also something of a novice. For Captain Henry George Kendall had taken command of the pride of the CPR's Atlantic fleet only four weeks earlier, at the beginning of May. In this time he had completed in her only one round trip, from her winter terminal of Halifax, Nova Scotia to Liverpool, and then back up the newly-reopened river to Quebec. This would be the first time that Kendall had ever commanded the great liner on a voyage down river from Quebec. At thirty-nine, Henry Kendall was a man who by any standards was near the top of his profession. Moreover, he had reached that position after a career that sounded like a cross between a boys' adventure story and a detective thriller.

Although he was born in Chelsea, Kendall had passed his boyhood in Everton, Liverpool, and it was in the river Mersey that he had undergone a brutal introduction to the sea aboard a floating hell of a nautical training ship designed to produce young officers for Britain's mercantile marine. As a boy of fifteen, Kendall had sailed as an apprentice aboard a big square rigger called the *Iolanthe*, bound for Normanton on the desolate shores of the Gulf of Carpentaria in Australia's Far North. The *Iolanthe* was a tough ship; her captain was a hard-case Nova Scotian Bluenose, and her crew were mostly West Indians. It was not long after the *Iolanthe* reached Australia that Kendall met with his first and most hair-raising adventure. A member of the crew had been murdered by a psychopathic shipmate. Kendall was one of two witnesses. Shortly afterwards, he became the only one; the other died suddenly and unpleasantly. Kendall jumped ship and headed inland at a steady trot, bent on putting as many miles of dusty outback as possible between himself and his prospective assassin. He reached the gold mining centre of Croydon, Queensland, one hundred miles inland before he decided it was safe to stop running. Australia was in the grip of gold fever, and young Kendall decided to try his hand, but nuggets proved unaccountably hard to come by.

He stowed away on a coaster in search of more promising horizons, but the skipper found him and threw him ashore on the remote pearling settlement of Thursday Island, far out in the Torres Strait between Cape York and New Guinea. Young Henry was set to work aboard the pearling luggers that worked the Arafura Sea, but pearls proved to be as hard to come by as gold. Ashore in New Guinea, Kendall found a berth aboard a tiny 350 ton tub of a Norwegian barque, bound for Britain with a reeking cargo of guano, the nitrogen-rich harvest of seabird droppings that was eagerly sought in Europe as fertiliser.

It was not a happy return. The old barque leaked like a shopping basket; she lost her mizzen in a southerly gale off New Zealand, the main topgallant jumped ship and went overboard off Cape Horn, and the salt pork and hard tack ran out in the Roaring Forties. The insalubrious ruin floundered into Falmouth under jury rig after 195 days at sea, her starved and stinking crew labouring at the pumps to prevent the wretched vessel from foundering beneath their feet. Kendall trudged home to find his family mourning his death.

Undismayed, he went back to sea, finished his apprentice time in sail, and rose to be first mate of the crack Mersey square rigger *Liverpool* before leaving sail for steam, and joining Elder Dempster's Beaver Line. After it was bought by the CPR, Kendall worked his way steadily up. He had served them for eleven years, the last six in command of one or another of the CPR's smaller ships. For the past dozen years he had held his Extra Master's Certificate, the highest qualification a British merchant seaman could attain. There was no question of plodding seniority in his promotion to the *Empress*. Kendall had vaulted ahead of many far older men. It was one of the most senior positions the company could offer, and if the responsibilities of the post were great, the rewards were equally so. As master of the *Empress*, Kendall earned around £850 a year. In 1914 this was a princely salary in its own right, quite apart from the perquisites of the lonely and Olympian position of master of a great Atlantic liner.

Had no element of drama ever entered Kendall's professional life, he could still have been remembered as a model of what the world expected a British seaman to be. Adored by his passengers, respected by his officers and crew, he was a first-class master mariner. His guiding star in life was the simple faith propounded in Kipling's poem 'If'. It was not only his favourite poem, which he loved to recite at ship's concerts in aid of seamen's charities, but it was the stoic creed by which he sought to live his life. He sent a copy to his young son, urging him not only to learn it by heart, but to live by it.

Although a rigid teetotaller, Kendall was no killjoy; hundreds of passengers remembered him for his breezy and genial personality. It was that talent for geniality, combined with an acute and perceptive mind, that had led Kendall to the most remarkable episode of his career. For by an extraordinary accident of history, Henry Kendall was already a name on both sides of the Atlantic among tens of thousands who had never set foot on a ship in their lives.

Some four years earlier, when master of the small CPR liner *Montrose*, Kendall had grown curious about the identity of a couple, supposedly 'Mr and Master Robinson', whose conduct on the slow crossing from Antwerp to Canada was not that which he would have expected from father and son. Kendall was an alert and well-informed man, who read carefully the copies of the *Daily Mail* brought aboard by his steward. Again and again, he studied the newspaper pictures of a heavily-moustached man. Then, with a piece of chalk, he blanked out the moustache on the picture; the resemblance to the clean-shaven Mr Robinson became even more striking. Still, Kendall was not quite sure enough to act. The man whose mild features stared myopically forth from the newspapers was said to have gold fillings in his teeth. Had Mr Robinson gold teeth and how was Kendall to find out?

The *Montrose* was neither a large nor a fashionable ship. It occasioned no particular remark among her nondescript collection of passengers when Kendall exercised the age-old privilege of the sea and invited the Robinsons to dine at the captain's table. There, he set out to entertain his guests from the fund of funny stories gathered in a lifetime at sea and of which he was an acknowledged master, until Mr Robinson threw back his head and roared with honest laughter. And Henry Kendall, with a gentle smile upon his lips, gazed down his guest's open throat until he saw within it the dull gleam of gold. The comedy was over. Kendall used his ship's wireless telegraphy system to convey secretly his suspicions to the authorities in Britain. In one of the most dramatic episodes in criminal history, Chief Inspector Dew of Scotland Yard hurried aboard the fast White Star liner *Laurentic*, overtook the *Montrose* with hours to spare, and was waiting at the little St Lawrence riverside town of Rimouski to arrest a mild-mannered Michigan dentist named Hawley Harvey Crippen for the murder of his wife in a respectable villa in Camden Town. Crippen and his girl friend, Ethel Le Neve, were taken back to England, he to the scaffold, she to a merciful obscurity.

Henry Kendall's alertness and initiative earned him a police reward of £250 for his role in the capture of Crippen. It was a very substantial sum in 1910, not least to a young shipmaster with a wife and three small children to provide for. Characteristically he never cashed the cheque; instead he had it framed, and hung it on his stateroom bulkhead. In any event, Kendall's fortunes had prospered since then. His wife and family were installed in a comfortable home in the smart Liverpool residential suburb of Blundellsands, where he returned at the end of each voyage.

Some two years after the Crippen affair, Kendall's nerve and skill as a seaman had earned him high praise when he had taken the *Lake Champlain* to the aid of the Allan liner *Corsican* after the latter had hit an iceberg off Belle Isle. On that occasion, Kendall's men were said to have put fifteen lifeboats into the water in twelve minutes.

On 28 May 1914, The *Empress* sailed with a crew of 420, including nearly a dozen stewardesses. Then, as now, passenger liners carried a high proportion of crew to customers. Even with a full complement of passengers, the proportion would have been about two crew to every seven passengers. On this particular voyage, the proportion was nearer two to five. In First Class, it was far higher.

To navigate the ship, Kendall had six watchkeeping officers, four of whom held master's tickets. Steede, the chief officer, had served in the *Empress* for eight years, ever since she was built. Only thirty-six or so of the crew were seamen. By contrast, no fewer than 130 worked in the engine-room department. Sixteen of these were certified engineers. Most of the rest were firemen and trimmers, seagoing labourers who earned their bread by the sweat of their brows and by the strength of trained muscle and sinew. In 1914, a big steamship was still almost as labour-intensive as a Roman galley. The whole process of raising steam, from the initial coaling of the ship in harbour to the feeding of the furnaces, was achieved with human labour. True, a rival had arisen to challenge the supremacy of coal, and the first oil-fired battleships were even then fitting out in British shipyards. But for the moment coal was king, and the steamships of the world still advertised their passage across the waters by the endless coils of dense black smoke that poured from their funnels.

The coal consumption of a large steamer was enormous, and storage space for fuel constituted quite a large part of her internal arrangements. For the six-day Atlantic crossing the *Empress* carried about 2,600 tons of coal. Her furnaces ate the stuff at something like a quarter of a ton a minute. To hold this mountain of coal the *Empress* had six huge vertical coal bunkers, one running along each side of the boiler-room, the others arranged transversely along the bulkheads at each end of the boiler-rooms. The side bunkers, 175 feet long and 14 feet broad, held about 900 tons of coal each while the remaining 800 tons were distributed among the thwartships bunkers. The liner started her voyage with these monstrous cupboards crammed with coal from deck level down to stokehold floor, where the black torrent spewed out through seven big bunker doors on each side of the ship. To keep it flowing freely and easily was the task of the trimmers, raking and shovelling in a perpetual haze of coal dust high up in the bunkers. Below them, the sweating firemen fed the coal to the white-hot furnaces glowing and flaring in the nine cylindrical boilers. Traditionally, firemen were the toughest men afloat. Their work was killingly hard, frequently dangerous, and extremely skilled. To keep the furnaces burning evenly at precisely the right temperature demanded judgment and delicacy of touch, as well as strength and stamina. The firemen fought as hard as they worked, and when they could, they drank as hard as they fought. Predictably, those aboard the *Empress* were almost exclusively Liverpool Irish.

The purser's department was by far the biggest in the ship: 240 men and women, or well over half the entire crew, were there solely to look after the passengers. Their muster roll sounded like the establishment of a large hotel, which was exactly what the *Empress* was. There were stewards – saloon, cabin or deck – of numerous grades; there were barmen and storemen, cooks and bakers, pastrymen and confectioners, butchers and bellboys. There was a boots and an assistant boots, and a whole battalion of scullions. There was a barber, a printer and even an interpreter. Considering the number of foreign immigrants the ship carried, he was no doubt in steady demand.

Aboard the *Empress* were two young men whose positions

were slightly ambiguous, for while they were responsible to the captain in day-to-day matters of discipline they were employed, not by the CPR, but by the Marconi Company. Like most of those who practised wireless telegraphy, the *Empress's* two operators were young men. Ronald Ferguson, the senior, was 23, but had had three years at sea, and had sailed in five ships, including the current queen of the Atlantic, the *Mauretania*. Like almost every other man and woman in the liner's crew, Ferguson was from Merseyside. He had spent his boyhood in New Brighton. His junior, Edward Bamford, was a Mancunian who had thrown over a safe but unexciting career as a clerk with the Lancashire and Yorkshire Railway in favour of a life at sea. Although he had been out of the Marconi Company's school for only six months or so, he already had made several voyages. He was on the homeward leg of his first voyage in the *Empress*.

In 1914, wireless telegraphy was perhaps the most widely employed and widely discussed of all the new technologies of the early twentieth century. For over a decade after its birth at the turn of the century, it had struggled to gain recognition, and the Marconi Company had poured money into its development with little return. It might have taken decades more to gain acceptance, had it not been for the Titanic disaster in which wireless had played so vital a part. A Bill was at that very time before the British Parliament requiring all British-registered ships carrying fifty or more passengers to be equipped with wireless. By the summer of 1914, the Marconi Company alone had 1500 trained operators at sea in nearly 900 ships. Hardly a month passed without a further demonstration of the matchless power of wireless to lessen the perils of the sea, even if it could never completely remove them. The *Empress of Ireland* herself had just given a classic illustration of the fact. Inbound to Quebec on 21 May, she had encountered heavy ice floes in the Cabot Straits. Her urgent ice warning, flashed out by wireless to every ship within range, was picked up by her competitor, the Canadian Northern Railway liner *Royal Edward*. The next day, moving cautiously through the danger zone at reduced speed, her captain saw a long, menacing floe stretching nearly half a mile across his ship's course. Rather than risk the fatal glancing slash that had gutted the *Titanic* like a herring, Captain Wotton turned his bows toward the floe and hit it head on. His ship reached Avonmouth with a slightly buckled stem.

Success had not been without its problems. Ten years before, Guglielmo Marconi observed bitterly to his British shareholders in 1914, it had been difficult to get anybody to take any interest at all in his invention. Now, when the company had turned the corner and was returning a modest profit, Members of Parliament were beginning to allege that it was a monopoly. Monopoly or not, the company continued to advance enthusiastically into new and exciting fields of technology. Already, the human voice had been transmitted more or less successfully through the ether by the new technique of wireless telephony, and the company proudly demonstrated a gramophone record of music that had been transmitted from Berlin to London by radio, and there recorded. Marconi himself intended in the summer of 1914 to attempt to broadcast the human voice across the Atlantic from a transmitter in Ireland. At sea, the Canadian Northern liner *Royal George* was about to conduct experiments with a new device, designed to establish a ship's position by taking bearings on shore stations, and called a direction finder.

Marconi was not the only inventor working in the field. In May 1914, a young visionary named Dr A. M. Low claimed to be able to transmit images, based on the use of selenium cells, along a telephone wire for a distance of fifteen feet. He was confident, he said, that one day he would be able to transmit images by wireless, without any physical link at all. He called it Televista.

CHAPTER 3

The Passengers

All that afternoon, the passengers filed up the gangways of the *Empress*, while porters and stewards followed with loads of baggage. There were 1057 passengers, for it was approaching the high season for transatlantic travel. The spring was almost over and the pleasures of the European summer attracted those with the taste and the means to enjoy them. Moreover, the *Empresses* had always been popular ships.

First Class, uncharacteristically, was some two thirds empty; there were only 87 passengers to occupy about 300 berths. At least three ladies brought their own maids with them, a normal feature of transatlantic travel at the time. Second Class was just over half-filled, with 253 passengers. And Third Class was nearly full, with 717 men, women and children.

The passengers were of many nationalities. While Canadians and Britons predominated in the First and Second Class, the St Lawrence route was also popular with Americans from the Middle West. There were passengers from New Zealand, Hong Kong, Japan and Fiji who had elected to travel to Europe via the CPR's far-ranging services, with good reason. Only the maddest of dogs and Englishmen chose to sail the length of the Red Sea in summer. About half the passengers were Canadian, with the Province of Ontario, and particularly the city of Toronto itself, well represented. Altogether, there were about 200 Torontonians of all ages and both sexes. The First and Second Class passengers were a cross section of middle-class Canada. Many were men travelling on business, but by no means all. Links with the British Isles were still extremely strong, family ties were close, and Canadians (the English-speaking variety, at any rate) referred openly and proudly to Britain as the Mother Country. Many middle-class Canadian husbands could afford to send their wives and children off for a visit to relatives in the United Kingdom, out of the sweltering heat of a North American summer. Later, if all went well, father might make the crossing himself for a brief holiday in Britain before he escorted his brood home again. There were many women and children aboard the *Empress* who were making the crossing on their own.

The passenger list of any popular Atlantic liner could be expected to include at least a scattering of celebrities, and the *Empress's* was no exception. The most notable in the eyes of both Canadian and British newspaper readers were undoubtedly Mr and Mrs Laurence Irving. For a generation Laurence's father, Sir Henry Irving had dominated the English stage as the greatest theatrical figure of his age. After his death in 1905, the name of Irving lived on, for both his sons were notable stage figures in their own right. They had become so in spite of their mother's efforts to divert their talents elsewhere; one actor in the family, she felt was enough. Harry, the elder, was set to studying law. Laurence, slightly younger, was sent to Marlborough, and thence into the Diplomatic Service. A year in St Petersburg left him with no taste at all for diplomacy, a passion for Russian literature, a fluent command of the language, and a determination to make his career on the stage.

At forty-two Laurence Irving's career promised, in the opinions of critics, to equal that of his father. He possessed two of his father's characteristics; the inimitable voice, and a driving determination to reach the top, shared by his wife, who was almost as famous under her own name of Mabel Hackney. Iriving had made his way into the first rank of a glittering generation not only by talent, but by sheer hard work. He had played every role from Hamlet to Captain

Brassbound, and adorned them all. His recent work, *The Stage* said, was not untouched by greatness. It was typical of Irving that when his career on the legitimate stage had languished after his father's death, he and his wife had worked up a dramatic act, and taken it round the English music halls. The theatrical Establishment was speechless. Irving did not care. He needed money to launch himself upon the career he dreamed of as dramatist and actor-manager, and if the music hall audiences had the money, that was where he would get it.

It was as a dramatist as much as an actor that Irving had become one of the great names of the contemporary London stage. In 1910 he had written and produced an adaptation of Dostoievsky's *Crime and Punishment*, under the title of *The Unwritten Law*. With Irving as the fiery student Raskolnikoff and his beautiful wife as the heroine, Sonia, the play had appeared at the Garrick Theatre. It took London by storm. Fortified by that success, Irving had followed it up with a play called *Typhoon*, in which he played the sinister Japanese secret agent, Takarama. His wife played the subtle enchantress who brought him to his doom. It ran for over 200 performances.

Miss Hackney was a worthy foil to her husband. She was the archetype of the fragile, 'English Rose' type of beauty that the English theatregoer adored. Phrases like 'wistful', 'gentle' and 'plaintively appealing', rang like a recurrent theme through contemporary accounts of her work. All those things she undoubtedly was, but it had taken more than an ingenue charm to carry Miss Hackney from a modest role in Sir George Alexander's company to stardom. She had already played opposite Sir Henry Irving himself as his leading lady in some of his most famous performances before she became his daughter-in-law. She was clever, temperamental and exceedingly able.

It was not without some justification, perhaps, that her husband himself had referred to her affectionately in a speech from the footlights as 'The Holy Terror'. Irving himself had a power of mordant utterance. On one occasion, for instance, he had advanced to the footlights of New York's Comedy

Theatre and delivered himself of an undertaking publicly to chastise a particular critic and rival named Dale if he ever again dared to speak disparagingly of Miss Hackney's talents. The critic was not heard from again. Irving was also the scourge of inattentive first night playgoers. If anyone in the fashionable audience was ill-advised enough to cough, Irving was liable to stop the play and courteously offer the offender a mentholated jujube. Not many people coughed during Laurence Irving's plays.

The Irvings had been married for a little over a decade, and to all appearances it was not only a brilliantly successful professional partnership, but a genuine love match. They were, it was said, 'the best suited couple imaginable'. They had no children. As a substitute, perhaps, they shared a passion for dogs. When Mabel Hackney was working and Irving was not, he and the dogs would be waiting patiently outside the stage door for the moment when she would emerge after the performance. Then they would walk home together through the crowded streets of Edwardian London, Irving, his lanky frame clad in his wing collar, soft felt hat, smoking his inevitable cigar. Their talent was a real one, and the affection in which they were held by English audiences was genuine.

Irving, clad appropriately in an astrakhan-collared overcoat, had led his troupe of twenty talented actors and actresses on a three-months tour of Canada. Predictably, their repertoire of four plays included both *The Unwritten Law* and *Typhoon*. It was the great age of the English touring company. The reputation of the London stage stood as high then, perhaps as it does today. Great cities such as Montreal, Winnipeg and Vancouver had fine theatres, and such distinguished actor-impresarios as Martin Harvey, Forbes-Robertson, Frank Benson and Cyril Maude had all appeared there recently. Flushed with enthusiasm for their efforts, a *Times* correspondent said that they had done more to nourish Imperial sentiment in Canada than any British statesman since Joseph Chamberlain.

FOURTEEN MINUTES

The Irvings had brought their Canadian tour to a triumphant conclusion in Winnipeg the previous Saturday. True, there were carping voices. To be honest, the *Toronto Globe* reported, the tour had not been wholly a success. The newspaper feared that the subtle innuendoes of *Typhoon*, which had so engaged the interest of London theatregoers, had gone largely over the heads of Canadian audiences. Even if this was true, the reaction to *Typhoon* in Vancouver must have been most gratifying to Irving. His performance as Takarama had been received with much enthusiasm by the city's Japanese community. Certainly, Irving himself was said to be very enthusiastic about the success of the tour. His wife in particular, the critics said, had won the hearts of Canadian audiences by her charming and unaffected manner. And whether they appreciated all the nuances of *Typhoon* or not, there must have been many in Irving's audiences who remembered his closing line as the final curtain fell: 'What is death? Death is nothing but the passing to another life'.

The Irvings' presence aboard the *Empress* was fortuitous. Originally, the whole company had been booked to return aboard the liner, but shortly before departure, the bookings were switched to the White Star line *Teutonic*, due to sail three days later, because scenery and costume hampers would not be packed and ready in time to be embarked upon the *Empress*. The Irvings were anxious to reach England without delay. The reason probably was Irving's newly-completed play, a drama about Napoleon, and Irving was anxious to get it into rehearsal at once, for it was due to have its provincial try-out in Blackpool in September, before moving to the West End in October. Irving had no doubts about its merits. 'This,' he told his agent in Canada, 'will make me a great man.'

Of all their company, the Irvings took with them only their juvenile lead, Harold Neville, and his actress wife, Elsie Vron. They, too, wanted to return without delay for their three small children were waiting for them. The youngest was just eleven months old. Mrs Irving took her maid, Hilda Hagerson, with her. Hilda was a reluctant passenger; she feared a lonely crossing with none but her employers as company, and would have preferred the companionship aboard the *Teutonic*. Mrs Irving insisted. Irving himself was less demanding. He allowed his valet to follow him later aboard the *Teutonic*.

The Irvings were not the only passengers of note. Sir Henry Seton-Karr was what the early twentieth century called a sportsman, largely because it was difficult to categorise him with any greater precision. Sir Henry had been enjoying his passion for the outdoor life up and down the world for forty years, and at the age of sixty-one he was still enjoying it. Seton-Karr had been born in India, and as a small boy had lived through the horrors of the Mutiny. A Scot, he had received the customary education of an English gentleman, and had qualified as a barrister. It was not, however, a profession to his taste; instead, he had advanced his fortunes by marrying into the wealthy and influential Pilkington glass dynasty. The Pilkingtons owned and ran the Lancashire town of St Helen's. When Sir Henry aspired to a Parliamentary career; he was duly elected for St Helen's in the Unionist interest, and was the sitting member for over twenty years. 'Sitting member' was not perhaps the most apposite of descriptions, for Sir Henry rarely sat. He rode, walked, cycled, climbed, crawled and if necessary swam in the furtherance of his insatiable appetite for hunting, shooting, fishing and exploring. He had climbed everywhere from Norway to the Rockies, he had explored in some odd corners of the earth, and on one occasion in East Africa he had announced proudly that he had discovered the site of the Garden of Eden. When not roaming the earth, he was to be seen, knickerbockered and Norfolk-jacketed, striding the fairways of the Royal Wimbledon Golf Club. He was, of course, the captain. With a pair of shrewd eyes twinkling in his weatherbeaten face, and a luxuriant walrus moustache to match, Sir Henry Seton-Karr was a splendid specimen of the British sporting gentleman in an age when the earth was milord's and the fullness thereof.

Sir Henry was on his way home from one of his numerous business trips to the New World, for much of his time was spent afloat. As a young man, he was an enthusiastic canoeist; he was quite fearless on or in the water, and even some dangerous accidents in swift-running rivers did not deter him. He did not readily disclose his adventures to his family, however. In his boyhood, his two elder brothers, along with their tutor, had died tragically in the waters of a Swiss lake.

There were other distinguished passengers; for instance there were Mr Leonard Palmer, a noted British financial journalist and his wife, and Mrs Hart Bennet, wife of the British Colonial Secretary in the Bahamas.

Among the Second Class passengers were a group of about 170 members of the Salvation Army. They were in holiday mood, for they were one of the five Canadian contingents, 400 strong in all, who were on their way to the Great Salvation Army Convention about to be held in the Albert Hall in London. At their head was a man who was one of the best loved in all the Army of the Lord. He was David Rees, the sixty-year-old Commissioner for Canada, Newfoundland and Bermuda, a patriarchal figure with a fine white beard. David Rees had once been a baker in Huntley and Palmer's biscuit works at Reading before he was called to the Lord's work by a young lady Salvationist named Ruth Babington. So strong was the conviction borne of her preaching that David Rees had embraced not only the lady's principles but the lady herself. In the course of a vocation that had taken them from Sweden to South Africa, they had raised three children, all of whom grew up to be members of the Army. The whole Rees family were aboard the *Empress*. Also in the party were thirty-nine men of the Canadian Salvation Army band. Not only were they to play for their fellow Salvationists, but by kind permission of the London County Council, they were also to play in the Embankment Gardens in June.

The Third Class passengers did not feature in the society pages. They were among that huge army of men and women of many nations who moved restlessly back and forth across the Atlantic during the heyday of the greatest population movement in history. While the bulk of that tide was normally westbound, there were plenty who took ship back to the continent of their birth. For some, it was *wanderlust*; others, disenchanted by the new continent, or simply content to have seen a little of the world before they settled down, were returning home with enough dollars sewn into the linings of their jackets to pick up the threads of life a little richer than when they had left. Others simply wanted a holiday with their families. For some, the cause was a tragedy; a husband, a father had died, and his dependents were forced back to the only home, the only relatives they knew.

Not all of them started their journeys in Canada. From all over the Great Lakes area, from the northern and midwestern USA, from as far away as California, they gathered on the quayside in the afternoon sunlight. About 300 of them were Ford car workers from Detroit, laid off for the summer. Unable to find other jobs, they were heading home to Europe, some for good, some for a holiday before returning to the assembly lines.

Among the passengers who filed down the steep companionways into the crowded Third Class quarters were Russians, Ukranians, Poles, Swedes, French, Italians, Irish, Scots, and English. Undistinguished by and indistinguishable to the world at large, they were lost in the vast anonymity of their kind. They were immigrants; they were the working class; they were Third Class passengers.

At least three intending passengers did not sail at all. Mrs Joseph Pencerick, a Cornish lady, had cancelled her passage at the last minute. Her two children had developed measles.

The *Empress*'s freight that afternoon was not composed entirely of human beings. Apart from about 1100 tons of general cargo, she was carrying in her strong room a considerable quantity of bullion. Just how much was uncertain, and still is. A million dollars in silver from the Ontario mining town of Cobalt, said one report; two million, said another. According to a Reuter's news agency report, there were no fewer than 163 bars of silver in the liner's strong room, worth $1,099,000 in all. One package, the report said, contained $275,000 worth in silver. The other, much larger, contained the balance of $824,000. A rival report said there were 78 bars of specie. Everybody was at least agreed on one fact. It was a lot of silver. There were also four railway wagon-loads of sacks stowed in the *Empress*'s mail room containing, it was estimated, at least 13,000 dollars' worth of money orders in over 800 registered letters. Most of them were on their way from settlers in Canada to their dependents spread across Europe from Donegal to the Urals.

At 4.27 p.m. on the afternoon of Thursday, 28 May, the last mooring line splashed into the St Lawrence. Slowly, inching away from the wharf, the big liner slid out into the stream, turned, and began to head smoothly downstream, her bows pointing towards the open sea many hundreds of miles ahead. The departure was a happy affair. Apart from the usual knot of well-wishers, seers-off and assorted stay-at-homes who by tradition attended the departure of any ocean-going liner, there was a substantial contingent of Salvationists. The voyagers replied in kind; to their farewell cries were joined the strains of the Canadian Salvation Army Band. High on the promenade deck, they were cheerfully pumping away at the Army's favourite hymn; 'God be with you till we meet again'. They were still playing as the big liner slipped out of earshot under the powerful beat of her twin screws, and the crowd of well-wishers turned their backs and began to drift away from the wharf.

Almost any ocean-going departure could provide its quota of minor incidents, and this one was no exception. For instance, four members of the crew had failed to rejoin at the appointed hour; they had jumped ship in Quebec for reasons of their own. It was not an unusual occurrence. There had been another and more curious desertion. A few minutes before the *Empress* sailed, her cat, a yellowish tabby of doubtful antecedents, threw aside the well-fed rewards of two years' faithful shipboard service, and fled down the gangway. A kindly steward raced after her, scooped up the fugitive and carried her back aboard. The cat again sprinted lithely down the gangway, and disappeared into a freight shed. The ship's siren was squalling its warning of departure, the gangway was about to be hauled ashore, and the steward had other tasks to attend to. The cat stayed ashore until the gangway was down. Then, as the big liner slid almost imperceptibly away from the quayside, the cat reappeared among the well-wishers on the wharf, and added to their cries of farewell her own melancholy valedictory.

Nobody took any particular notice at the time.

CHAPTER 4

The Gulf of St Lawrence

Between the Quebec quayside and the deep Atlantic there lay an inland voyage of almost unparalleled length, for the Gulf of St Lawrence is some seven hundred miles from end to end. A ship leaving Quebec would steam down the great river, leaving the shore of the Gaspe Peninsula close on her southern or right-hand side, while to the north of her the river widened imperceptibly into a great inland sea. Some 200 miles from Quebec, just past the little white riverside port of Rimouski, she would stop her engines briefly off a remote point of land where stood a pier, a lighthouse, and a recent addition to the scene – the tall slender mast of one of the Marconi Company's wireless telegraphy stations.

The lonely little settlement, some four miles downstream from Rimouski, was called Father Point, and it was the place where the Canadian Government river pilots joined ships bound upstream and left them again at the end of their journey downstream. There, the outbound vessel would conduct her last transactions with the land. The Government postal tender from Rimouski, the *Lady Evelyn,* would probably steam out with the final bags of foreign mail. Simultaneously, the little tug *Eureka,* which doubled as the pilot cutter, would come alongside to disembark the pilot. The landing of the pilot was in a sense symbolic. From then on, a ship's navigation was completely in the hands of her own officers and traditionally, with the departure from Father Point, the ocean voyage was reckoned to have begun. Already a vessel would be steaming down an inland sea more than 25 miles wide, and yet she was still several hundred miles from the Atlantic Ocean proper.

From Father Point a ship would by custom steer about north-east from Father Point for a few miles until she had made her offing from the shore. Then, with deep water under her keel, she would turn about east-north-east and settle on a course designed to skirt the southern shore of the estuary, keeping a comfortable five or six miles from the land as she slipped past the little townships and landmarks of the Gaspe Peninsula – Metis, Matane, Cape Chatte, Martin River, Fame Point. On and on the ship would steam, the northern shore of the great estuary long lost to sight, until at length, she swung south-east past Cape Gaspe and into the open sea. Even then, she had perhaps 250 miles to go before she passed Cape Breton, guarding the Cabot Straights, and stood out into the Atlantic. Moreover, a ship bound for Liverpool, say, would still have several hundred miles to steam past the southern shores of Newfoundland before she rounded Cape Race, the last toehold of the North American Continent on the ocean.

No finer or broader highway into the heart of a continent exists than the St Lawrence River and Candians were duly anxious to see that commerce flourished upon its waters. To that end they had lavished millions of dollars upon navigational facilities; lighthouses, automatic light-buoys, pilot stations and the like. They were sensitive about the St Lawrence because the river's reputation in past years had not been unspotted. Fierce gales could blow up with terrifying speed and the waterway was notoriously liable to fog, particularly when the warm spring air met the river water chilled by the newly melted ice. Maritime accidents had been frequent and although the casualties were often the fishing vessels and other small sailing craft that thronged the waters, there had been larger victims. Fog was a particular peril and there had been an embarrassing incident about two years before when the *Empress*'s sister, the *Empress of Britain*, had sunk a Norwegian collier called the *Helvetia* in a fog bank off Father Point.

FOURTEEN MINUTES

The collier was inbound for Montreal with a cargo of Nova Scotia coal when she encountered the St Lawrence fog. Her third mate, who was officer of the watch, suddenly saw the huge bulk of the *Empress of Britain* looming out of the fog. There was no chance at all of avoiding collision; the collier's bows were pointing directly at the liner's side. With great presence of mind, the mate swung the *Helvetia's* wheel hard over and put his own ship across the liner's bows, an action that sent his ship to almost certain destruction, but that also saved countless passengers from injury and death. No lives were lost, but the *Empress* impaled the collier neatly across her bows where she stayed, like a pair of spectacles across the liner's nose, for half an hour before she slid off and sank. The subsequent inquiry found both ships to blame. Murray, the liner's captain, later became harbourmaster of Quebec.

Despite the Canadians' protestations as to its safety the St Lawrence had an evil reputation among those who sailed it. There was hardly a seaman who could not retail a story, frightening or funny as the case might be, about its peculiarities. Not least of these was the fact that the river ran deep right up to its banks, so that the traditional precaution of sounding with the lead line was of little avail; a ship could be perilously close to the shore before the leadsman's cry brought warning of danger.

Not long before, a British vessel had been groping her way upstream in a fog under the guidance of a St Lawrence pilot when her master became disturbed by a pervading scent of new-mown hay. The lookout reported that he could hear a cow mooing. Overruling the pilot's assurances that they were simply passing a cattle boat, the captain insisted on stopping his ship. The fog rolled away, leaving cow and captain to regard each other across the narrow strip of water which separated the ship's bows from the meadows of the Gaspe shore.

Understandably, the St Lawrence was not popular with the Imperial Merchant Service Guild, which calculated that in the previous two years it had spent more money hiring Canadian lawyers to represent its members after St Lawrence accidents than it had spent on legal fees in any other part of the world.

Although the southern shore of the river from Father Point eastwards was well provided with lights and buoys, there were no individually-marked channels to separate vessels steaming upstream from those bound down river to the sea. The river's protagonists argued that there was no need for them. The river was deep and free from shoals, and with the better part of 30 miles of open water to the north, there was no lack of sea room. Ships had ample space in which to pass in safety, with no need to do more than observe the normal rules of the road at sea.

Those rules were to assume a particular significance in the lives of a great many people over the next few hours. Accordingly, they must be considered, in particular with regard to the arrangement of lights that the *Empress* would bear that night to display her presence and her intentions to other ships.

The navigation lights displayed by a steamship were arranged according to a simple formula. They were intended not only to advertise her presence to other vessels, but to reveal at once to a trained eye the direction in which the ship was travelling. On each side of the bridge was a navigation light, red on the left-hand side, green on the right. Each was screened so that it was visible only through an angle from dead ahead to roughly abeam. From dead ahead, both red and green would be visible, indicating the moment when the vessel was pointing exactly at the onlooker. But the moment the ship's course was altered even slightly, the light on the far side would disappear and only the nearer one would be visible. In theory at least, the observer could be in no doubt that such a vessel was coming towards him, and about which side of her bow she was presenting to him. In addition, a steamship under way must carry two white masthead lights, called range lights, of which the after one must be at least 15 feet higher than the forward one. Burning high on the masts, they would be visible long before the coloured sidelights came into view. Like the sidelights, they served not only to reveal the ship's presence. To the trained eye, they would reveal a great deal about her course. From dead ahead, the two white range lights would appear directly in line, one above the other. As the oncoming ship altered course, the lights would move further and further apart, the after one always higher than the leading one. While the coloured sidelights would tell only the direction in which the ship was moving, the range lights, by their apparent distance apart, would tell the experienced onlooker a great deal about the angle at which the ship was approaching. Close together, they meant she was pointing nearly directly at him. Wide apart, they meant she was presenting herself at a broad angle. Like all good safety systems it was essentially simple, and given reasonable visibility, it was tolerably easy for an experienced seaman to gauge the course of an oncoming ship, and decide whether to hold his course or alter to avoid the stranger.

Which course he adopted depended upon a code of practice, accepted by all maritime nations and known as the Rule of the Road. The underlying principle when two ships approach each other is simple. Provided the two ships are on roughly parallel courses in open waters, then they may pass safely either right-hand to right-hand ('green to green') or left-hand to left-hand ('red to red'). Only if they are approaching left-hand to right-hand on converging courses does it become the duty of the vessel showing her right-hand green light to keep clear of the other. When two ships approach each other exactly head on, there is a simple safety rule: each must alter course to the right, so they pass left-hand to left-hand, 'red to red'.The same applies in narrow waterways where there is insufficient room to manoeuvre. There the rule is that vessels should each keep to the right-hand side of the channel and pass red to red. This body of rules, refined by generations of experience, endorsed by every nation whose ships sail the seas, is known by heart to every officer who stands watch upon the bridge of a ship. Applied with essential alertness, caution and common sense, they make possible the safe navigation of ships of every flag, in every part of the world. With their aid, thousands of ships every day meet and pass safely both on broad oceans and in narrow waterways, each confident that however the other vessel may approach, the man in command of her will react in accordance with a set of clearly understood rules.

The greatest peril that a well-found and powerful ship could encounter was fog. Even with the help of radar, fog at sea remains an unnerving experience. Without it, navigation in fog is among other things a simple test of nerves. Wrapped in an impenetrable blanket of moisture, the mariner is like a blind man trying to cross a street. He may think he knows what is approaching, but he cannot be sure. The only way in which a ship may warn other vessels of her presence is by her siren, and every seaman soon learns that in fog, sound is a totally unreliable method of judging the bearing of another ship. Fog plays strange tricks with sound waves. The note of another ship's siren may seem to come first from one side and then from the other. Even an experienced sailor, straining to catch the eerie moan of the siren of another vessel, can soon convince himself that the sound is coming from almost any point of the compass he chooses.

No set of rules could eliminate the hazards completely, and collisions in fog were among the commonest causes of marine accidents. But the Rules of the Road laid down prudent procedures to reduce those hazards. Where the ships had been in sight of each other before the fog descended, and were known to be steaming on safe courses without risk of collision, the rules said, each should continue on the course it had been following before the fog descended, sounding long, single blasts of its siren or whistle to tell the other; 'I am holding my course and going ahead.' Only if one ship heard the call of another whose whereabouts had not been positively established should she stop completely. There were recognised siren signals to indicate what a ship was doing. Three shorts blasts meant: 'I am going astern on my engines' – a manoeuvre usually employed, not to move a ship physically backwards through the water, but to stop her forward movement as rapidly as possible. Once she had stopped completely, two long blasts in succession meant: 'I am motionless'. The unavoidable weakness of fog signals of course was that while they might indicate what the ship was doing, they did not necessarily help to establish exactly where she was.

One principle of great importance underlay all the rules for navigating in fog. While it was safe for two ships to steam slowly ahead when they already knew each other's respective courses, it was essential that each should then hold that course. To alter direction in fog when another ship was nearby was recognised by seamen as a thoroughly dangerous procedure.

CHAPTER 5

First Evening at Sea

Afternoon lengthened into an early summer evening as the *Empress*'s passengers settled into their cabins and prepared for the pleasant ceremony of dinner at sea. On the *Empress*'s bridge, Adelard Laurier stood with Kendall and the officers of the watch. Laurier was a professional St Lawrence pilot, a veteran of the waterway who was pilot of choice to the CPR, that is, he had been specially selected by them to pilot their ships whenever he was available. To be a pilot of choice to one of the great Atlantic shipping companies was a coveted position, earned by years of skilled service, for apart from the prestige of the position, the fees earned were the highest aboard the big, deep draught liners.

On the bridge there was silence, save for the occasional quiet order from the pilot. Then the wheel spun in the quartermaster's fists, and the vessel's bows swung obediently on to her new course. From time to time, a drifting patch of fog moved across the liner's course, and each time she slowed to half speed, or to slow, until she was clear of the clinging hazard. Then, to a shrilling of engine-room telegraphs, the great engines swung again into their regulation pace, measuring off the miles with the revolution of the spinning shafts. All evening and late into the night, the *Empress* beat her way steadily down river. It was a fine, clear night, with little or no wind and a young moon. One by one the lights of the little townships on the river bank dropped astern into the darkness.

The first evening at sea was a cheerful affair. The great

majority of the passengers had every reason to look forward to their voyage and to the prospect of a summer season in London or a family reunion in a Manchester parlour.

Dinner for the First and Second Class passengers was served at 7 p.m. By tradition, First Class passengers were not required to dress for dinner on the first or last nights of the voyage, (on any other night, it would have been unthinkable to fail to do so). Despite that, many chose to dress; Henry Seton-Karr was among them. The sound of the string orchestra rose discreetly above the murmur of conversation, and the chink of crystal. Beneath the baroque dome of the great white and gold dining-saloon, the Irvings, seated at one of the long tables, chatted agreeably with their neighbours across the snowy napery and the gleaming silver.

At least two of their fellow diners remembered the encounter clearly, for a little later that night, they were briefly to get to know each other a great deal better. Clayton Burt was the works manager of the Toronto Factory of the Russell Motor Car Company, the manufacturers of an exclusive, very expensive and long-forgotten vehicle called the Russell-Knight. Burt, a big, burly man who was also an excellent swimmer, was crossing to Europe. He had sent his wife and two children to their family home in Indiana and was off for a tour of Europe's car factories. The other passenger was unlikely to have been forgotten by the gentlemen of the party. She was a tall auburn-haired beauty of seventeen named Tiria Townshend. Miss Townshend came from Blenheim, New Zealand, and she was on a world tour, escorted by her aunt, Mrs Wynn Price. Like many young ladies from that land of outdoor living, Miss Townshend was an athlete. In particular, like Mr Clayton Burt, she was an excellent swimmer.

After dinner the passengers dispersed, some to their cabins, others to the library or to the music-room. A number of the gentlemen, predictably, headed for the smoking-room for a drink or a hand of cards before bed.

Dinner in the Second Class dining-room was an equally pleasant if less ceremonial occasion. Many of the Second

Class passengers were members of the Salvation Army contingent, and they were in festive mood. Among the passengers at the long tables, Miss Alice Bayles was thoroughly enjoying her first meal at sea. Young Alice, on her way home to South Bank, Middlesbrough after a holiday in Canada, was in no mood to be put off by her table companion, a woman who seemed downcast and ill at ease. 'I don't like this boat at all,' she kept saying. 'I don't feel safe.' Alice, who was a sensible young woman, took no notice of her. After dinner, she left the table and her melancholy companion, and headed sleepily for the cabin she was sharing with two other girls. She never learned the unhappy woman's name, for she was never to see her again.

For the Third Class passengers there was no dinner. Nothing marked the social distinctions of the early twentieth century more indelibly than eating habits. First and Second Class passengers dined at seven; Third Class passengers ate high tea at 5.30. It was a substantial meal. There were smoked herrings and cold meat and pickles, with bread and jam to follow. However, even if there was no string orchestra, the Third Class passengers were not denied the pleasures of music. The Salvation Army band gave an impromptu concert, which was much appreciated.

After dinner, there was a general movement towards the promenade decks to watch the shoreline, silvered in moonlight, as it slipped astern. For those prepared to brave the chill of the evening air a little longer, there was a memorable sight. The Allan liner *Alsatian*, her promenade decks ablaze with light, went forging past in the darkness, bound upstream to Quebec. As she swept astern in the darkness, most of the passengers turned thankfully back to the light and warmth of saloon and cabin. It was not a late night. Most of the passengers would no doubt have been up early, and the start of a transatlantic crossing was an exhausting as well as an exciting experience.

The CPR, as a well conducted company, required that the liner's cabin decks, like her public rooms, must never be unattended. There were two or three stewards on duty in each class from late evening until 6 a.m. the following morning. They spent their lonely watch cleaning shoes, checking that the night lights were burning properly, and listening for the occasional call-bell froma a restless or queasy passenger. Moreover, they were required to report to the bridge by telephone every half hour to confirm that all was well. Soon after 10 p.m. the night stewards were reporting thankfully that most of the passengers were in their bunks.

At 10 p.m. too, the night stewards made their final rounds of the passenger cabins, closing and locking with their brass keys the long rows of portholes that pierced the liner's steel sides. According to the regulations, the stewards were required to lock the portholes whether the passengers liked it or not, and some of the stronger-minded did so. Others, faced with the protests of angry passengers who objected to being hermetically sealed into small, crowded cabins for ten hours or so at a stretch, simply reported to the night watchmen the numbers of those cabins whose portholes were still open to sea and sky. If the night blew up rough, there would be plenty of time to close them after a few cupfuls of rain and spray had persuaded the occupants that the Anglo-Saxon passion for fresh air need not be carried to extremes.

Probably very few of the passengers, as they climbed into their bunks, had any clear idea of the layout of the ship or even of how to find their way from cabin to deck. There would be plenty of time for that in the long days ahead at sea. Meanwhile, they would sleep well tonight. It would take a great deal to wake them.

While his fellow-passengers slept, Colonel David Creighton, of the Salvation Army, sat up late writing a cheerful note to his fellow Salvationists back home in Toronto. After a strenuous day of toil and excitement, he said, the Army contingent was asleep, 'having partaken, rather more sumptuously than is the accustomed habit of the members, of the festive board.' He can hardly have meant liquor; perhaps he was referring to the tapioca pudding served to the Second Class passengers. At least one traveller subsequently expressed gratitude for it, claiming that it had kept him awake. Then

FIRST EVENING AT SEA

David Creighton sealed his letter, scribbled the address, and dropped the letter in the ship's post box, just in time to catch the outgoing mail that would be taken ashore by the pilot boat at Rimouski.

They were the last words he ever wrote.

From time to time that night the liner passed another vessel bound upstream. There is no record that anybody on the liner's bridge took any particular note of them. 'Ships that pass in the night' is a phrase well chosen. Few things can be less memorable than such a passage in the darkness; a twinkle of mast head and side lights passing safely on the opposite course, to be replaced by a glimpse of a white stern light disappearing into the blackness. If the passing vessel is some obscure collier or cargo ship, it is unlikely that anybody will ever know her name. The *Empress*, by contrast, was clearly identifiable, if not by name, then at least as a big passenger liner, decks a blaze of light. The men on the bridge of a collier, say, would be unlikely to forget passing such a ship on a particular night. Upon that particular May evening, the crew of one such ship remembered the *Empress*'s passage very clearly indeed.

By midnight the *Empress* was largely a silent, ship, save for her crew on watch. One passenger, said to have been Thomas Smart, remained on deck because he was not feeling well. Perhaps he was a poor sailor; perhaps he found the cool night air on the promenade-deck preferable to the smoking-room. About 1.30 a.m. Mr Smart was seated in his deckchair enjoying the night breezes, and listening to the steady, comforting beat of the engines far below, throbbing like a human heart as they drove the big ship smoothly through the hissing water. Mr Smart's reverie was interrupted when Captain Kendall passed him on his way to the bridge. For a few minutes, the two men chatted on the otherwise-deserted promenade-deck. They spoke, as strangers will, of the weather. 'It is nice and light, but it looks to me as if a fog is coming up. You never know when fog is going to drop its pall at this point of the river,' Kendall was reported to have said. Then he climbed back to the bridge.

FOURTEEN MINUTES

It was a prophetic conversation, if it ever took place. Unfortunately there are grounds for doubting whether it did, or indeed if Mr Smart himself ever existed. There was certainly a Mr Smart on the First Class passenger list, but he rejoiced in the memorable Christian name of Bogue, not Thomas, and at 1.30 a.m. he was asleep in his bunk. Moreover, there was clear evidence that Captain Kendall never left the bridge that night except to visit his own adjoining quarters. Perhaps there really was a passenger on the promenade-deck at that unlikely hour, and the newspapers got his name wrong. Perhaps it was some other officer who took a turn round the promenade-deck. We do not know.

One man was not in bed early that night, or most other nights. Augustus Gaade, the *Empress*'s Chief Steward, held a post of considerable importance. Around him revolved the smooth functioning of the great retinue of stewards and stewardesses who ministered to the passengers' needs around the clock. It was a post that called for the deftness of a maître d'hôtel, the alertness of a seaman, and the cool eye for detail of a born organiser. Gaade was a man who combined them all, for he had learned his skills in a lifetime of service at sea. This was to be one of his last transatlantic trips, for he was shortly to take up a new post ashore as the CPR's port steward at Liverpool. Gaade's last duty of the day was to make a final tour of inspection around his floating parish, assuring himself that all was shipshape for the night before he retired to his own bunk. At 10 p.m. precisely, he made his rounds of the Second and Third Class quarters. The public rooms in both classes were practically deserted. At 11.30 p.m. Gaade started his tour of inspection of the First Class quarters, where passengers traditionally kept later hours, but by then the reading-room and the music-room, too, were deserted. Only in the smoking-room a handful of men lingered over a final rubber beneath the gaze of a heavy-eyed steward. Gaade headed for his bunk.

Gaade's official cabin was modest and close to the First Class dining-saloon, and he tended to use it more as a day office than as living-quarters. Whenever there was a First

FIRST EVENING AT SEA

Class stateroom vacant, Gaade slept there instead. On this occasion, there were plenty. Gaade headed for stateroom Number 218, an inside cabin on the right-hand side of the saloon deck. Gaade's was a demanding job. Bad weather, a delayed arrival, any one of a hundred things could test Gaade's skill and tact in dealing with a shipload of queasy, fractious passengers. On this occasion, Gaade noted with relief, there were no signs of headaches ahead. The voyage had started well, the weather forecast was good, and the passengers seemed a contented and good-natured crowd. Gaade's last conscious thought, as he turned out the light, was that it looked like being an unusually trouble-free trip.

CHAPTER 6

Fog

At 1.30 a.m. the beat of the *Empress*'s engines died away and the big ship slowed to a halt. She had just passed the port of Rimouski, and now the pilot station at Father Point was almost abeam, a mile and a half away. The halt was not a long one. Within about five minutes the little pilot cutter *Eureka* had swirled alongside, pilot Laurier had climbed nimbly down the swaying Jacob's ladder to the cutter's deck, and the last bags of mail had been handed over. Kendall and Laurier exchanged a farewell salute and the *Eureka* forged away into the darkness towards Father Point. With a clamour of engine-room telegraphs the liner's engines resumed their rhythmic pulse of 72 revolutions per minute and the big ship began to forge ahead through the water. For the next eighteen minutes or so she would head diagonally out across the river, her course almost exactly north-east, until she had gained a safe distance from the darkened shore. The long voyage to the Old World had really begun.

Kendall was still on the bridge. The captain had had a long day, but he would stay in command until dawn when the ship would be well on her way in open water and he could safely relax. Then Steede, the Irish Chief Officer, now asleep in his bunk, would come on deck to relieve him for the morning watch. Apart from the custom that the captain should be on the bridge so long as the pilot was aboard and so long as the ship was in narrow waters, Kendall had perhaps a further and very human motive for remaining there. He was the new master of one of the finest ships in his company's fleet and this was the first time that he had ever taken her down the St Lawrence. Professional caution may well have been mixed with a natural pride in his position.

There were five men and a boy on the *Empress*'s bridge. Although Kendall was still in command, Edward Jones, the First Officer, was on duty with Alwyn Moore, the Third Officer. Like Kendall, Jones was fairly new to the ship. Although he had held his master's ticket for about twelve years, he had been with the CPR for only three years or so. He had sailed in the *Empress* on two previous voyages as Second Officer, but this was his first voyage as First Officer. There were two Quartermasters, Sharples and Murphy, and there was a ship's boy as bridge-messenger. Far above Kendall's head, Seaman John Carroll was keeping his lookout in the crow's nest on the foremast. A bell shrilled once throughout the silence of the wheelhouse. Lookout Carroll was signalling: 'object on the right'. Far off to the eastward, where the blackness of the river met the dark night sky, two pinpoints of light were climbing over the horizon about eight miles away.

To a man on the shore watching a ship sail past him, eight miles may seem a great distance. That same man, standing on the bridge of a fast-moving ship and watching another such vessel steaming towards him will gain a different impression. The *Empress* was working up to her normal cruising speed of about 17 knots. Assuming that the newcomer was approaching at a modest 10 knots, then the two ships would be approaching each other at close to 30 miles an hour. In fifteen minutes or a little over, those two frosty sparks of light on the horizon would be alongside the *Empress*, gliding past in the darkness as the stranger made her way upstream against the current. Another ship that would pass in the night.

The stranger's masthead range lights were almost dead in line, broad on the *Empress*'s right hand, perhaps 45 degrees off her bow. That meant that the liner was crossing diagonally across the other ship's path. Accordingly, the newcomer had right of way, but that was no problem. The *Empress* was a fast ship. She had ample time in which to cross the stranger's path and settle on her new course before the two ships met. Another light was flashing in the darkness on the *Empress*'s right side. It was the Cock Point gas buoy and traditionally it marked the point where outward bound ships set course down river.

For a quarter of an hour the liner had been moving diagonally away from the shore and now, with the invisible shoreline a comfortable distance away, Kendall ordered Quartermaster Sharples to put the wheel over. The liner's stem swung eastward on to her new heading of north 73 east. The *Empress* was now heading almost exactly east-north-east, the course she would hold for the rest of her journey down river. The change of course had brought the other ship on to a track more nearly parallel with that of the liner. The *Empress* had crossed the newcomer's course now and the oncoming masthead lights were twinkling a little to the right of the liner's bows, perhaps 11 degrees off. As the two ships forged closer, Kendall climbed up to the upper bridge, above the wheelhouse, and squinted at the other ship's lights through the sight of the prismatic compass. For a few moments he watched her, carefully checking her bearings. Then, satisfied, he returned to the wheelhouse. There was no danger. Kendall was satisfied that the stranger's masthead lights were open for a right-hand passage, green to green. The two ships were in clear sight of each other and so long as they kept their present courses, Kendall would steam past the other vessel to the northward of her, with ample room to spare.

But now something else had caught Kendall's eye. Something equally common in the St Lawrence, but less reassuring. Moving out from the shore like a ghost upon the water was a long, low bank of fog. It was moving north-east, spreading lazily across the river. It had materialised at precisely the time and place calculated to carry it between the two ships. As the minutes passed, Kendall felt his first twinge of concern. The oncoming ship was very close now, perhaps a mile and a half away. Kendall was sure that he could see the other's green right-hand light, but even as he watched, the stranger's lights were growing misty; the fog was closing in. Kendall made up his mind. He reached for the handle of the engine room telegraph and rang down: 'Full astern'. Then he reached for the whistle cord and sent three short blasts shrieking through the night. To the other ship, indeed to any seaman within earshot, the message was clear: 'I am going astern on my engines.' The order did not mean that Kendall meant to drive his ship backwards through the water. His ship had no brakes; the quickest way to stop her was to set her screws in reverse, clawing at the water until they pulled the ship to a halt. Then he would stop his engines before the ship began to gather sternway.

As the *Empress*'s engines swung into reverse, sending the water boiling and heaving under her counter, a single long wail pierced the fog that now swirled dankly around the *Empress's* bridge windows. The other ship, Kendall concluded, was acknowledging his signals and indicating that she was holding her course.

Kendall walked to the bridge wing and gazed down through the fog at the black river below. It was no longer swirling past. Instead, it slapped and eddied against the steel hull plating. With no point of reference to guide him, it was hard for Kendall to be sure that his ship had lost all way, but once he was satisfied that the water was no longer moving aft along his ship's side, he called for the order: 'Stop engines.' Then he sounded two more short blasts. 'My ship is not moving.' Again, the eerie shriek of a whistle sounded through the fog. The invisible stranger was answering Kendall's signal, but the sound of her whistle was much louder now, and it no longer seemed to be coming from ahead. As nearly as the men on the *Empress*'s bridge could tell, it was about 45 degrees off the liner's bow. Kendall checked the standard compass again. Although he believed his ship was motionless, it was crucially important that she did not swing in the fog. He stepped back reassured; her head was still pointing east-north-east. If the stranger was holding his course, he should be groping his way down the *Empress*'s right-hand side out there in the fog, close perhaps, but passing safely on a parallel course. Kendall stood alone on the right-hand bridge wing of the silent liner, staring out into the fog, eyes and ears straining for the first sign that the stranger in the night was safely past.

Perhaps two minutes passed. Through the night, a light glimmered mistily. Then another. One was red, the other was green. As Kendall stared in shocked disbelief, the sidelights of a steamer swam out of the murk. Like the eyes of some creature in a nightmare, they glared at him, glowing brighter each second. Above them, dead in line, shone two white masthead lights. Kendall was gazing at the steaming lights of a ship. And she was heading straight for him.

CHAPTER 7

The *Storstad*

All that night, the collier *Storstad* had churned her way stolidly upstream towards Father Point. There, some time around 2 a.m., she would pick up her river pilot for the long inland voyage upstream to Montreal. Although she wass Norwegian-owned, registered and manned, the *Storstad* was on time charter to the Dominion Coal Company of Canada and earned her living carrying heavy cargoes of coal from Sydney, Cape Breton Island to the furnaces and fireplaces of Canada's heartlands.

The *Storstad* was a powerful modern 6,000 ton ship built some four years earlier at the Armstrong Whitworth yards on the Tyne. She was a big, lumpy flush decker, her hull painted as black as the cargoes she carried. On each side of her tall black midships funnel was emblazoned a large white 'K'. Her owner was a Norwegian named Klavenes. Hauling coal up the St Lawrence was a summer trade for the *Storstad*. During the winter, she usually earned her living carrying Newfoundland iron ore to the Cape Breton Island railhead, but sometimes she migrated to warmer climates. In the spring of 1914, she was newly returned to the St Lawrence from the Mediterranean by way of Venice and Algiers. This was her second St Lawrence voyage of the summer.

The *Storstad* was built upon what was known as the Isherwood system, which meant that instead of her ribs being arranged vertically in close-set rows from keel to deck, her main frames ran horizontally from stem to stern. Such ships were immensely strong, particularly in the event of a head-on impact of the kind that would often crumple the bows of a conventionally-designed vessel. It was a very sensible arrangement in a ship which, like the *Storstad*, spent much of her working life plying in icebound waters. Unhappily, the heavy stem and thick shell plating that could slice through pack ice and shoulder it aside without damage would be equally effective at piercing steel plate. Her sharp vertical stem and massive frames made her in effect an immense cold chisel. With 11,000 tons of Nova Scotia coal under her hatches, the big collier could be a lethal weapon aimed at any vessel that crossed her path, a weapon made even more formidable by the fact that at full load the unyielding knife edge of her stem reached down fully 25 feet below the water line. The inherent danger was no secret to the men who designed and built the *Storstad* and her like. They also knew that a raked, overhanging stem and a 'soft' bow that would crumple safely back to a reinforced bulkhead would do much to lessen the risk of serious damage in a collision. There had been plenty of object lessons in the past. In 1895, for instance, the German immigrant ship *Elbe*, a modern 5,000 tonner, had sunk in minutes when rammed by a British coaster, barely a tenth of her size. As late as 1922, the P & O liner *Egypt* was to sink after being rammed by the small French coaster *Seine*. Again, reinforced ice-breaking bows were the weapon that was to send 86 people to their death. But in 1914 the classification societies that laid down construction standards for insurance purposes, refused to change construction rules that made straight stems virtually obligatory. It was to cost many lives, and many fine ships before reason prevailed.

Of the thirty-six men in the *Storstad's* crew, only five were on deck that night. The captain, Thomas Andersen, was where any sensible man might have preferred to be at nearly two o'clock in the morning, which was in bed with his wife. Andersen was the archetypal collier-shipper of his day, a burly, bull-necked man in his mid-forties, broad-shouldered, red-faced and heavily-moustached. Colliers were not elegant ships. A battered peaked cap and a blue serge suit were

Andersen's version of uniform. Andersen had been at sea for thirty years. He had been in command of the *Storstad* for the last three of them.

There was nothing particularly unusual in Mrs Andersen's presence aboard the collier, for it was an era in which many captains followed the time-honoured custom of taking their wives to sea with them. Mrs Andersen was a large, matronly lady with a round face and determined features. As the Norwegian winter had lengthened into spring, she had left their two children behind, and journeyed south from her home in Arendal to join her husband. She had passed the winter making herself a new wardrobe for her summer journeying up and down the St Lawrence, and she had brought so much that Andersen had grumbled good-naturedly that it was impossible to move aboard the ship for his wife's trunks. Once aboard, Mrs Andersen had set to work, like a good Norwegian housewife, to make a cheerful home out of the captain's quarters, and now their cabin was bright with new curtains. She was particularly proud of the new chenille drapes that hung round their bed.

The Andersens had retired to bed four hours earlier. Andersen had given orders to be called when the ship was some six miles below Father Point and now, fully dressed except for trousers and boots, he lay in his bunk, awaiting the call to the bridge immediately above his cabin. Already, the *Storstad* had steamed some 250 miles upstream from Sydney, and in a few minutes she would be abreast of Father Point pilot station, where she would pause briefly to pick up her river pilot. There, Andersen would leave his bunk and climb to the bridge to take command for the most difficult part of the four-day passage.

While Andersen dozed in his cabin beneath the bridge, the collier was under the command of the First Mate, a tall, fair-haired young man named Alfred Toftenes. Andersen had complete faith in Toftenes, for the two had sailed together for three years. At thirty-three, Toftenes had been at sea for nearly twenty years, and had held his master's ticket for seven of them. He had joined the collier when she was nearly new, some three and half years earlier. Since then, under Andersen's fatherly eye, the younger man had risen from third mate to second mate. Then, a few weeks before, he had been promoted to the position of Andersen's second-in-command. Toftenes was sharing the watch with Jakob Saxe, the Third Mate. Saxe was a much younger man of twenty, but even so, he had eight years' sea time to his credit, as deckhand and as certificated officer, and he had sailed in the *Storstad* for over a year. On watch with the two officers were three seamen. According to custom, they divided their four-hour spell of duty into three 80-minute tricks, one at the wheel, one on lookout up on the fo'c's'le, and the third as extra lookout, or simply grabbing a quick smoke between spells at the wheel and on lookout.

With the enormous weight of a full cargo of coal under hatches, the *Storstad* was right down to her load line, with only a few feet of freeboard between waterline and deck. For all that, the big collier was steering easily enough against a gentle current of one or two knots. It was a fine, clear night for a river passage, as she ran smoothly towards the brightly winking light of Father Point lighthouse, flashing rhythmically across the dark river.

A bell rang twice, sharply, in the darkened wheelhouse. The lookout at the stemhead was signalling: ship in sight to the left. The officers on the bridge could see her too. Six or eight miles away up the river, a pair of white masthead lights were crawling steadily up over the horizon. Toftenes sent Saxe aft to attend to the patent log. By the time the third mate returned to the bridge, the lights were much closer. The stranger was only about three miles away now, and Saxe could clearly see her green right-hand navigation light, low down on the water. By the glow of light from her hull, she was obviously a big ship, probably a transatlantic liner on her way down river to the sea.

Both Saxe and Toftenes would see something else. A long, hazy band of fog was rolling out across the river toward the two ships. The *Storstad*'s officers had standing orders to call the captain in the event of fog. But the fog was not upon them yet, and the captain would be coming up to the bridge in a few minutes anyway, when the *Storstad* stopped her engines off Father Point to pick up the pilot. Perhaps – and this is pure speculation – perhaps Toftenes decided to leave his commanding officer to enjoy a few more minutes' rest with Mrs Andersen before his long vigil. The speaking-tube to Andersen's cabin was close by Toftenes' hand, but he did not lift the brass cover.

The big liner forged steadily down through the darkness towards the little knot of men on the *Storstad*'s bridge. Below her white masthead lights, the single green eye of her right-hand navigation light burned clearly through the darkness. The stranger's lights were still showing slightly to the left of the *Storstad*'s bow, Toftenes reckoned, but she was crossing ahead of them at a slight angle, on a course not far off parallel. The big ship was going to hold her course to seaward, Toftenes decided, and pass, green-to-green, down the collier's right-hand side. And then Toftenes changed his mind. Even as he watched, the liner's white masthead lights moved closer together until for a moment they were dead in line, one above the other. Out of the darkness, a red light winked into life, twin to the green light slightly to its left. Toftenes stared at the approaching lights. Beside him, Saxe was also watching the approaching steamer. Fremmerlid, the lookout, huddled into his heavy sea jacket at the stemhead, was also watching the newcomer warily.

If their sworn testimony is to be believed, all five men on watch aboard the collier that night saw exactly the same thing. For a few moments the approaching liner was pointing directly at them, her navigation lights staring unwinkingly at them across the rapidly narrowing strip of river that separated the two ships. And then the green sidelight snapped into darkness, leaving only the red warning eye of the left-hand navigation light glowing at her bridge wing. Above it, the white range lights had opened a fraction, the high mainmast light now slightly to the right of its twin on the foremast. For perhaps two minutes, the men on the *Storstad* watched that single red eye. Some of them later claimed that it was much longer, nearer five minutes than two. Nobody could later say for certain, for none of them noted the times by the wheelhouse clock, and estimates of time, particularly in darkness, can vary widely.

Toftenes and his shipmates felt no particular concern. The liner was still a couple of miles or so away, and there was plenty of room for her to pass safely down the *Storstad*'s left-hand side, red light to red light, as the Norwegians were now convinced that she had decided to do. No problem at all on a broad, deep river on a clear night. But it was no longer a clear night. That long, insidious belt of fog had moved well out into the river now, threatening to drop like a veil between the approaching ships. Already, the lights on shore were growing dim. And so were the lights on the oncoming steamer. Toftenes slowed his engines. As the liner faded like a ghost into the fog, Toftenes and his colleagues caught their last glimpse of her lights. The sidelight, they were sure, was still showing red.

Through the mist, Toftenes could hear the moan of the liner's siren. It sounded to Toftenes like the single blast of a running signal, and it was coming, he was convinced, from the collier's left-hand side, which was exactly where he expected it to be. From the high black funnel astern of the wheelhouse, the *Storstad*'s whistle shrieked in reply as Saxe tugged the whistle cord tied to the compass binnacle. Toftenes moved to the brass engine-room telegraph and swung the pointer to 'stop'. Beneath their feet, the men on the bridge felt the throb of the engines die away, and the silent ship moved hissing through the fog-shrouded water. The *Storstad* was still moving forward, but her speed was dropping off, for her big single screw was no longer turning. Silence fell in the wheelhouse, broken only by the ticking of the bridge clock. Outside, the fog was becoming thicker.

Toftenes was growing uneasy. The collier, her engines silent, was moving more and more slowly through the water as she lost way, and soon, the current sliding invisibly down river under keel would begin to exert its subtle force on the ship's hull. If it pushed the *Storstad*'s bows off to the left, it could begin to carry the collier into the course of the big ship they had been watching minutes before. For of one thing, every man on the *Storstad*'s bridge seems to have been totally convinced; the great ship they had seen bearing down on them was now moving irresistibly through the fog, somewhere close off their left-hand bow.

Peter Johannsen, the helmsman, was at the wheel, hands grasping the spokes, eyes fixed on the glowing compass bowl before him. Toftenes spoke softly. 'Wheel a little right' he ordered. The wheel spun under Johannsen's fists. But the *Storstad* was not answering her wheel. She had finally drifted to a halt in the water, and with no water moving past her rudder, she had no steering way. To keep the bows pointing straight, safely out of the way of that menacing hull somewhere in the fog outside the wheelhouse windows, the ship must have enough speed to give steerage way. Toftenes moved the pointer on the engine room telegraph to 'slow ahead', and a moment later, the engines beneath his feet began their slow, rhythmic beat.

Toftenes put his mouth to the speaking-tube that led down to the head of the captain's bunk. 'It's getting hazy,' he said. Andersen's voice replied at once: 'Can you see Father Point light?' The light was just disappearing into the fog, Toftenes told the captain. Andersen climbed from his bunk, pulled on his trousers, and headed for the cabin door with his slippers in his hand. He was moving fast, and Mrs Andersen asked if he was nervous. 'Yes,' her husband replied. 'I don't know why, but I am.' He headed for the bridge. Normally, Mrs Andersen would have stayed in bed, but instead she got up, and pulled a skirt on over her nightdress.

Andersen paused for a moment in the cool night air to glance over the ship's side at the black water of the river. The ship did not seem to be moving. Andersen swung himself up the ladder on to the right-hand side of the bridge and strode into the wheelhouse. From force of habit, his first move was to walk to the compass binnacle and check the ship's course. What his next action would have been, we shall never know. Perhaps he would have asked if any other ships had been in sight when the fog fell, for up to that moment, nobody had told the captain of the presence of a ship. But at that moment, the horrified Andersen saw something that drove every other thought from his mind. Through the fog a bright white light was shining, above 30 degrees off the *Storstad*'s left bow. Below it and to the right shone a single hazy green light. Ahead of him, not more than 300 yards away in the fog, was a big ship. And she was heading right across the *Storstad*'s bows. Andersen grabbed the engine-room telegraph and slammed it to 'full astern'. He had no time to see if the engine-room responded, for his gaze was fixed on the ship ahead, but from the vibration of the deck planking beneath his feet, he believed that the engine-room had responded.

Andersen snapped an order to Saxe, and the third mate yanked hastily at the whistle cord. Three short blasts yelped through the fog. It was the correct order to give, but it was of no more than academic interest. The *Storstad*, her whistle shrieking, slid like a gigantic battering ram into the towering black hull ahead of her. Fremmerlid, still standing at the stemhead in the extreme eyes of the ship, flung himself to safety, and the men on the bridge braced themselves for the shock of the inevitable collision.

But there was no staggering shock, no screech of twisted metal. There was the slightest of jars as the collier's bows hit the black cliff of the liner's side, a ragged flash of flame as metal ground against metal, and that was all. The shock was no greater than the slight jar that Andersen would have expected to feel as he brought his ship alongside a dock wall. Andersen did not know it at that moment, but there had been no shock because there had been virtually no resistance. The *Storstad*'s bows had gone between the liner's steel ribs as smoothly as an assassin's knife. Andersen heard a man's voice bawling through a megaphone into the night: 'Keep your engines ahead'. Andersen had the best reason in the world to obey.

The main hope of safety for both ships was to keep the collier's bows wedged in the wound like a cork in a bottle to staunch the flow of water. It was not just a question of keeping the other vessel afloat. If his own bulkheads had crumpled under the shock, then his own ship, monstrously burdened by 11,000 tons of Nova Scotia coal, would go down like a stone if she drifted free. Andersen had no megaphone, but he yelled back in English at the top of his voice to say that he was going ahead on his engines.

The captain's fist was clenched on the brass handle of the telegraph. As the two ships touched, he slammed the pointer to 'full ahead'. The *Storstad* had hit the liner at something approaching a right angle, her bow pointing slightly towards the *Empress*'s stern. Driven on by her tremendous weight, the Norwegian's bows had forced their way deep into the liner's side, about half way between the funnels. For four seconds or so she remained there, her bow locked inside the wound she had made. But then despite all Andersen's efforts to keep his ship in place, the *Storstad* began to slide out of the wound, swinging astern as she did so. She was being forced out, Andersen believed, because the liner was still moving ahead and the collier, broadside on to the current of her forward movement, was being thrust backwards and sideways like a gigantic crowbar. The collier's crumpled bows wrenched free from the hole in the big liner's side, and Andersen felt his ship swinging round so violently that for a few moments he thought that the two ships were going to collide again, this time stern to stern.

Mrs Andersen had hurried on deck and was standing at her husband's side, staring in amazement at the high black wall of steel looming ahead of her in the fog. 'What are you trying to do?' she asked. He was trying to get his bows back into the hole, her husband replied grimly. But it was too late for that. The big passenger ship was slipping away from them into the swirling fog, leaving the collier wallowing further and further astern. As the astonished Andersens watched, she vanished completely into the clinging murk.

The *Storstad* was alone. Outside the wheelhouse windows, there was nothing to be seen except darkness and fog. The other ship had disappeared as completely as if she had never been. Andersen's immediate concern was for his own ship.

For all he knew, she was even then sinking under him as the water poured in through her crushed bows.

It was Mrs Andersen who voiced her husband's fears for him.

'Are we going down?' she asked.

'I think so,' Andersen replied grimly.

'Take it easy, dear,' said Mrs Andersen soothingly. 'Don't say a word to anyone.' She told her husband calmly that she was going to stay on the bridge so that they could go down together.

Andersen sent Toftenes and a party of seamen scrambling forward to the wrecked fo'c's'le to sound the forward holds and see how much water the colllier was making. Obviously his ship was badly damaged, her fo'c's'le swept clean of deck fittings as it sliced under the liner's decks. Saxe was sent running aft to the boat deck to get the crew mustered and the *Storstad*'s four lifeboats cleared and swung out. Toftenes made his way back to the bridge to report: 'She still floats.' The fo'c'stle was a wreck, but the bulkheads seemed to be holding. These tremendous Isherwood frames were to be the salvation of the *Storstad*, no matter what they might have done to the big liner.

At that moment, however, nobody on the collier's bridge was particularly worried about the ship they had so briefly and disastrously encountered in the fog. They were angry that the big liner had apparently ignored the age-old custom of the sea by failing to return to offer them assistance. It was odd, Mrs Andersen remarked to the puzzled men around her, that the big liner had not come back to help, especially as the ship was apparently in no particular trouble herself. The speed at which she had disappeared into the fog seemed to prove that.

Having satisfied himself that she was seaworthy, at least for the moment, Andersen's next task was to get his ship under control. The *Storstad*, still steaming slowly ahead had been swung so wildly off course by the collision that she had described a complete circle and was heading erratically towards the shore. Andersen not only had to get his ship back on to a safe course, but he had to try to find out where the mysterious liner was. Fog still blanketed the river, and Andersen did not want a second encounter like the first. With his hand on the cord, he kept the collier's whistle shrieking intermittently into the night, but he heard no reply.

Perhaps ten minutes had passed since the collision, and the little group on the collier's bridge were still peering anxiously into the fog when Mrs Andersen heard noises coming from the water, low down on the collier's left-hand side. It was the sound of screaming.

CHAPTER 8

Collision

For a moment, Kendall gazed in horror at the apparition that loomed at him out of the fog. Not much over 100 feet away, the blunt chisel bows of a ship were bearing down on the *Empress*, aimed directly at her bridge. The stranger, he was convinced, was moving fast, for he believed that he could see a white moustache of foam curling away from her bows. Two thoughts filled his mind. The first was to stop the stranger. The other was to get his own ship out of the way of those deadly bows. Both were forlorn hopes.

Kendall leaped to the engine-room telegraph, grabbed the handle, and rang for full speed ahead on the engines. In the same breath, he ordered the wheel hard over to the right. He had virtually no chance at all of moving his ship out of the way of those terrible bows, but if he could move the point of collision as far aft as possible, he might at least lessen the seriousness of the blow. Moreover, by putting the wheel hard over, he might just begin to swing his ship over to the right, so that the blow would be a glancing one as the two ships crashed, right-hand to right-hand.

His second and even more slender hope was to stop the stranger, to ward off somehow that fearful blow. Kendall must have known, even as he grabbed the bridge megaphone, that the task was a hopeless one. Nonetheless he raised the megaphone to his lips and roared at the top of his voice: 'Go astern'. Several times he bellowed into the night, but he heard no reply. Even as he called, Kendall was not to know horrified men on the bridge of the other ship had already thrown their engines full astern, and that the newcomer's screw was thrashing the water, trying unavailingly to check the great steel mass as it slid towards the *Empress*'s side. As the collier bore down, Kendall turned to First Officer Jones. 'Get away,' he shouted, 'get all the hands, and get the boats ready.'

Kendall's main concern, now that a collision was unavoidable, was to make sure that the stranger kept her bows firmly wedged into the hole that she was inevitably going to make. Provided the two ships stayed locked together, it might be possible to beach the liner on the shores of Gaspe, so close to the liner's right side. As the stranger nosed her way into Kendall's ship with a gentle jar, Kendall grabbed the bridge megaphone, and roared into the night: 'Keep going ahead on your engines.' He yelled as loudly as he could, several times, but he heard no reply from the other ship. Instead, a few seconds after the collision, the other ship started to back away from the liner, swinging out and astern, her lights growing dim as the swirling mists closed round her. And then she was gone.

The *Storstad*'s reinforced steel stem sliced into the *Empress*'s unprotected side like a chisel into tin. From stemhead to forefoot, the collier's bow was some 46 feet tall, and the whole knife edge of the stem went through the liner's side, cutting her open vertically from shelter deck to double bottom, and penetrating many feet into her hull. The wound was monstrous. At the most conservative estimate, the collier cut a hole below the liner's waterline, 25 feet deep and 14 feet wide. The *Empress* started to fill with water at the rate of 60,000 gallons a second. Worse, much worse, than the size of the hole was its location. For the *Storstad* had hit the *Empress* alongside the after-boiler-room, perhaps 15 feet astern of the bulkhead that separated it from its forward twin. Fifteen feet was much less than the width of the collier's bows, and it is almost certain that as they tore their way into the big ship, they crushed the watertight bulkhead between the two boiler-rooms. In four seconds, both those huge compartments had been laid open to the river for at least 20 feet below the waterline.

The *Empress*'s designers, pondering the subtleties of buoyancy and stability, had designed her to stay afloat in the worst possible case that they could envisage, which was one in which both boiler-rooms were flooded. Now, the worst had happened. Had that been all, she might just have stayed afloat. But as the icy cataract swept into the liner's hull, she listed beneath the weight of water. As she listed, more of the great gash slipped below the water, and the torrent increased. Swiftly, irresistibly, the great ship began to slide over on to her right-hand side. The *Empress*'s side, like that of all large liners of her day, was pierced with row upon row of portholes. The lowest were only 5 feet above the waterline. It needed a list of less than 10 degrees to submerge them. That in itself would not have mattered much, had all the portholes been closed. But not all the portholes were closed.

The waters of the St Lawrence swept into the sleeping ship like the bursting of a dam. Within seconds, a tidal wave was crashing and surging through the lower decks, sweeping into cabins and passageways, higher and higher. Over a thousand passengers were asleep in the great hull. A great many, perhaps the majority, were drowned in their bunks. Those on the lower decks, on the right-hand side of the ship, probably never even woke up before the water swept over them. Of those who lived to tell of the liner's last minutes, nearly all were agreed on one thing; it was a very gentle collision. Many only awoke when the waters started to pour into their crowded cabin, or when the increasing list shot them out of their bunks on to the deck.

Those who were not drowned outright had at best a few minutes, at worst a few seconds, in which to struggle from their cabins, bewildered, terrified, still half asleep. Lost in the passageways of a ship they had seen for the first time a few hours before, they struggled towards whatever safety might lie on the open deck far above. Old men, women with children, began to claw their way along listing passageways, up reeling flights of stairs, as the river waters swirled along the decks at their heels. And then the lights went out.

The crew, as far as anybody was ever able to say, did all they could to help the passengers far below decks. But of three duty night-stewards in the Third Class quarters, not one survived. The Second Class night-stewards, further from that cataract of water, had time to race along at least some of the lines of cabins, yelling a frantic warning to the sleepers, hammering on a door and racing on to the next as the deck began to slope ominously beneath their stumbling feet.

A night-watchman named Leonard Powell managed to run part of the way round the upper deck, placing and lighting his emergency oil lamps as the ship's own electric lights flickered and died. So did another named William Morl. Between them, they got eight lamps alight. There were emergency lamps in the Third Class quarters as well, and it was the duty of the night-stewards to light them in a crisis. Whether or not any of them were ever lit we do not know, since none of the men who should have lit them lived. It seems unlikely.

Some of the passengers swiftly found life-jackets. In many cases, there were stewards on hand to help them into the cumbersome cork jackets, and tie the tapes around them. Many passengers helped each other to find and put on the jackets. Many never found them at all. In the First and Second Class cabins, the jackets were normally stowed in cupboards or above their bunks. In Third Class, they were kept in racks overhead. In many cases, although the jackets were there in plenty, the passengers, stumbling in the dark, did not even know where to look for them, let alone how to put them on.

For passengers on the lower decks, survival depended, as much as anything, on whether they were sleeping on the right or left-hand side of the ship. For those whose cabins were on the right-hand side, the chances of survival were slender indeed, and for this there was a tragically simple reason, apart from the sheer speed of the disaster. Some of the *Empress*'s companionways did not open directly upon the deck like a simple staircase. Instead, they rose to a little landing and then split into two short sideways flights, leading up to right and left. Even if the passengers on the right-hand side reached the landing at all, they could go no further, for as the ship listed the fan of steps to the left of them reared up past the vertical, so that it was impossible to climb them, while the torrent at their heels was rising so fast that the steps to the right of them simply led back down under water. The men and women struggling up towards the deck were doomed as surely as if they had been trapped at the bottom of a well. For those placed on the left-hand side of the ship, the chances of survival were slightly better, for the companionways on the left were still above water. For those who grasped the chance early enough, it was still possible to scramble up them to the comparative safety of the upper deck. But for everybody berthed low down in the ship, the act of reaching the upper deck, if they reached it at all, was a simple and brutal struggle for survival in which a difference of a few feet in height above the rising water could decide the issue of life or death.

For those sleeping higher up in the ship, particularly in First Class, the motive for going up on deck, initially at least, was often one of curiosity rather than despair. They were the lucky ones. It was to become an article of faith among those who lived through that night that many passengers tried to return to their cabins to fetch their wives and children, or to dress, or to collect their valuables. A few, a very few, did so successfully. It was also an article of faith that many women, unwilling to appear in public in their nightgowns, stopped to dress. Again, it is probably true for with one or two exceptions, those women who were still alive twenty minutes later were in their nightgowns, if they were in anything at all. There were even reports that some passengers, having gone on deck immediately after the collision out of pure curiosity, decided that there was nothing to be alarmed about, and returned to their cabins. One fact is fairly certain. Very few people who were not on deck, or at least on the final flight of steps, within five minutes of the collision were ever seen again.

* * *

COLLISION

High on the liner's bridge, Kendall swung the handle of the engine room telegraph to: 'close watertight doors'. Then, to make sure his order was understood, he picked up the engine-room telephone, and repeated the order to the engineer who answered. The man's reply was reassuring; the order had been given, and far below the waterline the doors were going down.

The mysterious Mr Thomas Smart later claimed to have been close at hand. Kendall, he said, was leaning over the bridge wing, looking down on a little knot of seamen who had been brought running to the liner's side by the collision. 'Keep your heads there,' he was shouting to his crew. 'Don't get excited.' But already the liner's deck was beginning to list under Kendall's feet. Kendall ordered the emergency signal on the *Empress*'s siren, a single blast, calling all hands to the boats.

Kendall then ran from the bridge to the boat-deck and began throwing off the gripes of the first four boats on the right-hand side, the lashings that held the boats snugly in their chocks against the rolling of the ship at sea. Kendall ran back to the bridge. He still clung to the forlorn hope that he might be able to drive his ship ashore, and turned again to the engine-room telephone. 'Give me all you can, I'm going to try and beach her,' he called. The reply that came back from the engine-room was the death knell both of Kendall's hopes, and of his ship. 'The steam is gone,' he was told.

Steede, the liner's Chief Officer, had been in his bunk when the collision occurred. Now, clad in pyjamas, he was at Kendall's side. Kendall told his deputy to get an SOS off. Steede replied that it had already been done. Instead, Kendall told Steede to get the boats away as fast as possible. The boat-deck was swarming with passengers by now, crowding round the crew as they swung themselves against the heavy boats, pushing them forward and outwards, clearing away the massive blocks and tackles for lowering. Steede pushed his way into the crowd, and disappeared. Kendall was never to see him again.

FOURTEEN MINUTES

Mr Thomas Smart, still at hand, takes up the story again. Kendall was shouting through a megaphone to the crew, though he was having difficulty making himself heard because of the noise on deck, Smart said. Kendall was calling: 'There's no time to lose. Send stewards through the corridors, and if there are doors locked, break them in. Get the people out, and don't forget that women and children come first.' A little later, Smart heard Kendall again shouting through his megaphone to the crew working at the boats: 'Hurry up there, everybody. There is not much time to lose.' Smart could hear nothing more of what Kendall said. By that time, there was so much screaming and shouting on the deck that the captain's words were drowned.

Despite the crowds that milled around them, trying to find places in the boats, and despite the appalling and ever-growing list, the crews at the boats were working calmly and well. Kendall had retreated to the left-hand wing of the flying bridge and from there, his last vantage point on his dying ship, he saw at least three boats full of people being lowered smoothly into the water from the right-hand davits. There were certainly other right-hand boats lowered that night, successfully or otherwise, but nobody was ever completely certain how many boats were launched altogether. Probably five or six boats were launched, plus at least one of the Englehardt collapsibles. One boat almost certainly reached the water intact, and with a full load of passengers, only to be overwhelmed as the ship rolled over on top of them. In any case, it swiftly ceased to be a question of lowering the boats into the water, for the river rose to meet them where they lay in their chocks. Within minutes, the boat deck, normally forty-five feet above the waterline, had heeled over until the water was lapping round the feet of the davits, so swiftly did the great ship roll over. Most of the left-hand boats, rising higher and higher above the water line as the ship listed, probably never left their davits. Certainly, they were never lowered into the river because try as they might, their crews could not swing them out against the list of the ship.

Ten minutes after the collision, as nearly as anybody could

establish, the *Empress of Ireland* lurched violently and fell on to her side. Kendall's last sight of his command came as her twin funnels hit the water together. He saw no more, because at that moment Kendall, along with scores of other survivors, was flung out into the night by the force of the ship's fall. Once again, Mr Thomas Smart was there to record the moment. As Kendall and Smart were flung together into the river, Smart claimed to have heard Kendall's last despairing cry as his ship capsized beneath him: 'Heaven help us, for we cannot help ourselves.'

The final agony did not last long. The dying ship lay for a few minutes completely on her beam ends, her left side almost flush with the water. Then, at about nine minutes past two a.m., she lifted her graceful counter stern wearily above the surface of the river, and slid below the dark waters of the St Lawrence. It was just fourteen minutes since the *Storstad* had struck her. Down to the river bed 150 feet below went the liner. With her went the dining-room, the table silver and the potted palms. With her went the popular café, the music room, the children's sand pit and the Salvation Army's trombones. With her, trapped below decks, went also some 800 people, most of whom had probably never even got clear of their cabins. Their voyage from Quebec had lasted for just nine hours and forty-two minutes.

As the *Empress* lay on her side in the calm water, at least 700 men, women and a few children were clinging like ants to her superstructure, or standing on her horizontal hull-plating. So still did she lie that several of the crew raised a shout: 'She's aground.' One man claimed that two of the ship's officers had told him that the great liner was lying on a shoal in the river, and would sink no further. But there was no shoal: beneath her lay 150 feet of cold, black water.

Those minutes while the dying ship hung motionless upon her side were described by scores of survivors. None did so better than Mr Cunningham, from Winnipeg: 'The boat did not seem to be sinking. The water was just creeping up. The side was at a gentle angle with the water. It was just like sitting on the beach watching the tide come in. The waves came splashing up the slope of steel, and then retired one after the other. But each came a little higher than the last.'

There was even time in those minutes for people to do strange things. One man walked down the ship's side, along her bottom, climbed round her vast, motionless bronze propeller, and calmly dived into the river from her overhanging counter.

As the ship rolled over, the few boats safely afloat, already filling to the gunwales as men and women scrambled aboard, faced a new menace. One crew had to fend themselves off with an oar as one of the vast funnels swung down closer and closer, until it almost touched them. Clear of that menace, they faced another; the *Empress*'s wireless aerials were so close to the water now that they stretched like a huge wire fence across the path of the boats, entangling oars and rowers as they tried to force or squeeze their way under the deadly strands that threatened to drag them down. Somehow, hacking and twisting, they made their way out of the deadly trap.

The ship sank. As she did so, a great and terrible cry arose from 700 throats. As the *Empress* went under, one of the Salvation Army officers claimed, the men and women clinging to her turned to the water, and then, with a kind of desperate resolve, they leaped into the water with an agonising shout. Singly or in groups, they jumped or fell or slid or simply walked into the river. The temperature of the St Lawrence that night was a few degrees above freezing. Where the ship had been was a struggling, screaming mass of men, women and children, 'as thick as bees'. One man said it put him in mind of the flooding of a village. Many of the survivors had lifejackets; others, perhaps a majority, had not. Those who had jackets found themselves dragged down by those who had not. Sometimes, those who lived had literally to fight their way through the drowning men and women around them, feeling the dying clutching at their limbs, feeling the bodies of the dead under their feet as they tried to swim away. It was not totally dark, for many of the *Empress*'s lifebuoys were fitted with chemical flares. As they hit the water they burst into a faint bluish glow, casting what one survivor called a kind of 'creepy light, like bugs on a pool'.

The fog rolled away as suddenly as it had fallen. It was then that the survivors saw, most of them for the first time, the ship that had sunk them. She was brilliantly lit, the amber light from her portholes streaming out across the calm black water. She seemed a very long way away.

CHAPTER 9

Last Message from the *Empress*

The *Empress*'s wireless room, like that of many liners of her time, was a little deck-house astern of the after-funnel. There her two young operators lived and worked. The right-hand half of the deck-house was the operating room while the left-hand side was their living quarters. Ferguson and Bamford worked watch and watch, six hours at a spell, around the clock. There was nothing unusual about that. No British ship in 1914 carried more than two operators.

Ferguson had just handed over the long night watch to his junior and retired to his bunk when he heard the *Empress*'s siren squalling into the night. In his pyjamas, but not yet asleep, he looked out of the left-hand window of his quarters to spot whatever ship it was that the liner was apparently trying to avoid, but could see nothing. Seconds later he felt the collision, but it was a very gentle jolt. Up on the boat-deck, he felt practically nothing. There was very little noise, and no sensation of crashing or tearing.

In the adjoining wireless room, the astonished Bamford looked up from his morse key to see the *Storstad* in the very act of ramming the *Empress*, before her lights drifted aft and out of his line of vision. 'Here she is,' he shouted to Ferguson, and with that, his pyjama-clad chief hurried into the operating room. He told Bamford to get him some clothes, picked up the headphones and reached for the transmitter key. It was more than Ferguson's job was worth to send a distress call on his own initiative, for the Marconi Company's rules threatened with dismissal any operator who sent an SOS without direct instructions from the bridge. But he could and did send out the vital 'stand by' message to any wireless station within range. 'Stand by for distress call' was the burden of the message he tapped out on his key. 'We have hit something.'

The *Empress*'s transmitter was a powerful one and the big Marconi shore station at Father Point was only a few miles away. Whatever problems Ferguson had, weak signals were not among them. Almost before Ferguson's fingers had finished clicking the morse key, the reply started to crackle comfortingly back through the night from Father Point. 'OK,' the message read. 'Here we are.'

Bamford came back carrying Ferguson's jacket, trousers and overcoat, and Ferguson put them on. At that stage it had not occurred to him that he might have to swim in them.

Steede, the chief officer, appeared in the doorway of the wiress cabin and told Ferguson to get off an SOS, for the ship was sinking. Ferguson could have been in little doubt about it any longer, for the growing angle of the deck beneath his feet told its own story. Struggling to keep himself in his seat, he tapped out: 'SOS, we have hit something, sinking fast, send help.'

Any operator might have been forgiven if in that desperate emergency, he had fumbled with the key, or sent his message out at top speed, but Ferguson not only refused to be hurried, he deliberately sent the vital morse groups more slowly than he would usually have done. 'I knew that there would be no senior operators on watch,' he explained later. 'So I sent it out very slowly to give the junior operators a chance to understand.' It was the only SOS message that left the *Empress* that night, but it was enough.

Time was running out for the *Empress*. So heavy was her list by now that Ferguson, still at his key, was working with one foot on the deck and the other braced on the bulkhead to stop himself from toppling over as a reply from Father Point to his SOS began to crackle through his headphones. The shore station was asking the *Empress*'s position.

FOURTEEN MINUTES

That was precisely what Ferguson could not say, for nobody had come from the bridge to tell him, nor could he leave his post to go and ask. Even if he had, it is doubtful if anybody could have told him with any exactitude. Knowing that the *Empress* had dropped her pilot at Father Point about half an hour before, and with a fair idea of the ship's likely speed, Ferguson did some quick mental arithmetic, and replied: 'Twenty miles past Rimouski.' It was not right by several miles, but at least it gave his colleagues ashore something to work on. There was to be no further chance to tell anybody ashore where the liner was. The dynamos that drove the transmitter were dying. Nonetheless, Ferguson knew that his message had been received and understood, for Father Point came back at once: 'OK, sending *Eureka*, *Lady Evelyn* to your assistance.'

That was the last message ever to reach the *Empress*. Ferguson was still trying to get confirmation of the ship's position when the power supply failed, the set went dead, and for good measure, the wireless room lights went out. From the time of the collision until the complete failure of the ship's power supply, exactly eight minutes had elapsed.

Ferguson was not diverted from his task by the fact that his power supply had failed, the lights were out and the list was now so steep that his manuals and pads and pencils were cascading on to the floor. His emergency transmitter, powered by primitive wet cells, had enough strength to raise Father Point. He was still trying to check the ship's position when a couple of officers told him to clear out and get to his lifeboat. Instead Ferguson went back to his emergency transmitter, but the list was now so great that the acid had run out of the standby batteries. Ferguson finally abandoned the wireless room and headed for the rail where he shouted to the milling survivors on deck the only words of comfort that he could bring. Rescue ships were on their way, he told them.

The final lurch of the dying liner flung him into the water where he struggled to keep afloat for about fifteen minutes, he reckoned, before a lifeboat found him. By that time, the overcoat that Bamford had so thoughtfully provided was threatening to be the death of him. When the lifeboat found him, its sodden weight was pulling him down and it took him all his failing strength to pull himself out of the water. Later, Ferguson found himself among the survivors aboard the *Lady Evelyn*. Considering that he must have been nearly frozen, extremely tired and probably suffering from shock, Ferguson might have been forgiven for calling it a night. Instead, on finding that the *Lady Evelyn* had a wireless aboard but no operator, Ferguson broke into the wireless room and started transmitting to Father Point, calling for clothing, medical supplies and a special train for the survivors.

Bamford, the junior operator, also survived, to share in due course in the lofty commendation bestowed upon them by the chairman of the court of inquiry. 'You young gentlemen,' they were told, 'did great credit to the service you are in.' It was no less than the truth.

Ferguson had been right in supposing that only junior operators would be on duty at that hour of the morning. The assistant operator on watch at the Marconi station at Father Point was Crawford Leslie, and he was nineteen. Leslie had been at his post for less than an hour when Ferguson's first message came: 'Struck a ship,' Ferguson's morse key was spelling out. 'By; get officer in charge.' The single word 'By,' Leslie knew, was operator's jargon for 'stand by'. Leslie did what he was told. He woke up William Whiteside, the Marconi Company's superintendent at Father Point, shouting: 'The *Empress* is in distress.' Then Leslie bolted back to his headphones. By the time Whiteside reached the operating room, Ferguson was reporting that the *Empress* was listing terribly. Whiteside tapped back the vital question: 'What is your position?' 'Twenty miles from Rimouski,' Ferguson replied. Whiteside tried to get Feguson to verify the position, because he was not sure whether Ferguson meant 20 miles upstream or downstream. He was too late, for even as Ferguson tried to reply, Whiteside could hear the shrill morse note dying away, and knew that the liner's power supply was failing under the operator's hand. Many years later, Ferguson told how he had conveyed his plight more dramatically than any words could have done. As the power failed, he simply held his key down so that Whiteside could hear the whine of the signal fading into silence. But Whiteside knew that even if Ferguson could no longer transmit, he could probably still receive. Moreover, so long as the ship was still afloat, he would be standing by his set. 'Am sending *Lady Evelyn* and *Eureka* to your assistance,' he tapped out.

Then Whiteside sent out a 'CQ' – a general alarm call to any ship within range. It was a forlorn hope that another vessel would be near enough to help, but Whiteside was trying to reach the Norddeutscher Lloyd liner *Hannover*, which he knew should be somewhere near Rimouski, on her way upstream on her first voyage to Montreal. But the *Hannover* did not answer. In 1914, even those ships fitted with wireless did not always carry enough operators for a round-the-clock watch, and at two o'clock in the morning, the *Hannover*'s operator was probably asleep.

Leslie, meanwhile, was busy on the telephone. He quickly reached François Pouliot, the captain of the *Lady Evelyn*, which by then was back alongside the wharf at Rimouski. Whiteside took the telephone from Leslie, and told Pouliot that the *Empress* was sinking, but he did not know exactly where. Moreover, the *Eureka*, which had taken off Laurier, the *Empress's* pilot, and would best know the liner's position, was somewhere out in the darkness off Father Point again, collecting a pilot off another ship. Pouliot took the news calmly. There was time to find out, he said, because it would take him some minutes to get steam up. He would be off as soon as he could.

Leslie ran to the house that served John McWilliams in his various capacities as manager of the Great Northwestern Telegraph Company, meteorologist, signals officer, light-housekeeper, and general factotum to the big liners that passed Father Point. McWilliams had had a busy day. He had made up the local outgoing mail for the *Empress* and sent it aboard by the pilot cutter, and made sure his landlines were switched through for the Marconi Company's night traffic. Then he retired thankfully to his bed long after midnight. An hour and a half later, he was jerked from sleep by Leslie ringing 'SOS' on his doorbell. McWilliams ran downstairs in his night clothes to hear Leslie's dramatic story. Even as McWilliams looked out into the night, he could see the steaming lights of the *Eureka* as the cutter returned to her berth. He ran to the quay to meet her. As the little boat bustled alongside the quay, the quayside telephone was ringing frantically. Jean Baptiste Belanger, her captain, strode ashore and picked it up. 'The *Empress* is sinking, rush,' Whiteside was shouting.

Belanger was not altogether unused to dramatic instructions in his job. It was he who four years before had lent his blue serge uniform and white-topped cap to Chief Inspector Dew of Scotland Yard so that he could be smuggled aboard the liner *Montrose*, disguised as a pilot, for his confrontation with Dr Crippen. But he had never been more shaken than by the apparition in a striped nightshirt that ran onto the little pier at Father Point at that same moment, shouting hysterically: 'For God's sake get downstream. The *Empress* has gone under.' Belanger moved so fast that he left the earpiece of the telephone swinging on the end of its cord. Over the open line, Whiteside at the other end could hear him shouting: 'Cut those ropes, let's get away quick. The *Empress* is sinking.'

The *Eureka* went foaming into the night. Later, Whiteside saw more lights out in the river, racing downstream past Father Point. The *Lady Evelyn*, too, was on her way. Belanger had his ship clear of the dock at Father Point in about two minutes. With her bow wave curling back from her stem, and the wake boiling under her low counter, she raced off eastward as fast as her powerful screw could drive her. The *Lady Evelyn*, some time behind her, was running blind at full speed through the fog to reach the *Empress*, the glow of her navigating lights reflecting eerily off the swirling blanket around her. Her crew took their lives in their hands that night. Never, one of them recalled later, had a ship been steamed through fog in that part of the river at the speed they made that night. They had been told to drive the little mail tender for all she was worth, and they did. For all their frantic haste, it was a long run down river. It took the *Eureka* about three quarters of an hour to reach the scene of the disaster, the *Lady Evelyn* rather longer.

The *Lady Evelyn* found her first evidence of tragedy when a lifeboat loomed out of the fog. 'For God's sake hurry up,' a man was yelling as the mail steamer swirled alongside. 'There are thousands drowning just ahead.' Tragically, it was no longer true. The two little ships had run a gallant race against time, and they had lost. By the time they arrived, the *Empress* had gone, and there was nobody left alive in the river.

CHAPTER 10

The *Storstad* to the Rescue

As the *Storstad* inched forward in the fog, the sounds that Mrs Andersen had first heard were becoming hideously clear to the men beside her on the bridge. The shocked listeners could hear individual shouts and cries now, rising from the hundreds of human beings struggling in the water. A high, wailing cacophony of sound rose from the mist-shrouded river. Andersen stopped the *Storstad's* engines. Then he rang down to the engine room for 'slow astern', and began to ease his battered ship slowly backwards towards those terrible cries, edging her in as near as he dared, for if he came too close the *Storstad's* great single screw, churning beneath the water like a giant scythe, would simply add to the casualty list.

Toftenes, no longer needed on the bridge, was sent hurrying aft to the collier's overhanging counter stern to guide the ship in towards the survivors with shouts and hand signals. By the time the big collier had come to a halt in the water, Toftenes was later to maintain stoutly, he was so close to the first of the swimmers in the dark water below him that he could not only hear them, but could see them as they splashed towards the ship's side.

By now, young Saxe had completed his task of clearing away the boats. They dangled awkwardly in their davits as they hung out over the side of the collier's low superstructure, ready at the word to drop the short distance into the river below. Their crews of startled, half-dressed seamen and stokers waited for the orders to lower away. The *Storstad* had four boats. Three were regulation wooden lifeboats, designed to hold about thirty men each. The fourth was a little gig, which doubled as the collier's tender and maid of all work. At a considerable squeeze, she could hold about fifteen people. As the *Storstad* eased to a halt. Andersen ordered the boats away. One after the other, they splashed raggedly into the river and began to pull into the fog towards the shouts and screams that echoed across the water. They started the search pretty well together, for the Norwegians' boatwork had been good. All four boats were in the water within about three minutes of Andersen's order to lower away.

Despite the cold, the half-dressed Norwegians were sweating as they dragged at the heavy ash oars. None of the boats had more than four rowers, and it was hard work to move the big, double-ended lifeboats at any speed. Even so, with four men at the oars of each boat, and an officer at the tiller, well over half the collier's crew were actually out on the river, racing against time to save the men and women struggling around them before the icy water froze the life from them.

Einar Reinertz, the *Storstad's* second mate, had been asleep in his bunk when the collision came. Reinertz was new to the ship, so new that when Andersen ordered him away in charge of one of the ship's boats, Reinertz did not even know the names of the men in his crew. The only one he could put a name to was Jensen, the cook. Not that it mattered, for anybody who could pull an oar was welcome at that moment, and the Norwegian was not born who could not handle a boat. Reinertz and his men were working against time as they splashed into the river, unhooked the falls, and began to pull through the darkness towards those terrible cries. They had not far to go, for the liner was still afloat, though she was on her side. Even as he watched, standing in the sternsheets of the long wooden boat with his hand on the tiller, Reinertz saw the last moments of the big liner. She rolled over, further and further, until her masts were under water. Then she lifted her counter stern clear of the water and slid beneath the surface.

As she went, Reintertz claimed, there was a violent explosion; he believed it was her boilers bursting.

The *Storstad* was lying very close to the spot, not more than a couple of lengths away, Reinertz reckoned, so that it took the lifeboat only two or three minutes to reach the first of the survivors. Reinertz and his men believed that they saved about fifty people on that first trip. Nobody kept count, for there was no time. The men at the oars were too busy reaching out into the darkness, grabbing at frozen, gasping bodies who had to be dragged from the water like so many sodden bundles. However many they picked up, it was far more than the thirty or so that the boat should have carried, so many more that the survivors themselves were crying out to Reinertz not to take any more aboard. Considering how close they had come to drowning, their desire not to find themselves back in the river was understandable. But Reinertz and his men went on dragging people from the river until the boat was too crammed to hold any more, for he dared not lose the chance to save a single survivor, in case it was too late by the time he returned. He was right. By the time his boat had unloaded her survivors and set off back for a second load, there were few left to save. On that second trip, they found only about twelve or thirteen still alive. The third journey was even worse. For all the Norwegians found was a little knot of people standing on an upturned boat, and a man sprawled across it, half dead from exhaustion and exposure. The *Storstad's* men saved them all, and they also brought back some passengers who were past human aid, for although they were wearing life-jackets, they were already dead, their heads drooping limply beneath the surface.

Reinertz, like virtually every other rescuer, stayed out in the river until there was no possibility of finding further life to save. In Reinertz's case, that was a considerable feat of endurance. He had rushed from his bunk when the ships collided and manned his boat so fast that he was almost naked as he led his crew through the chill Canadian night. In the darkness and confusion, it is doubtful if anybody noticed. If they did, it is even less likely that they cared.

FOURTEEN MINUTES

Jakob Saxe, the young third mate, had little enough time to reflect upon that appalling encounter in the fog in which he had unwittingly played so significant a part. He was working frantically at the head of a scratch party to clear the collier's boats away for lowering, and by the time he had finished, Andersen was shouting to him to get the boats into the water. As the junior officer aboard the ship, Saxe's command was the little gig. As the rope falls squealed through the heavy sheaves, Saxe leaped into his boat, grabbed the tiller and steered his crew out into the night. His men, he said later, rowed 'like demons' to reach the source of those terrible shouts and screams. Like Reinertz, Saxe soon had his little lifeboat so full of survivors that she was in danger of swamping. As she headed back towards the collier's side after her first rescue trip, however, Saxe heard a woman's shrill cry echoing across the water close astern of the retreating boat. It was more than Saxe could do to leave her to die in the freezing river. 'Boys, turn the boat round,' he shouted. 'There's a woman calling.' The passengers jammed into the little gig protested bitterly at the order. If anybody else was taken aboard, they would all die when the boat swamped. Saxe, barely out of his teens, was master of the situation. 'I'm in command of this boat,' he shouted back angrily, 'Turn her round.' The gig crawled back on her tracks to where the faint cries could still be heard. The woman was hauled gasping into the boat, which then headed back to her parent ship. She made it with a few inches of freeboard to spare.

Kendall, wrenched from his grip on the bridge rail as the ship rolled over, was flung into the water and carried down deep. When he rose to the surface, his ship had gone; instead there was a frothing line of water where the waves of her passing swept inward and fused momentarily into a ridge over her grave. At that moment a loose grating rose to the surface directly underneath Kendall, and he grabbed it thankfully. A boat full of survivors was bobbing in the water nearby, and a voice shouted: 'There's the captain.' Kendall was grabbed by strong hands and hauled over the gunwale.

Kendall had lost his ship. Now, he took command of the lifeboat and started to rescue the struggling human beings who, minutes before, had been his passengers and his crew. Toiling in the darkness, his men hauled in survivor after survivor until about sixty men and women were in the boat, and there was no room for more. Many others were clinging to the lifelines looped along the side of the boat, the thin ropes twisted around their wrists. Kendall told the survivors in the boat to keep a grip on their less fortunate comrades in the water in case they slipped away and drowned from cold and exhaustion.

Some distance away, Kendall could see the lights of a ship. Painfully his overloaded command pulled towards the stranger. On the way, they passed two of *Storstad*'s boats. In one, a single passenger was sprawled across the thwarts, while the crew were pulling another survivor into the boat. In the second boat, about three survivors were huddled, and another was being hauled in to join them. As Kendall's boat wallowed alongside the collier, he could see several more of his own ship's boats alongside her, together with one of the *Storstad*'s. The Norwegians, those who were not out on the river looking for survivors, were hauling passengers to safety. They lowered six or seven wooden companionways, rope ladders and anything else they could find. Mercifully, the sheer weight of the collier's cargo made their job easier, for she was so low in the water that her rails were only a few feet above the surface. Even so, some of the survivors were so far gone from cold, exhaustion and shock that they had to be hauled bodily up the ship's side, suspended like sacks from the end of a rope.

Kendall put his own survivors aboard the *Storstad*. Then he called for volunteers from among his crew to go back and search for more. Ten of his men offered to go with him. Kendall kept six who had got into the boat without swimming for their lives, and who were at least dry. He threw all the boat's sails and rigging into the sea to make more room for survivors. Then, although he was soaked and exhausted, Kendall took an oar and helped to row the lifeboat back towards the spot where the *Empress* had gone down.

Altogether, it was said, Kendall and his crew spent three hours rowing back and forth across the river, and in that time, they saved no fewer than 73 lives; 75 according to another report. It is doubtful in fact if Kendall or anybody else could have said exactly how many human beings they dragged alive from the river. Had there been more to save, Kendall and his men would have saved them. But there were no more; just dark bundles, drifting sluggishly downstream on the gentle current. Painstakingly, Kendall hauled each bundle alongside, searching vainly for a spark of life before abandoning it and moving on to the next. Kendall made one final effort. Some distance away he could see one of his own ship's lifeboats, and he took his own boat alongside it. But it was empty, smashed and half full of water.

Kendall's men rowed slowly back to the *Storstad.* and Kendall climbed to the collier's bridge. There, as the dawn light spread across the broad river, the two captains came face to face.

'Are you the master of this ship?', Kendall demanded. Andersen agreed. 'You have sunk my ship,' Kendall accused the Norwegian. 'You were going full speed ahead, and in that dense fog.' 'I was not going full speed,' Andersen retorted. 'You were going full speed.' The argument developed no further. The *Storstad's* own river pilot, Lachance, had arrived aboard the collier from the *Eureka*, and he intervened between the two angry men. 'Don't say anything,' Lachance told Kendall. 'You had better go below.' Kendall walked from the bridge into the chart room, and there he collapsed. He remembered nothing further for a considerable time.

CHAPTER 11

The Crew in Action

Nearly forty men were on duty in the *Empress's* machinery spaces when the collision occurred. All but a handful were working in the two great boiler-rooms, amid the blinding glare and leaping shadows of the stokeholds. Two engineers, two leading firemen, fifteen firemen and twelve trimmers were needed to keep the steam gauges steady at the 220 lb mark. Astern of them in the engine-room, separated from the boiler-rooms by the massive thwartships coal bunker, only eight men were on duty, three engineers and five greasers.

Two of them, engineers Robert Brennan and Robert Liddell, were each in charge of one of the main engines. Their function was to act as a human link with the bridge far above, turning the throttle valves and moving the engines ahead or astern as the telegraph directed them. James McEwen, the *Empress*'s junior fourth engineer, was on duty in Number Three stokehold in the after-boiler-room when the collision came. The shock was not even hard enough to make him lose his balance. But it was sufficient to fill the stokehold with a choking, swirling black cloud of coal dust. McEwen could see nothing through the murk, but he could hear a deep roaring sound. Something, he decided, was blowing off fairly hard – possibly escaping steam, or boiler feed-water under pressure.

Cautiously, McEwen inched his way into the coal dust to see if he could find the cause. What he saw, as he moved through the choking dust, was a wall of uater, leaping and crashing through the bunker door on the right-hand side of the stokehold. He turned and ran for his life, the flood swirling at his heels, towards the narrow tunnel that led deep under the great thwartships bunker to the comparative safety of the engine-room on the other side of Number Six bulkhead. At the far end of that tunnel was a watertight door, and McEwen's life hung on his ability to get through that tunnel before the watertight door slammed down before his eyes and left him to die in the darkness of the tunnel. McEwen burst through the tunnel, swung himself up on to the engineers' control platform, and yelled to the men standing there that the stokehold was flooding. Already, a shallow tide was flooding through the tunnel into the engine-room. A greaser threw himself on to the operating lever of the door, and McEwen saw the great steel door begin to slide down across the mouth of the tunnel, cutting off the flow of water. That hole, at least, was stopped up. But there were many others.

McEwen swung himself up the tall engine-room ladders, and out into the working passageway that ran overhead, linking the access doors to the boiler-rooms. He knew that the after-boiler-room was flooded, but was the forward-boiler-room dry? As he headed for the door leading down to the forward-boiler-room, he met his colleague on duty there, George O'Donovan, hurrying towards him. O'Donovan told McEwen that the forward stokeholds, too, were deep under water, and th whole boiler-room was flooding.

O'Donovan had much the same story to tell as McEwen. He had been standing his watch in the Number Two stokehold, twenty-three feet below the waterline, when a terrifying jet of water burst from Number Two bunker door, crashing and thundering into the narrow stokehold like the bursting of a dam. No power on earth could close the bunker door against that jet of water hurtling from the door as from the nozzle of a gigantic hose. O'Donovan yelled to the men on duty to get out before they drowned where they stood. Flinging down their shovels and slices, the firemen leaped for the ladders leading to whatever safety they might find on deck.

O'Donovan, having reached the temporary refuge of the working passage overhead, shouted down to the men in the engine-room that his boiler-room was flooded. Then he headed back to shut off the great ventilation fans that fed air to the furnaces. One was still thundering away in the darkness, but now it was sucking, not air, but salt water. O'Donovan switched off the fans he could reach, and returned to the engine-room. By the time he got back, his colleagues there were scrambling frantically up the ladder to the surface.

McEwen had taken a different path. Both boiler-rooms might be flooded, but there was still a watertight door between them, and it was his job to try to close it. If that door could be closed, it might stop or at least slow the water rushing through the ship. The levers operating the watertight door in Number Five bulkhead were situated by the third class dining-saloon, forward of the working passage. Already the passage was listing ominously, but McEwen lurched his way along it, determined to drop the door if he could. By the time McEwen had stumbled along the passageway to the third class saloon, a swirling tide was lapping across the passageway. McEwen tried to cross the flood, but he could no longer keep his footing on the sloping, half-submerged deck. If the water had reached that level, it meant that it was already within eight feet of the top of the *Empress*'s bulkheads, and once it lapped over the top, flowing uninterruptedly along the deck above, there could be only one end. McEwen abandoned his hopeless task. So far as he knew, nobody else reached the levers that night.

McEwen was a brave man, and so were his colleagues. He struggled back along the reeling passageway, not to the comparative safety of the deck, but down the long ladders to the control-platform far below. The engineers and greasers were still standing at their posts on the platform, but the great engines were still now, and the lights were dying to an eerie glow. McEwen heard a voice call to them to clear out. They had done all they could to save the ship, and now they were free to save themselves. If they could.

FOURTEEN MINUTES

The man who ordered the abandonment of the engine-room was William Sampson, the *Empress*'s Chief Engineer. Sampson was an Irishman, a veteran of his trade with a third of a century at sea behind him. He had commissioned the ship eight years before; this was his 96th voyage in her. All the way from Quebec to Father Point he had stayed on duty. Then, at Father Point, he had headed thankfully for his bunk. But he had barely reached his cabin, astern of the engine-room, when he felt the shock of the collision. Sampson hurried back towards his post on the control-platform, calling to everybody he met to get the bulkhead doors closed. The men on duty below, with the black tide swirling through the tunnel from the after-boiler-room, had needed no orders. Even as Sampson lowered himself down the ladders, he could see the vital door to the boiler-room rumbling down on its guides.

The ship was listing horribly, but the engine-room itself was dry, save for a small quantity of water from the boiler-room, already draining off into the bilges. For a few moments, Sampson did not think the situation was hopeless or even particularly dangerous. But then he realised that everything in the engine-room was falling silent and the needles of the steam gauges were dropping ominously back towards their stops. Sampson picked up the bridge telephone. Kendall's voice answered him. 'For heaven's sake try and beach her,' Sampson urged the captain. Kendall's reply was terse. 'Do the best you can,' he replied.

For a few desperate seconds, Sampson and his men tried to drive the dying ship towards the shallow water of the Gaspe shore, but it was too late. The great cranks swung over wearily five or six times, and then hissed sullenly to a halt. There was no steam coming from the flooded boilers, and the engine-room lights, too, were flickering out like tired glow-worms as the dynamos whined to a halt. Sampson ordered his men out, and turned his back for the last time on the machinery of which he had been so proud. Reaching safety was no easy task. There were three tall ladders and platforms to negotiate, the ship was rapidly rolling on to her side, and the lights were almost out. Sampson was not a young man, and left to himself, he knew that he could never have negotiated them alone. But the younger men stayed with him. Patiently, they shepherded their old chief up the high ladders and across the tottering platforms to whatever fate lay above them in the night.

They reached the deck, Sampson recalled later, 'like flies crawling up a wall'. By the time they got there, the liner's list was so steep that there was no longer anything to stand on. Instead, Sampson and his men crawled out along one of the tall steel kingposts that supported the ship's cargo derricks. The kingpost, normally vertical, now reached out horizontally across the river as the engineers inched their way along it, straddling it like a greasy pole. Sampson never reached the end of the post, for a mass of loose gear, breaking free from the left hand boats now high above his head, came crashing down and swept him into the river. When he came gasping to the surface, he found himself trapped in a mass of wreckage underneath an upturned lifeboat. Somehow he fought his way loose from the trap, swam to another boat, and clung to the gunwale, shouting feebly for help. In the darkness and the uproar, however, he was neither seen nor heard. Sampson, too weak to pull himself to safety over the boat's side, felt his numbed grip loosening. 'If you can't save me, then goodbye,' he called despairingly, and began to sink for the last time. As he did so, the ship's butcher heard his faint voice, and pulled Sampson to safety. When the old man came to, he was stretched out on a bunk aboard the *Storstad*. Appropriately, it was that of the collier's chief engineer.

How many of the *Empress*'s bulkhead doors were closed that night, and how many were left open to the inrushing water, was never positively established. Altogether, 32 men should have been standing by those watertight doors and hatches. Just thirteen of them lived, and of those, only five were from emergency stations on the right-hand side of the ship. It seems all too certain that of the rest, many died at their posts in the darkness, struggling with the heavy doors, until it was too late to escape.

At least one man lived to tell the tale. His adventures were probably typical of what happened below decks in those critical minutes. Joseph Hayes was an assistant chief steward in third class. Clad in trousers and slippers, he left the stewards' sleeping quarters after the collision, to find the working alleyway filled with smoke, and the evil stench of hot coals doused in water. It was rising from the stokehold access doors, for far below his feet, hundreds of tons of icy water were hissing into the white hot furnaces. Hayes' emergency station was at the controls of Number 78 watertight door, which separated the Third Class saloon from the sleeping quarters. Hayes ran to the lever which operated the door on the deck below, and tried to crank it closed. He strained at the handle, but he could not close the door, for it ran horizontally, and as ill luck would have it, the door worked from right to left. Against the fearsome list, Hayes was trying in effect to force the heavy door uphill, and strain as he might at the crank handle, it would not shut. He might have succeeded, he believed, if he had had more time. It will never be known for certain, but it seems likely that all over the ship, doors were left open to the cascading waters because men had neither strength nor time to crank them home against the increasing list.

Second Class steward Frank Harrison also tried to close his allotted door Number 86, and like Hayes he failed. It is doubtful if either man realised the fact, but the doors that Hayes and Harrison were trying to close were at that moment, the two most important in the *Empress*. Given the kind of damage the *Empress* had suffered, it is doubtful if she would have been kept afloat for long. But had those two doors been wound securely home, they might at least have slowed the fatal inrush of water for those few vital minutes while the men on deck swung out the boats, and while the passengers trapped below struggled along darkened passageways and up the crazily leaning companionways to the chance of safety. Harrison, like Hayes, failed because of lack of time. He scrambled to the operating gear and took the key from its bulkhead clips, fitted it over the head of the winding shaft flush with the deck, and painstakingly cranked the door closed. It does not seem as if Harrison ever discovered that it was difficult if not impossible to wind the door closed against the list of the ship. The darkness, and the steadily deepening water, beat him before he could even try.

When Kendall told him to see to the boats, First Officer Jones peeled off his uniform overcoat, threw it aside and ran down the bridge companionway to the boat deck. Above him as he worked, the *Empress*'s siren was bellowing into the night a single unbroken blast: 'All hands to the boats.' Already, half-dressed men were clattering up the companionways from the crew quarters, throwing themselves on the laced boat covers and the cleated falls, working with desperate speed in the gloom as the teak deck listed ominously beneath their feet. Discipline was good, Jones noted. These interminable boat drills were paying a handsome dividend.

Jones and his men got three right-hand boats cleared and lowered, and were starting to work on a fourth boat, Number Seven. But by that time, the list was so great that they could not work without something to hold on to. Jones lost his grip, and simply slid down the deck into the river. Gasping in the cold, he was trying to swim clear of the tangle of ropes and tackle dangling from the davits when a lifeboat bobbed alongside him, and the men in it hauled him from the water. Jones, too, began frantically fishing human beings out of the water until the boat could take no more. Whether the people aboard were crew or passengers or both, Jones did not know, for it was too dark to see. Clumsily, for the boat was full of sodden, exhausted men and women, Jones's scratch crew rowed their way slowly towards the lights of the nearby steamer. They unloaded their survivors aboard the *Storstad*, and rowed back towards the spot where the *Empress* had gone down. That second trip they rescued eight men and three or four women. They could not save more, for the fog was still heavy on the surface of the water, and they could see the swimmers only when they were close alongside. Back they went to the *Storstad* with their haul, and off again into the night to try for a third load. But there was nothing to be seen in the river this time except dark, half-submerged bundles bobbing on the gentle swell. There were more lights on the river now, for the *Lady Evelyn* had arrived. Jones and his men paddled wearily alongside her, and climbed aboard.

John Murphy was one of the two quartermasters on duty on the *Empress*'s bridge. Each by custom spent two hours at the wheel and two hours acting as extra lookout, or at whatever task the officer of the watch set them. Murphy had completed his trick at the wheel and was standing by on the bridge when the *Storstad* struck. Murphy's last task on the bridge was to sound the emergency signal calling the *Empress*'s crew to the boats – a single prolonged blast on the siren. Murphy tugged at the siren cord and held it down, letting the great blast of sound roar on and on. Even before he let go, he could see men running to the boat stations. Then Murphy himself ran down the bridge steps to his own alloted boat. This was Number Twelve, on the left-hand side. There were three or four men there already, and together they laboured to clear the boat from her restraining chocks. But already, the terrible list was against them. They could not swing the massive boat out and up against the steadily increasing angle of the deck, so Murphy and the others crossed, or slid, to the right-hand side of the boat deck and helped to get Number Thirteen boat into the water. Like First Officer Jones, Murphy saw no signs of disorder. Everybody was doing what he could to help.

By the time Number Thirteen was launched, the water was so high up the side of the ship that Murphy could simply walk off the deck into the sea. He jumped in, and found himself clinging to Number Fifteen boat, which had capsized. He got alongside Number Thirteen, climbed in, and started rescuing survivors. When the boat was full, Murphy set out for the *Storstad*. Then, like Kendall and Jones, Murphy went back for more. His boat's second rescue mission was surprisingly successful, for they picked up another 30 people. But that was all they saved that night. On their third expedition they found, as Kendall had found, as Jones had found, that there was simply nobody left alive to save. The *Eureka* had arrived on the scene, so Murphy and his mates made their way alongside her. Murphy, like a good seaman, was making the boat secure alongside the little tug when somebody shouted to him to let her go, and indeed there was no more use for a lifeboat. So Murphy threw the painter aside and let the boat drift away into the dawn.

The fact that so many of the *Empress*'s seamen not only escaped alive from their crowded quarters in the big liner's fo'c's'le but were awake and at work within seconds was due largely to the quick thinking of a veteran seaman named Alec Radley. Radley was the *Empress*'s Chief Bosun's Mate, the senior petty officer responsible to the Chief Officer for supervising the day-to-day work of the seamen about the ship's decks. As the liner slid away after her brief halt at Father Point, Radley was on deck, making sure that everything was snugged down for the long ocean passage ahead, when he saw the *Storstad*'s bows looming through the fog. He lived to describe vividly the events of the next few minutes, exactly as he remembered them:

> Just before she struck, I ran forward and shouted a warning to the men off watch who were asleep, forty or fifty of them. Then I ran back to the boat deck to break out the lifeboats. The last of the boats swung back and forth and nearly threw me overboard. It was fouled. I passed two axes to somebody in the bows to chop the lines, but he let the axes fall overboard. The ship settled and pulled the boat under water until the lines broke. We all went under water. When we came to the surface, the boat was upside down.

At least one other man had a grandstand view of disaster. He was young Ordinary Seaman J.H. Pryce who had been standing the middle watch that night. Pryce's immediate task had been to haul in and secure the wire Jacob's ladder down which pilot Laurier had climbed to the deck of the *Eureka* a few minutes before. He was just finishing when the liner came to a halt in the fog. Pryce had looked up to see the *Storstad*'s bows bearing irresistibly down upon him. He was still watching astonished a few seconds later when the collier buried her chisel bow into the liner's side with a gentle crunch. 'She cut us,' Pryce said simply, 'as clean as a can opener.'

As it happened, only the previous year, aboard the Britsh liner *Devonian,* Pryce had been among the seamen of many nations who had watched helplessly while the little immigrant ship *Volturno*, packed with passengers, had burned like a torch amid mountainous Atlantic seas. Pryce had managed to save two lives on that occasion, and now he was on his way to England to receive the Albert Medal for his bravery. Pryce raced to his station on the boat-deck. He got there in time to see Number One boat being lowered. It had not taken long for her to reach the water, for Number One was the seaboat, the emergency boat always ready for instant launching when the ship was under way. It went down into the river so fast, Pryce recalled, that there was nobody ready to get into it as it splashed into the river.

Pryce was probably the last man to see Chief Officer Steede alive. Steede's death was, and still is, something of a mystery. According to several survivors, Steede was swept to his death when one of the left-hand lifeboats, possibly Number Eight, broke loose and crashed down upon him. Pryce's account was rather different. According to him, he and the Chief Officer, who was still in his pyjamas, were clinging to the coamings on the roof of the wireless cabin, feverishly trying to free the spare lifeboat gear lashed to the top of the little deckhouse where Ferguson and Bamford were crouched over their transmitter. Since it must have been at about that time that Steede had appeared in the doorway of the wireless cabin and told Ferguson to send out his vital distress message, the time and the place fitted neatly with Ferguson's own account. Steede and Pryce were still struggling with the lashings when a mass of heavy gear crashed down across the wireless cabin roof onto the men, and thundered across the deck. Steede was swept aside, and Pryce did not see him again. It is doubtful if anybody did. Steede's body was taken from the river a day or two later.

There may or may not have been another witness of those seconds when the *Storstad* bore down through the fog. According to one newspaper report, which was never confirmed, the other eyewitness was an amateur photographer, and he missed the picture of the year. The photographer, the story ran, was on deck, trying to take a picture through the fog with the aid of a primitive tray of flash powder, when the *Storstad*'s bows loomed through the fog. For a moment, the astonished cameraman thought that the *Empress* was passing very close to an anchored ship. He soon learned better. However, before the photographer could aim his camera and touch off his tray of flash powder, the collier struck. The jolt was just severe enough to knock the passenger off his balance, and his camera went flying. Nonetheless he survived to render up, not a photograph of that dramatic meeting, but a vivid word picture of the occasion. As the collier drifted away from the liner's side, he was quoted as saying, the water flooded round the *Storstad*'s bows into the gaping wound in the liner's side, 'like a millrace, frothing and hissing.'

Many of the events remain a mystery. For instance, nobody ever established whether or not there was an explosion aboard the *Empress* as the ship went down. Kendall himself denied it, and he was as well qualified as anybody alive to know. All that happened, he said, was that a great gush of escaping air burst from the ship as she plunged beneath the surface. Sampson, the Chief Engineer, also denied it and he, too, should have known. And yet survivor after survivor spoke of being hurled into the sea by a massive explosion, and several survivors were reported to have been scalded or burned by fire or by escaping steam. As with so many accounts of the disaster, the stories are irreconcilable.

Then there were the stories of the left-hand side lifeboats. Desperate attempts were made to lower them, and several at least must have been cleared from their chocks ready for lowering, for there were reports of the boats swinging in from their davits until they dangled over the heads of the men who were trying to launch them, so far inboard that they could not be launched down the sloping side of the ship anyway. Moreover, report after report spoke of them breaking away, killing and maiming all those unfortunate enough to be in their path. A Salvation Army staff Captain named McAmmond claimed that several boats filled with women and children broke away from their falls and fell across the deck to crash into the lower rails. McAmmond was a brave and capable man who saved not only his own life but that of many fellow beings by his exertions that night, and his account of the disaster was soberly matter-of-fact.

Unfortunately, it is not entirely clear if he actually saw the incidents with the left-hand boats, or had merely heard of them. Another survivor spoke of seeing women crushed against the right-hand rail by liferafts, presumably the Englehardt collapsibles, that had broken away. It seems extremely likely; a great deal of deck gear certainly broke loose from the *Empress* that night as she turned on her beam ends, and the collapsibles, designed to be quickly and easily released from their housings, may well have been among them. Indeed, a professional marine engineer named James Rankin, of whom more will be heard, claimed that as he struggled to reach the boat-deck from his Second Class cabin, he could hear the boats rumbling and slithering across the deck above him. The collapsibles were heavy objects of wood and canvas, and they could quite certainly have killed and maimed as they hurtled across the deck into the lower rails. Nevertheless they were featherweights compared with the regular lifeboats. The *Empress*'s steel boats weighed two and a half tons each. One of those, plunging across the deck would not merely have crashed into the lower rail; it would have flattened rails, davits and anything else in its path. We cannot be absolutely sure it happened. Significantly, Kendall, who from his precarious position on the left-hand bridge wing was in as good a position as anybody to see what was going on, was specifically to deny any knowledge of whether or not anybody was killed by boats falling from the left-hand davits. Equally specifically, he was to deny knowledge of what actually happened to Chief Officer Steede.

Augustus Gaade had been asleep in Cabin 218 for about two hours when the *Storstad* struck. The jolt of the collision woke Gaade, who was a light sleeper, and he put his head out of his cabin door in time to be told by a hurrying nightwatchman that the liner had been struck amidships. Gaade sent the watchman running with orders to call all the passengers, get them into life-jackets, and muster them on deck. Then Gaade put on trousers, jacket and shoes, and headed for his station at Number One Boat. Gaade met several women passengers, and told them briskly to put on life-jackets and go on deck. Instead, several of them clung to him and begged him to save them. Chief Stewards of Atlantic liners in 1914 did not lose their aplomb, even when the vessel was manifestly sinking under them. Nonetheless, Mr Gaade's professional patience was clearly under strain. 'No one will be saved unless you give us a chance to get out on deck and get the boats out,' he told them.

Gaade joined a group of men working feverishly to swing out Number One Boat, but already the fatal list was beginning to hamper their efforts. For a few moments they strained vainly against the chocks, and then the boat broke loose and swung violently out over the water, hurling six or eight men into the river before they could recover their balance. Another six who had been pushing frantically against the side of the boat were sent swinging wildly out into space, clinging to the gunwales like so many monkeys.

Gaade did not get into the boat. Instead, he yelled to the men clambering aboard her to pick up all the people they could, and keep the boat close to the ship's side. Gaade was joined by another figure on the listing boat-deck. It was his friend and shipmate MacDonald, the liner's purser. By common instinct, the two men headed for the traditional seat of authority, the liner's bridge. As Gaade and MacDonald crawled like flies along the deck towards the bridge, they saw

Kendall. The captain was still at his post of command, the extreme wing of the left-hand flying bridge, now pointing skywards like a dying finger. Kendall was hanging to the bridge wing with one hand, while with the other he bawled instructions through a megaphone to the men still struggling to free the left-hand boats. Even if they heard his orders above the uproar of screams and yells that filled the night, they could no longer carry them out. All they could do now was try to save their lives as the ship rolled over and flung them into the heaving river.

Gaade hauled himself up hand-over-hand until he was beside Kendall on the bridge-wing. 'I suppose there's no chance of running her ashore?' Gaade asked, but Kendall said no, for there was no steam. Gaade's professional self-possession did not desert him. 'Well, this looks to be about the finish,' he said, as the ship slid steadily over on to her beam ends, and the dark water climbed higher and higher up the deck. 'Yes,' Kendall replied shortly, 'and a terrible finish it is, too.'

Gaade was still on the bridge-wing with Kendall, clinging to the bridge rail as the great ship rolled further and further over. To his astonishment, Gaade watched the two great black and yellow funnels swinging over in a great arc until they slapped into the water together, and Gaade saw the black river begin to swirl down their enormous mouths into the boilers, like water down a gigantic plughole. That was his last glimpse of the ship, for at that moment Gaade, like Kendall, was hurled out into the river and was carried deep beneath its surface.

Gaade, who could not swim, very nearly drowned on the spot. He was going down for the last time, he believed, when he grabbed at an object in the darkness. He did not know what it was, but it was buoyant, and it at least enabled him to keep his head out of the water. He actually hung on, he believed, for about twenty minutes, before he realised that he was clinging to a corpse in a life-jacket. After a while, Gaade drifted among some floating wreckage, and he parted thankfully with his grisly supporter. Gaade later said he

THE CREW IN ACTION

believed the corpse that had saved his life was one of those killed before they ever entered the water, when masses of gear had been crashing down across the listing deck of the *Empress*. Gaade was one of hundreds who by pure chance survived. Although he could not swim a stroke, and had no lifebelt, he lived. Purser MacDonald, who was an excellent swimmer, did not.

Williams, the Chief Second Class Steward, had made sure that the night-watchmen were calling the passengers on the two lower decks before he scrambled to his boat station, clad simply in a pair of trousers. Trying to launch his own allotted boat on the left-hand side was clearly a waste of time, so he went to help Moore, the Third Officer, who had left the bridge and was trying to get Number Thirteen boat over the side. The men got it half way out, and then the boat jammed between the davits. Moore told Williams to climb in and try to twist the block of the falls to clear the boat. Williams did so successfully – so successfully that the boat broke free and swung wildly out into the darkness, flinging Williams flat on his back in the boat. The steward, bruised but alive, helped to fill the boat with survivors, and then headed for the *Storstad*. There, Williams left the boat and went aboard the collier. Any man would have understood and endorsed his reason for doing so. Williams, professionally attentive to the needs of a passenger even worse off than himself, had made the supreme sacrifice. He had given away his trousers.

One of the *Empress's* acknowledged characters was her First Class bar steward, a big, jovial man named Tom. Everybody aboard the ship knew Tom, and Tom, after the manner of his kind, knew everybody. For all his patrons he had a cheerful greeting; for his regulars, and the ship had many such, there was always a friendly welcome back when they came aboard. Curiously, nobody seemed to know his other name. That was how a passenger named Henderson was to remember him. Henderson struggled from his cabin towards the deck in the first chaotic minutes after the collision and there, battling his way on deck beside him, was Tom. The steward had a life-jacket in his hands; Henderson had not. Tom looked at the passenger's empty hands, and asked quietly; 'Are you married?' Yes, Henderson replied, he was. 'Well, then, take this,' said Tom, and before Henderson could reply, the big man had slipped the jacket over Henderson's head, and deftly tied the tapes. Then he turned, and in an instant was gone in the crowd. Henderson lived. Tom was not seen again.

Charles Spencer probably owed his life to his captain. Spencer was one of about a dozen bellboys aboard the liner, a seagoing pageboy on absolutely the lowest rung of a nautical career. As the *Empress* listed after the collision, young Spencer raced below to awaken his mates who slept down by the steerage quarters; by the time he got there, he was wading through water two feet deep. Two of his fellow bellboys, Charlie Baker and Harry Tunstall, were struggling to close the watertight doors nearby. Spencer never saw them again. By the time the boy reached the deck the *Empress*'s funnels were about to hit the water. One of them, he recalled, nearly sank a lifeboat. Charles Spencer found himself floundering in the river. He might never have emerged from it alive, but Captain Kendall grabbed the boy and helped him along. Together, captain and page were fished from the river by the men of lifeboat Number Three. Aboard the *Storstad*, Spender found another young shipmate Sam Baker. They were the only two bellboys to survive. There were no clothes to spare that night for shivering bellboys. However, Charlie Spencer and Sam Baker came ashore wearing old coal sacks, with the corners cut off to poke their heads and arms through.

CHAPTER 12

Struggle for Survival

Behind her, the *Empress* left perhaps 700 people struggling for their lives in water a few degrees above freezing. The number is an approximation, for we do not know, and never will know, exactly how many people got clear of the liner before she sank. We know only that about 490 people were dragged, or dragged themselves, more or less alive from the water, and that something over two hundred more were later taken dead from the river. Even of those who left the water alive, a number lived only for hours or minutes longer.

The Irvings were dead. Moreover, the manner of their death was attested in detail by at least one survivor. If his account was correct, and there is no reason whatever to doubt it, then their last minutes were both touching and gallant. Probably the last man to speak to the Irvings was a First Class passenger from Toronto named Frederick Abbott. It was in the passageway outside his cabin that he met the Irvings. 'Is the boat going down?' Irving asked him. Abbott did not know, but he said that it certainly looked like it. Irving turned to his wife in their stateroom. 'Hurry, dearie,' he called. 'There's no time to lose.' In response, Mrs Irving began to cry. Irving reached into the cupboard for the life-jackets stowed there. As he did so, the liner took that appalling lurch that so many survivors were to remember and describe. Irving was flung hard against the stateroom door, and when he straightened up, his face was covered in blood. Mrs Irving, nearly frantic with distress, flung her arms around her husband. Irving, master of so many dramatic moments on stage, was equally the master of this one. 'Keep cool,' he told his wife. Then, as she continued to cling to him, he forced a life-jacket over her head, pushed her through the stateroom door, and began to carry her up the companionway to the deck. 'Can I help you?' Abbott asked Irving. 'Look after yourself, old man,' the actor replied. 'God bless you, all the same.'

Abbott left the Irvings struggling up the listing companionway. He himself reached the deck and dived overboard. Struggling in the freezing water, Abbott grabbed a piece of timber, and as he did so, he looked up to watch the last moments of the *Empress*. Irving and his wife, Abbott said, were on deck. He was kissing her, and as the ship sank, the couple were clasped in each other's arms. They were not seen again.

A less romantic but almost equally specific account of the Irvings' last moments was given by Clayton Burt, the big factory manager who had been their companion at dinner. After the collision, Burt, hurrying on deck, had come across the Irvings. 'Save yourselves, for God's sake,' Burt had told them. 'We're sinking.' Irving, Burt said, went back to his cabin and got out two lifebelts. He put one on his wife, while Burt put the other on to Irving himself. Together, the three hurried on to the listing boat deck. Burt climbed the rail, and called to Irving to follow him over the rail and down the ship's side to the water's edge. Burt's last glimpse of the couple was of Irving helping his wife to climb over the rail. At that moment, Burt recalled, there was a tremendous explosion, and he was blown into the water. He did not see the Irvings again.

Tiria Townshend, the young lady from New Zealand, also saw the Irvings for a moment, as she struggled on deck against the increasing list of the ship. The Irvings were standing by the left hand rail and appeared, she said, to be 'conversing earnestly'. She did not see them again nor did she look for them again, for from then on Miss Townshend was to have troubles of her own. Another survivor told a similar story of seeing Irving trying to climb the rail. His name was James Galway, and he was one of the *Empress*'s quartermasters. Within the next few weeks Galway's reputation as a witness was to be such that it is doubtful if anybody would have believed him if he had offered to tell them the time. Nonetheless, there is no reason to suppose that his account of Irving's last moments aboard the ship was other than truthful.

Soon after the sinking, it was reported that Irving's body had been recovered. The actor had been identified by his ring, and clutched in his hand was a scrap of silk, presumably part of his wife's nightdress. Later the story was denied. The body, it was said, was not Irving's at all. Hilda Hagerson also drowned but her body was not found.

Sir Henry Seton-Karr, sportsman and traveller, was quite certainly dead. It was a splendid story of self-abnegation in a tradition that runs from Sir Philip Sidney to Captain Oates, and the world's newspaper readers loved it. Sir Henry, the story ran, had a stateroom right opposite that of a Mr Merton Darling, from Shanghai. As the ship began to roll over, the two men bumped into each other in the passageway. 'He had a life-jacket, but I had not,' Mr Darling was reported as saying. 'But seeing that I was empty-handed, he offered it to me. I refused to take it, but he said "Go on, man, take it. I'll try to get another." I again refused,' Mr Darling was said to have continued, 'and then he got angry, and pushing the lifebelt over me, pushed me along the corridor. He went back into the cabin, and I believe never came back again, for the ship sank in a few minutes. I owe my life to Sir Henry,' Mr Darling's narrative continued. 'He lost his because he insisted on me taking his lifebelt.'

It was a story to swell the English heart with pride. Unfortunately, Mr Darling's heart refused to swell. He did not wish to be cast as recipient of Sir Henry's final *beau geste*. Mr Darling issued an indignant denial. Sir Henry had indeed helped him on with a life-jacket, but it was the one Mr Darling was carrying anyway. Sir Henry, he maintained, was already wearing one.

Sir Henry's body, clad in evening dress, was recovered from the river a day or two later, some 40 miles downstream from the scene of the sinking. The records do not tell if Sir Henry's body was wearing a life-jacket. The body was identified by a handkerchief bearing Sir Henry's initials: his signet ring was reported to be missing. Later, Captain Belanger of the *Eureka* found his passport, and a letter of introduction signed by Sir Edward Grey, the Foreign Secretary. They were floating on a little raft of wreckage, where presumably Sir Henry himself had placed them. Sir Henry had left his widow a request that if he died on his travels, he should be buried in the land where he ended his days. His wishes were observed. Sir Henry lies today in the Mount Hermon Cemetery in Quebec.

The Irvings' fellow actors and travelling companions, the Nevilles, were also dead. So were Leonard Palmer, the financial journalist and his wife. So was Mrs Hart Bennet, from the Bahamas. The Salvation Army contingent was almost wiped out. Of more than 170 members just over two dozen were still alive. Commissioner Rees and his family were not among them. Of the 39 men of the band nine were still alive.

The death of Rees was something of a mystery. Detailed reports described how Salvationist Frank Morris had swum with the old man on his back until Rees, already sick before the journey began, slipped off and sank. Even then, it was said, Morris had dived again and again, trying vainly to find his old chief. It was all very circumstantial, and was repeated in many accounts of the tragedy. However, Morris himself was later reported to have denied the story completely. He had indeed helped the elderly Rees to reach the deck, he said, but then Morris himself had lost his footing and tumbled back down the companionway. By the time Morris struggled on deck again, Rees had disappeared. According to another report, Rees was last seen standing on deck, his arms folded, saying quietly; 'Thy will be done.' He had refused to be parted from his family, and was also reported to have given away his life-jacket.

Ruth and David Rees had not wanted to make the trip to Britain at all. Both of them were elderly, and neither was in

1. The *Empress* leaving the Mersey. Her promenade decks are almost deserted, but her fo'c's'le, well deck and poop are crowded with people. This picture was taken when the CPR adopted the livery of buff funnels with black tops.

2. The *Storstad*. This picture, probably taken on her builders' trials off the Tyne in 1910, shows the ship in ballast; note the high freeboard, compared with picture of her, no. 9.

3. (*above*) The First Class entrance lobby on the lower promenade deck of the *Empress*. The 'Fan' companionways, of which the *Empress* had a number, proved death-traps as the ship rolled on to her beam ends.

4. Mr Laurence Irving, the famous actor, and his wife, Miss Mabel Hackney.

5. (*above left*) Captain H. G. Kendall.

6. (*above right*) Thomas Andersen. A picture taken aboard the *Storstad* when she arrived in Montreal after the collision.

7. Doctor James Grant. A picture taken shortly after the sinking, probably in Rimouski.

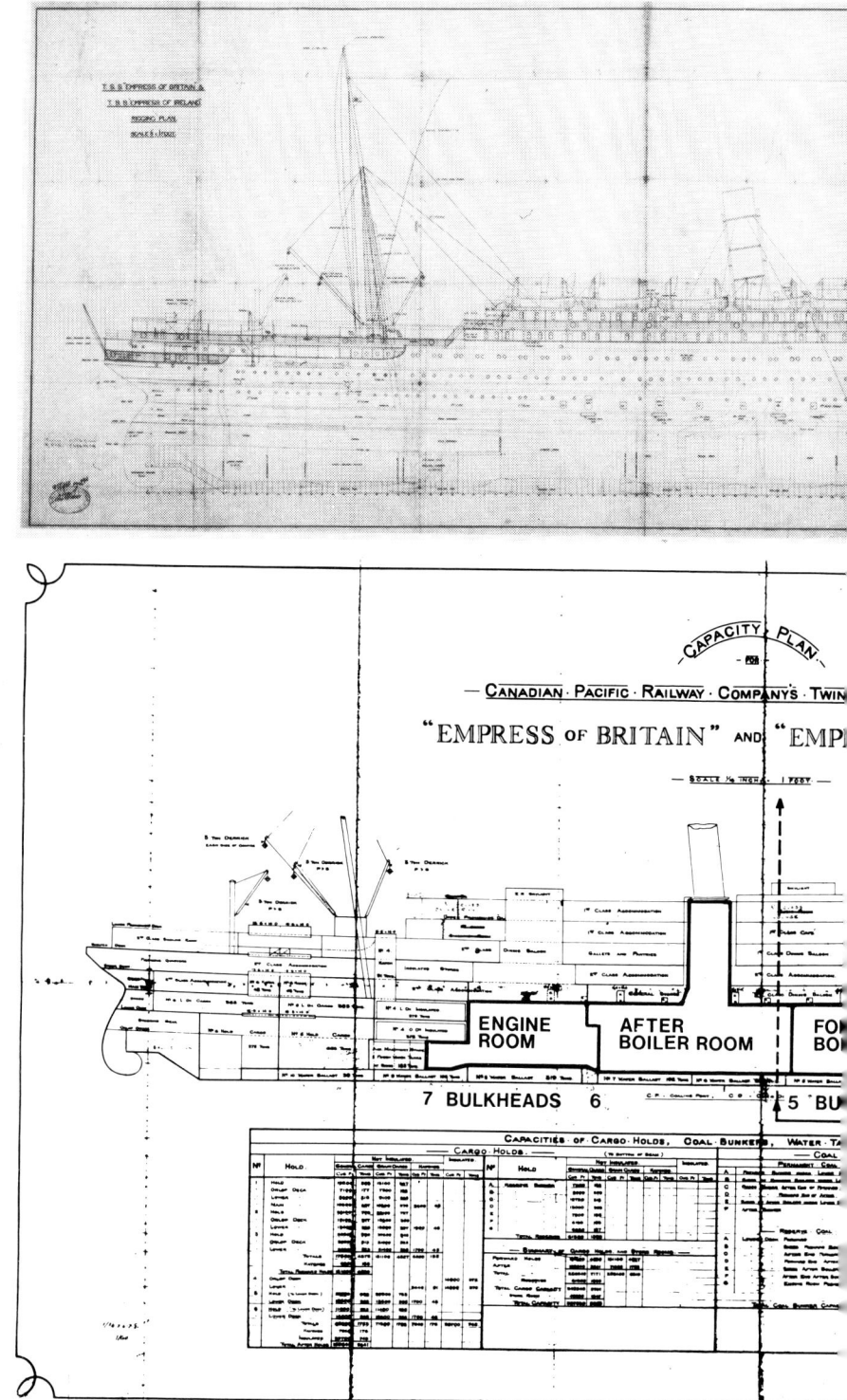

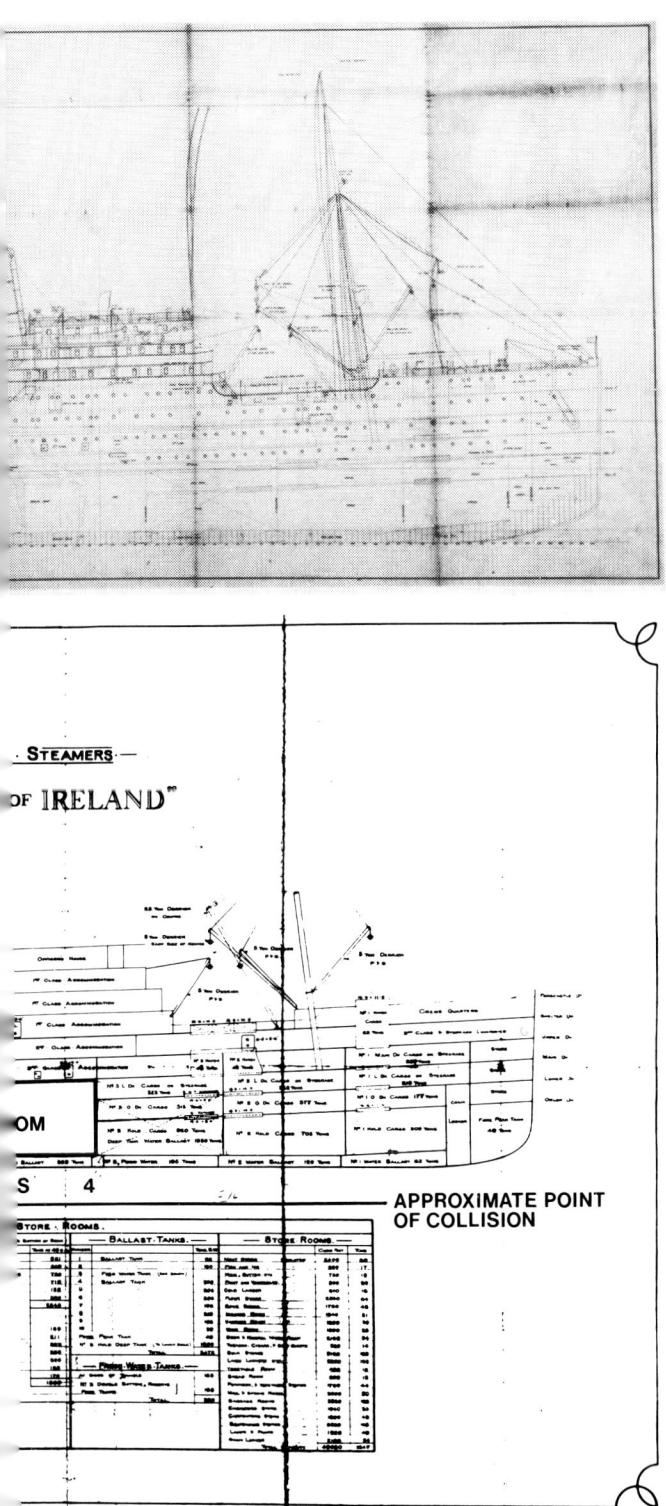

8A and 8B. The *Empress* as her builders envisaged her. Two of the original Fairfield drawings of 1906. The lower drawing has been amended to show the engine and boiler rooms and their bulkheads, and also the point at which the *Storstad* struck the liner, just astern of number five bulkhead.

9. (*above*) The *Storstad*, her starboard bow crushed and twisted, approaching the wharf at Montreal.

10. The vigil: crowds wait patiently outside the CPR's London office in Cockspur Street. Two bulletins about the disaster can just be seen in the nearest window.

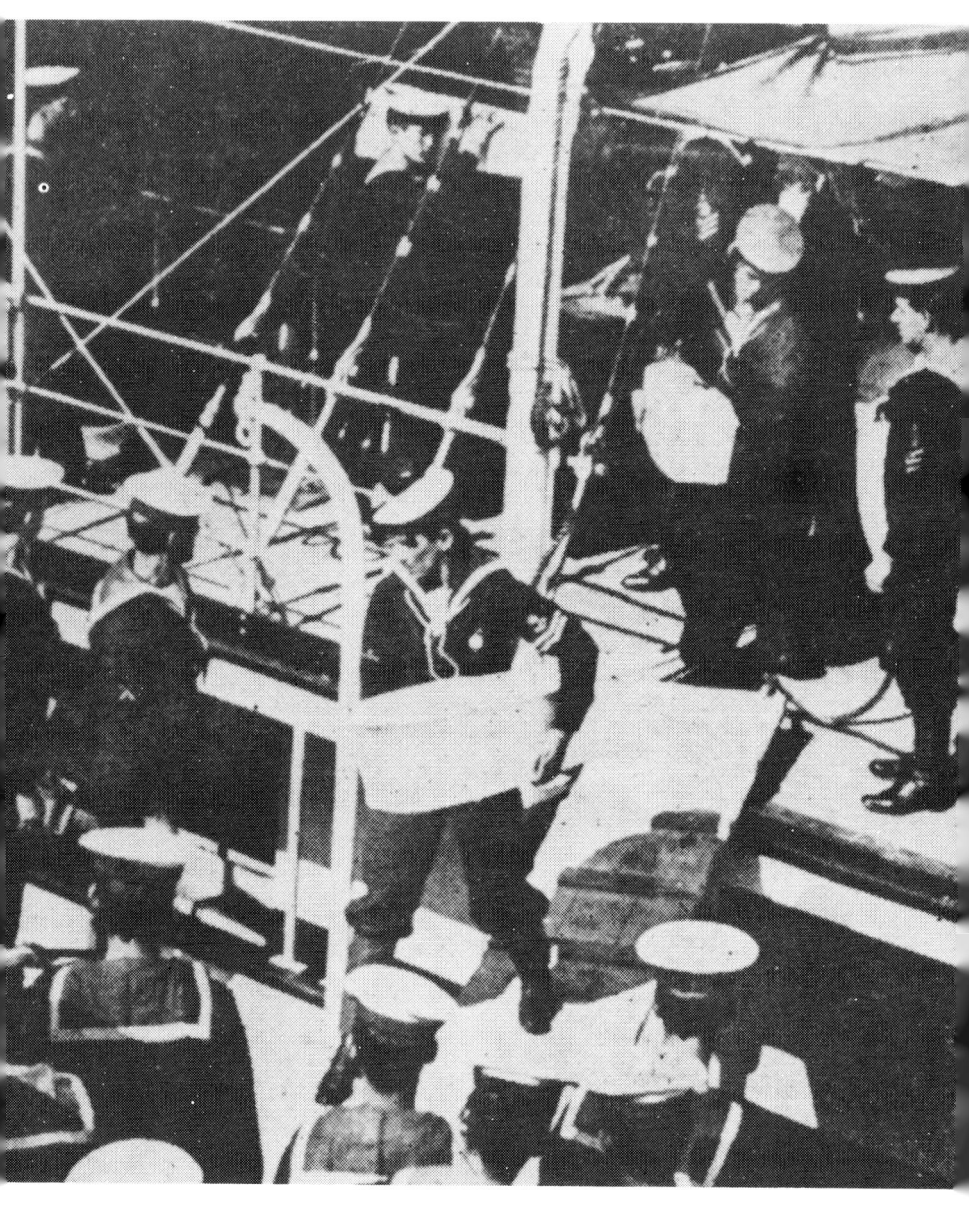

11. The aftermath. Men of *HMS Essex* carry the dead ashore from the revenue cutter *Lady Grey* at Quebec.

good health. But the Army had called them, and Rees, like a good soldier, had obeyed orders. Ruth and David Rees had never been parted in their married lives; they were not to be separated in death. The Commissioner and his wife were buried in the same grave in the Mount Pleasant cemetery in Toronto.

The Salvation Army died like heroes and heroines. Of the few men of the Army who survived at all, it was claimed, not one was wearing a lifebelt, and it was a source of pride that those who did reach a lifeboat before the ship sank were without exception the last to enter it. The surviving Salvationists were to give some of the clearest and most vivid accounts of the sinking of the *Empress*.

Less than twenty-four hours earlier, a young Army bandsman named Earnest Greene had eaten his last meal at home, in company with his parents and his sister, all members of the Army, and all booked to sail for the Albert Hall aboard the *Empress*. 'Well,' his father had said as they rose from the table, 'a whole lot will happen before we have another breakfast in this house.' By breakfast time the following day, Bandsman Greene was the only one of the four still alive. Greene's last glimpse of his family before the ship went down was of the three of them standing on the deck, where a little knot of Salvationists were singing; 'God be with you till we meet again'. Greene senior had turned to his son. 'Well, boy,' he remarked quietly, 'We're in God's hands.' At that moment, the little family was jostled apart in the crowd. Greene did not see his parents or sister again.

Later, Greene remembered how little panic there had been. Where there was any, he recalled, it was mostly among the foreigners. However, he did see one man in the water try to clamber into a lifeboat in front of a woman. Another man hit him in the face and made him wait his turn. Greene also had an odd recollection of those minutes in the water. When the ship sank, he said, it was pitch dark. But after a few minutes, it seemed to grow light very suddenly. The dawn, he was convinced had broken unusually early. Bandsman Greene believed it was a miracle from heaven.

Ensign Ernest Pugmire was also struck by the lack of panic. Even though the companionways leading up from below were jammed with people struggling to reach the open air, there was no shouting, and everything was orderly and quiet. This, he thought, was in part because unbelievable things were happening so fast that few people had time fully to take in what was going on.

Most surviving passengers, if they spoke of the crew at all, claimed that the *Empress*'s men had behaved splendidly. Not all took so charitable a view, however. The officers were not to blame, said one, but the crew nonetheless shifted for themselves. Another complained that the crew members grabbed the available life-jackets for themselves, and left the passengers to find their own. There were plenty aboard, he added, but the passengers did not know where they were, and there was no time for anybody in authority to tell them. Among the hundreds fighting for their lives aboard the *Empress*, or already struggling to survive in the water, Salvation Army bandsman Thomas Greenaway had firmly resolved to die because he believed he had been bereaved after a married life lasting about a week.

Young Mr and Mrs Greenaway had made their way on deck safely, but then Mr Greenaway went back to their cabin because, he said, he wanted to get her a wrap. Furthermore, he claimed quite seriously, he had wanted to close the porthole in their cabin to stop the water coming in and spoiling their new clothes. Many of the passengers, Greenaway reported later, did not seem to realise the danger the ship was in, and thought right up to the very moment of sinking that everything would be all right. One can only conclude that young Mr Greenaway was among them. Whether or not he ever reached the cabin is uncertain. It seems extremely doubtful, since very few who tried to do so lived to tell the tale. When Greenaway reached the deck again, he discovered to his horror that Mrs Greenaway had vanished. Convinced that she was drowned, and filled with remorse, her groom decided that the prospect of life without her was insupportable, and resolved to go down with the ship. To this end he grasped the rail tightly as the ship sank. But his resolution was foiled by an explosion that blew him to the surface again. There he found a table leg floating by, and having by this time reconsidered his attitude towards survival, he hung on to it until a lifeboat found him.

Despite the fact that her husband had vanished from her side young Mrs Greenaway was not particularly nervous. She found some friends on the crowded deck, and one of them gave her a lifebelt. As the ship rolled over, Mrs Greenaway climbed the rail, started to pray, and fell into the water. Although she had quite given up hope, she did not seem able to grasp the fact that death was very near. The same explosion that had thwarted bandsman Greenaway's efforts at self-destruction nearly finished his wife's equally determined efforts to survive. She was stunned by the blast, and when she recovered consciousness, she was lying across a deckchair, bruised and burned, and with a badly cut ankle. As she drifted on her deckchair, a raft floated towards her. On it were two men – 'a huge man', she was later to describe him, and another. The big man reached out towards her with a paddle, and called: 'Are you alive?' Cold, frightened and in pain, little Mrs Greenaway could only moan in return. The big man pulled her on to the raft, and said gently: 'Don't be afraid, little girl, my wife's gone.' Mrs Greenaway spoke. 'I've lost my husband,' she replied.

The big man opened his coat, drew the girl to his chest, and buttoned the coat around her. Frozen as she was by the bitter waters of the river, the shelter of the garment kept her warm and saved her life, she believed. Mrs Greenaway remembered nothing more until she found herself aboard the *Storstad*. She had not again seen the two men who saved her, and she feared they had drowned. There were few happy endings to any of the partings that night. The Greenaways were among the rare exceptions. Later that day, in the sunlight of Rimouski, the young couple found each other and wept with joy.

Mrs Greenaway's fear that her saviour had also perished was happily incorrect. He was a Norwegian named Magnus

Luren, and he was setting out on his first visit to his homeland in fifteen years of farming in the United States. But his wife, as he had feared, was dead.

Staff Captain McAmmond of the Salvation Army was trying to help with the launching of the boats. It was 'pitiful,' he recalled, to see how frantically the seamen went about their work, but despite their efforts, many of the boats could not be freed because the launching gear was foul of the davits. Even while the men struggled with them, McAmmond saw stewards cutting loose bundles of deckchairs and throwing them overboard as makeshift life-preservers. If McAmmond had had hopes of finding a place in one of the boats before he left the ship, they were swiftly dashed. It was not until he had been floundering in the river for several minutes that he found a lifeboat, but he could not enter it, for it was drifting bottom upwards. One man was already sprawled across its upturned bottom, and he helped McAmmond to reach the relative safety of its keel. Naked, huddled together for warmth, they drifted along, collecting two or three more survivors on the way, until they came to a collapsible lifeboat, still neatly folded and laced inside its canvas cover. That boat, too, had a man clinging to it. He turned out to be a member of the crew, and with the aid of his new-found companions, he had the strength to rip off the canvas cover and show McAmmond and his shipmates how to erect the boat. Then the men climbed in, shipped the oars, and rowed off to help others still in the water.

Whether McAmmond knew it at the time is doubtful, but one of his fellow oarsmen that night was another Salvationist, Captain McIntyre. The cold was the bitterest enemy of those still awaiting rescue, and the men in the collapsible boat found that the work of picking up the frozen men and women who eddied about them was desperately difficult. One man grasped the end of McIntyre's oar, but it slipped from his numbed grasp. McIntyre pushed the oar out to the man's hand again, but the swimmer sank out of sight. The men in the boat did not see him again. A woman was luckier. She finally got a grip on McIntyre's oar at the third attempt.

She was a foreigner from Third Class, McIntyre reported. He added that the lady was very grateful for being rescued.

Bandsman Fowler, was one of the few survivors who actually saw the collision take place. When he heard the sirens and whistles, Fowler put his head out of the cabin window, expecting to see another ship passing by. Instead, he saw the *Storstad* in the act of burying her bow in the *Empress*'s side. In those first terrifying moments, as the passengers below deck were trying to escape the inrush of water, Fowler did his best to calm and reassure them. He found a woman with a baby and a little girl, grabbed a handful of spare life-jackets, and put them on the children. But there was a great crowd of people trying to reach the deck, and Fowler lost sight of the family.

As he himself scrambled to the Second Class saloon deck, Fowler saw a young lady named Willmott. She was trying to climb the steps, but the list was too steep for her, and the passageway was filling with water. Fowler somehow got a rope from the boat deck, told Miss Willmott to tie it round herself, and pulled her up the stairs by main force. Together they reached the upper rail and walked down the ship's side as if it were a floor. Somebody grabbed Miss Willmott to safety, and Fowler swam off towards some distant lifeboats. After swimming for a considerable time he reached them, but they were crammed with people. Uncomplaining, Fowler swam off again towards another boat which had only eight men in it and which may have been Captain McAmmond's frail collapsible. The sailor in charge said they could not take any more people or they would sink, so Fowler clung to the side of the boat. After about ten minutes, the men inside let him come aboard.

Fowler was not the only man to find that his presence was less than welcome. James Johnston, one of Fowler's fellow bandsmen, tried to board a lifeboat, but the men already aboard the overcrowded craft beat the young Salvationist off with their fists as he tried to climb over the stern. The boat rowed away, but Johnston was not prepared to die that easily; he swam sturdily along in her wake until humanity prevailed, and he was hauled aboard.

FOURTEEN MINUTES

Dr James F. Grant was a dark-haired, cheerful-looking young man from British Columbia, who had graduated only the previous year from McGill University Medical School, Montreal. He had been an interne at the Montreal General Hospital, but his health had been bad. Sea air was prescribed, so Doctor Grant had joined the *Empress* as her surgeon. This was his second voyage. The doctor's quarters were on the right-hand side of the Upper Deck, in the forward part of the Second Class accommodation. Grant's cabin, therefore, was quite near the point of collision, but despite that, he neither felt nor heard it. Grant probably slept on peacefully for several minutes after the collision before he was rudely awakened by being rolled out on the deck by the list of the ship. He reached for the light switch, but it clicked uselessly under his hand, for the power had already failed. For several terrifying seconds Grant groped helplessly in the dark, unable to find the door of his cabin, while from outside he could hear the terrified screams of passengers and the roaring of water. Grant eventually found the door and scrambled out of his cabin, only to find a fresh terror in store.

The cross passageway outside his cabin, which ran across the ship to the left-hand side, was already at such an angle that he could not walk up it. Grant fell to his hands and knees and tried to pull himself up by digging his fingers in the carpet. But the carpet kept pulling away from its fastenings and falling back on him in great folds. Somehow, half-crawling, half-climbing along the steel wall of the passageway, Grant reached a porthole, now rapidly rearing itself above his head. He grasped the rim, pulled himself up, and put his head through.

To his astonishment, the doctor found himself looking at the left-hand side of the ship, which was crowded with people who were standing there as if they were on the deck. Grant rammed himself through the porthole and yelled for help. As he fought to get his shoulders through the narrow opening, somebody leaned down and obligingly hauled him out like a cork from a bottle. For a few moments Grant himself stood on the side of the ship, surrounded by a crowd that he put at at least one hundred people. Then, before he had time to think what to do next, or even to ask a question of his equally bewildered neighbour, the ship slipped away from under him. Grant described the moment vividly. He slid down into the water, he recalled later, as if he was walking down a sandy beach to bathe. It was an analogy that at least half a dozen survivors were to use in describing their experiences.

As Grant struggled in the water among hundreds of other survivors the fog rolled up 'like a curtain'. Low in the water, perhaps a mile away, Grant could see the lights of a ship, which he later learned was the *Storstad*. The doctor swam towards her, and while doing so was picked up by one of her boats, which was heading for the scene. Soon afterwards, Grant found himself aboard the *Storstad*. There, he borrowed a pair of trousers several sizes too large for him, tied a piece of string round the waist to hold them up, and went to work.

Mr George Bogue Smart was about as close as any living survivor could have been to the point of the collision. Even so, he remembered it as quite a gentle meeting, about as hard as the kind of jar one might experience when a couple of railway carriages were rather roughly shunted together. Mr Smart, who clearly was not the mysterious Thomas Smart who supposedly spoke with Kendall before the collision, ran from his First Class cabin on the saloon-deck, and put his head out of a porthole. To his astonishment, he saw a ship's bow up against the liner's side, so close that he felt he could almost reach out and touch her. There were men on deck and there was shouting, but Smart felt no particular sense of peril. Accordingly he pulled on his jacket and trousers over his pyjamas and started on deck to see what was happening, but neglected to take his life-jacket. By the time he reached the companionway the peril was all too clear for the ship was already listing dangerously, so that Mr Smart finished the ascent to the deck on his hands and knees. It was clearly far too late to think of going back for his life-preserver, so Mr Smart decided he would have to trust to providence.

The best place to await his destiny, he decided, was the left-hand rail, so he climbed it, put his arm securely around a stanchion, and sat there quietly while the *Empress* rolled over on her side. Mr Smart was shot into the water. By this time he had had bitter cause to regret the life-jacket he had left in his cabin, but his trust in providence was not misplaced. A deckchair floated past, and although by then he was very weak, Smart managed to grab it and pull it up against himself as a makeshift support. He clung on to it, he calculated, for about an hour. No doubt it felt that long, but it almost certainly was not. Few survivors lasted an hour in that numbing cold without a life-jacket, and indeed, many of those who were wearing them died of exposure long before that in water that was only a little above freezing point.

Smart seems to have been one of those who were saved by the single Englehardt collapsible that is known to have got away from the *Empress*, although he himself admitted that by the time he was picked up, he was so far gone that he was in no condition to take in technical details. What he did clearly remember, and lived to speak of with wonder and gratitude, were the order and kindness of all those who shared the experience of those harrowing minutes. Discipline aboard the *Empress* was 'really marvellous', he later told the court of inquiry. 'I never heard people who spoke with such tenderness to each other in that time of deep distress and danger, as there were there.' There was no panic, no violence and not even any bad language. Everyone was good-natured, and the man in charge of the boat that picked him up 'spoke in the kindest way to me. It was really delightful to me then under those trying circumstances.' Mr Smart's tribute to his fellow men seems to have been fully justified. While he may not have realised it at the time, the collapsible boat was largely manned by a scratch crew of Salvationists, and there was to be plenty of evidence that they were true to their calling that night.

One man claimed to have left the *Empress* that night without getting his feet wet. He was Mr Louis Gosselin, a well-known Montreal lawyer and political figure, and he was clearly accustomed to being the master of whatever circumstances he found himself in. Not only had he somehow managed to get himself decently attired by the time he came ashore at Rimouski, but when he boarded the special train that took the survivors back to Quebec, he claimed to be the only man aboard who had shaved.

Among his many other interests, Gosselin was legal counsel to a firm of manufacturers of industrial explosives called the Energite Explosives Company of Widdifield, Ontario. He and the Managing Director of the Company, Mr Lionel Kent, were travelling to Europe on business, and the two men were sharing one of the exclusive and expensive two-cabin suites on the liner's promenade-deck. To reach the open air after the collision, they had only to walk through the door of their suite. But escaping from the listing ship itself was another matter. They scrambled to the boat-deck, and tried to launch one of the lifeboats, but not surprisingly they failed to master the working of the davits and falls. While unhappily contemplating these nautical mysteries, Mr Gosselin lost his footing on the rapidly listing deck. He tobogganed down the planking, faster and faster, and was braving himself for the plunge over the side when one of the collapsible boats broke loose, together with a good deal of other gear, and went crashing past him into the sea, which must have been somewhere up to the level of the boat deck by that time. Mr Gosselin, by his own account of it, shot straight off the deck onto the collapsible boat. Later, he claimed to have take command of the boat and to have steered it for about half an hour, picking up survivors, until they reached the *Storstad*.

It may very possibly have been true. Stranger things happened aboard the *Empress* that night. On the other hand, Mr Gosselin was to have other things to say about that night which he no doubt believed completely, but which were nonetheless manifestly untrue.

Lionel Kent lived to describe vividly the chaotic scenes aboard the lifeboats wallowing amid the swimmers and the corpses. Kent had at first been reluctant to get up at all when Gosselin came into his cabin and told him the ship was in trouble. He thought it was a practical joke by Gosselin to get him to go out on the cold deck in his bare feet. He soon learned better. Had Gosselin not made him get up and go on deck, Kent admitted later, he would have drowned. His principal recollection of the next few minutes was that things weren't too bad while there was still light enough for the struggling passengers and crew to see what they were doing, but that once the dynamos failed and the lights went out, pandemonium broke loose. By that time, the big ship was very near her end anyway. Minutes later Kent, in his dressing gown, was swimming for his life. After a while, he became convinced that he was swimming through the darkness towards a low island set with tall pine trees. Only as he drew nearer did he realise that he was approaching a lifeboat, low in the water, and that the pine trees were men standing up in her.

As Kent bobbed alongside, a man in the boat offered to take his hand, but Kent could not so much as lift a hand clear of the water, for he was frozen past feeling. So he was hauled bodily into the boat, where another survivor began systematically to slap the life back into him. The boat was so crowded that Kent could not see if there was an officer aboard her or not. In any case, the yelling and moaning aboard were so loud that if there was indeed anybody at the helm giving orders, he was unable to make himself heard. The rowers at the oars were totally disorganised. On one side, men were pulling spasmodically, while those beside them were backing water or resting on their oars; the boat moved around in erratic circles, or revolved on its axis like a water beetle. It took them a long time to reach the *Storstad*.

Conditions aboard the other boats were probably very similar. A seaman named Shaun Downey recalled that there were so many people jammed into First Officer Jones' boat that the sailors attempting to row her could not drag the oars out from under the thwarts.

A Second Class passenger named Bernard Weinrauch told a hair-raising story of the launch of the boat in which he eventually escaped. Weinrauch had scrambled from his cabin to the lower promenade deck, a long, windy expanse of teak planking which ran along both sides of the ship from below the bridge to the extreme stern, and which was the principal deck area for the Second Class passengers. Two lifeboats, one on each side, hung on the lower promenade deck in the extreme stern of the ship, separated from the main boat deck, and it was to one of these that Weinrauch struggled across the sloping planking. Weinrauch and a group of fellow passengers boarded the boat, but then found there was no means of releasing the boat from the heavy rope falls that tethered it to its dying parent, for they could not free the massive hooks by which the boat was suspended. They searched in vain for an axe; desperate men hammered at the unyielding hooks with the butts of oars while Weinrauch saw other men trying to gnaw through the ropes with their teeth. Eventually, just as the frantic passengers thought they were going to be dragged to the bottom in the wake of the *Empress*, they managed to force the hooks loose, and the boat floated free.

A few passengers, probably very few indeed, actually reached the safety of the *Storstad* without getting into a lifeboat at all. One of them was a young Clydeside marine engineer named James Rankin. Rankin had served his apprentice time in the Fairfield yards where the *Empress* had been built, and had then gone to sea for a year in the CPR's newly completed liner *Empress of Asia*, which sailed on the Vancouver-Yokohama route. Now, he and a number of shipmates were taking passage home to Scotland in the *Empress* as supernumerary engineers. Rankin was an extremely fit young man in his early twenties, and an excellent swimmer into the bargain. He claimed, and there is no reason whatever to doubt him, that he had swum the whole way between the two ships. It was about a mile, he believed. He added that it felt like ten. He had no lifebelt.

Rankin almost certainly owed his life to the fact that he was suffering from the painful and disagreeable complaint prickly heat, an unwelcome souvenir of his spell in the Pacific. To ease its burning discomfort, he had smeared his body liberally with vaseline. Had he been preparing for a prolonged swim in icy water, he could not have hit on a more efficacious way of protecting his body.

FOURTEEN MINUTES

Rankin was lucky, as well as brave. A number of other passengers, despairing of being picked up by the few boats on the scene, set out to swim to the Norwegian collier. There were quite a number of them, at least to begin with, a passenger named Hutchinson was to remember. But as the labouring minutes passed, and the icy cold sapped the strength from their limbs, they grew fewer and fewer. The fact that there were any left at all, Hutchinson believed, was due to a fat man who swam ahead of them in the darkness and kept up a running chorus of encouragement. 'It won't be long,' he called to his fellow swimmers. 'We'll soon be there. You're all doing fine. The worst is over. You'll be there in a few minutes.' His cheery cries drove the struggling swimmers to a last effort. Later, when they were sprawled exhausted aboard the collier, they realised for the first time how few they were. The fat man did not seem to be among them.

A Salvation Army bandsman named Kenneth McIntyre also reached the *Storstad* by his own efforts. He had swum towards the collier until his arms were so numb with cold that he could no longer force them through the water. So he turned on his back and kicked his way there, and was denied even the illusory comfort of seeing where he was going, but McIntyre was a resourceful young man. As the fog rolled away he gazed upwards into the tranquil night and navigated his way to the *Storstad's* side with the aid of a couple of stars.

James Dandy was one of the many passengers who slept through the collision. So soundly did he sleep in his Second Class berth right aft that he awoke only when water started pouring in through the porthole. Dandy struggled back to consciousness under the vague impression that they were out at sea, and that the ship was in a desperate storm. Then someone produced a light, and a sleepy Dandy looked down to see somebody else's luggage floating across the floor. Dandy must have been among the last to reach the open air, for by the time he had fought his way on deck, the *Empress* was very near her end. He had been on deck only about three minutes he believed, when she sank.

A Third Class passenger named James Walker was actually

awakened when a jet of water shot through the open porthole of his cabin on to his bunk, and left him floundering sleepily amid the sodden ruin of his bedclothes.

Mr G. Dransfield probably owed his life to one of the Salvation Army passengers, who woke Dransfield to say that he had heard whistles, and feared that there was something wrong. Dransfield wanted to go back to sleep, but while he was still inwardly debating the issue, the liner lurched so hard the Dransfield was thrown out of his bunk. He climbed into his trousers and boots, and helped himself to a life-jacket from the rack. Then he tried to help the Salvationist who had awakened him. He failed, because by that time the man was on his knees, praying, and would not be moved. Dransfield left him, and joined the crowd trying to make its way up the companion ladder in the dark.

The Third Class passengers, many of them berthed far down in the ship, had in some cases to struggle up several flights of steps to reach their slender chance of life on deck. One of those who succeeded was named Bristow. With his wife, he battled his way as far as the Second Class promenade-deck. When they reached the side of the ship, they found lines of people hanging by their hands from the left-hand rail. Air was hissing from the portholes as the pressure built up inside the doomed ship, and Bristow could hear a load roaring, which he thought was the sound of steam escaping from bursting boiler tubes. Together, the Bristows scrambled over the rail and stood on the ship's side. Below them, a woman with two children was struggling up the sloping deck, trying vainly to reach the rail. Bristow tried to help them, but they slipped back down the deck into the angle between the deck and the side of the superstructure, and could not get out again. A little later, Bristow's wife also disappeared, and he did not see her again.

The nature of that terrible list that carried the ship over on to her beam ends was most graphically described by Martin Gill, who found himself one of a mass of passengers struggling to climb an aft-facing companionway to the boat-deck. It was so steep, he said that the passengers could no longer use the steps themselves. Instead, they were standing on the left handrail of the companion ladder, and hauling themselves along on the right handrail, which by then was amost vertically above their heads. When he got on to the boat deck, Gill joined some other men who were trying to launch one of the left-hand lifeboats, but as the list increased the boats, lifting free from their chocks, kept swinging further and further inboard until they were hanging over the men's heads. Gill gave up, and walked over the ship's side. He slid down the plating, bounded off the bilge keel, and shot into the water.

Another Third Class passenger, Bevan, was one of six men who were sharing a cabin. Bevan was a methodical man. Despite the confusion in the crowded cabin he took several minutes to dress himself and put on his life-jacket. That care nearly cost him his life, for by the time he reached the companionway, the lights had failed, and a mob of people was fighting to get up the stairs in the dark. Bevan managed to climb to safety, simply because one man struck matches and by their flickering light, Bevan and others found their way on deck. Once there, Bevan reached the fo'c's'le and climbed into the water.

Those few Third Class passengers who found themselves on deck at all had, in many cases, the easiest route into whatever safety might exist in the waters below them. The twin companionways leading from the forward exit in the Third Class quarters opened almost directly from the fo'c's'le on to the well-deck, which by that time was so close to the water that one could step straight off the fo'c's'le into the river.

Four children survived, out of 138 on board. Helen O'Hara, who was ten years old, lived because she had been taught to swim at school. She and her father ran on deck after the collision, but the child lost sight of her father in the crush, and she did not see him again. As the water closed over her, she struck out for a piece of wreckage, and clung to it until she spotted a lifeboat. She swam to it, and was picked up.

Gracie Hannagan was only seven, and she was travelling with her Salvationist parents, for Gracie's father was the conductor of the band that had so pleased the Third Class passengers so short a while before. Gracie and her parents had reached the deck alive. As the deck rolled beneath the surface of the river, Gracie saw what she described as a black rope, and clung to it like grim death. 'I went down deep, oh, so deep into the water,' the little girl said afterwards. 'When I came up again after a long time, I saw some lights in front of me. When I looked a second time I saw Mama and Papa. They were swimming.' Gracie went down a second time and swallowed a great deal of water, but she clung like a leech to the rope. When she came up a second time, she saw a light very near. A man in a boat pushed an oar out towards her, and yelled to her to hang on. Gracie Hannagan's principal concern afterwards seemed to be that in sliding down her black rope, she had got her hands covered in tar. Gracie told her story to reporters on the special train that took her back to Quebec. No, she explained to the adults around her, her parents were not on the special train with her. They would be coming on the next train. Did they think she would get home before Mama and Papa? Nobody thought it the moment to tell her that Mama and Papa would not be on the next train, after all.

Florence Barber lived. She was eight years old. Her immigrant father had died in an accident in London, Ontario. His widow was taking herself and her two little daughters back to Cumberland. Florence alone survived. She did so because Mr Robert Crellin, also of Ontario, laid the child across a piece of flotsam and paddled the child in front of him until they were picked up. Crellin, who was described as a well-to-do farmer, had been travelling with Florence's mother, whom he had been intending to marry. Now that she was dead, Crellin announced his intention of adopting the child. Later, another wealthy family named McQuillan had offered to do so in his stead. Florence, Crellin decided, faced a far better future in their care than he could offer.

Mr John P. Black, of Ottawa, saved his life by the same mixture of quick wits and good luck that had brought most of the survivors through the ordeal alive. In most respects, his story differed little from that of the others, but Mr Black was among the few people who claimed to have witnessed the terrible fate of one of the handful of lifeboats that was launched at all that night.

The Blacks were asleep in their Second Class cabin when Black was awakened by the impact of the *Storstad*'s bows. Looking out of his cabin door, he saw two stewards running down the passageway. He grabbed his wife from her bunk and hurried her on deck. There, Black asked a sailor what was wrong. 'Nothing,' the man replied, 'it's only a trifle.' He may even have believed it. But the deck was beginning to slope beneath their feet, and Black saw other seamen helping women into life-jackets.

The Blacks slid down the deck towards the river. Already, two boats were afloat, and seamen were struggling to free the boats from the heavy rope falls that tethered them to the rapidly sinking ship. Black took his wife in his arms, and leaped into the water. A boat was nearby. A seaman grabbed Mrs Black and hauled her aboard. Black himself, nearly exhausted, clung to the side of the boat. Aboard it, a seaman was shouting for an axe to free the boat from the entangling bow falls. Somebody passed him a hatchet, and the boat was hacked free just in time to prevent its being dragged to the bottom of the river by the sinking ship.

Just astern of them, close by the side of the dying liner, another boat was drifting towards them. Black estimated that it contained at least 45 people. Even as Black watched, what he described as a heavy mass of superstructure thundered from the decks of the *Empress* and landed with an appalling crash on top of the second boat. Black, still clinging to the lifelines of his own boat, closed his eyes in horror; when he opened them again, the boat and all aboard her had vanished. Where she had been, a few scraps of wreckage were bobbing on the surface. Moments later, Black himself was pulled from the water, and taken to the *Storstad*. There, he rejoined his wife.

The heavy piece of superstructure that Mr Black said he

saw crashing down on the neighbouring lifeboat may well have been one of those left-hand lifeboats that so many reports said had broken loose from their davits. If it was, Mr Black did not say so, and indeed he may not have known if it was or not. But another account of what was amost certainly the same incident came from a man who not only saw it, but actually claimed to have been one of the occupants of the sunken boat. He was a steward named Percy Gee, and he reported that the boat had been entangled by wreckage – whether by floating fall-ropes or by ship's wireless aerials, he did not say. While the occupants were still struggling to free the boat, Gee said, he looked up to see one of the left-hand boats crashing down upon its luckless sister. Gee had the presence of mind to throw himself overboard and so avoid being crushed to death. Unfortunately, Gee did not say which lifeboat he had been in. Very possibly, in the darkness and the confusion, he did not know. Nor did he say whether the boat that fell was one of the regular steel boats, or one of the collapsibles. Again, he may not have known.

Falling wreckage of one sort or another undoubtedly accounted for a substantial number of casualties that night. A passenger named Peter Rusk was also a witness to the fact, for he, too, saw it happen. Rusk was among the passengers milling around on deck when the liner went under. 'They were clinging to anything they could lay hands on,' he recalled later. There was practically no light, and the waves were washing up over the deck, which by then was nearly as steep as the side of a house. Many of them just let go their hold, and slipped into the water. 'I believe it was the best thing they could have done, for it was a marvellous thing that anyone who was in the ship when she went down came out alive at all.'

As the ship rolled over, there was an appalling crash, and what Rusk described as much of the rigging and part of the foremast plummeted into the water, killing many of the swimmers struggling in the river underneath. Rusk was no seaman, and he did not describe the scene any more exactly. We may speculate that what Rusk saw was one or more of the

Empress's cargo derricks breaking loose from its housing, and falling into the river like an enormous steel flail. If it was, it would undoubtedly have killed or destroyed anything in its path. According to another report, a falling derrick actually killed one of the *Empress*'s officers on the bridge.

Rusk hung on to his precarious handhold on deck, thinking that the ship would stay afloat for a while longer. He was swiftly disabused; the dying liner gave a horrible lurch, and sank beneath him. In a second, Rusk found himself in a whirlpool, buffeted by bodies living and dead, by wreckage, and by what he described as enormous waves. Twice he was dragged below the surface and all the time, heavy spars and pieces of timber seemed to be grinding him to fragments. He was swirled round and round for what felt to him like hours before he found himself in relatively calm water, with his arms wrapped round a piece of timber. He had absolutely no recollection of having grasped it.

Fergus Duncan was a young London solicitor, and he, too, witnessed one of the subsidiary disasters of the sinking of the *Empress*. Duncan himself probably owed his life to the fact that he was one of the few who could afford one of the luxury cabins on the *Empress*'s promenade-deck, high above the waterline. It was that height which saved him, for Duncan's right-hand cabin was midships, directly above the spot where the *Storstad* struck. Because the collier was so low in the water, her chisel bow passed directly beneath the stateroom where Duncan lay. Only feet below him, the more modestly priced cabins on the upper and main decks were crushed like eggshells.

Duncan had already been awakened by the sound of the liner's siren. When the collision came he climbed from his bunk, pulled on his life-jacket, and walked out on to the promenade-deck in his pyjamas. Even though his cabin was only feet away, he never returned to it. The ship was already beginning to roll over, and then the lights failed. By then, the first lifeboats were being lowered from the boat deck above him. As he watched the boats going down, disaster struck. Even as one of the boats was being filled and lowered, one end dropped sickeningly, the boat flipped on end, and the occupants were spilled into the river. However, Duncan had not had his fill of horrors that night. He was one of the survivors, and there were many of them, who reported seeing women hanging by their hands from the rail until they lost their grip, dropped down the sloping deck, and crashed sickeningly against the sides of the superstructure, now many feet below. It was not surprising that doctors were later to comment on the high proportion of bodies taken from the river who had died, not of drowning, but of physical injury.

'It was pretty rotten on deck,' he was to remark later, with what sounded like a masterpiece of British understatement. 'We simply stood there. We knew we were going down. There was no question about that from the first, and it was no good struggling. The poor women were hysterical, but there was no chance to do anything for them.' Another of Duncan's memories was of the sudden, uncanny silence which fell as the ship's engines thudded slowly to a halt when the steam failed, and of the darkness that followed as the electric lights died. But then followed the single, high-pitched shriek of despair that rang out from the hundreds of survivors standing on the ship's side, or clinging to the superstructure, as the liner rolled over and took her final plunge.

Duncan was flung into the river, and rose gasping to the surface to find himself in the centre of a churning, screaming mass of people thrashing about in the water over the spot where the ship had gone down. Although he was one of the lucky ones with a life-jacket, Duncan had to fight to stay alive, for at one time he had no fewer than five men and women clinging to him and threatening to drag him down. One by one, as Duncan clawed his way towards clear water, the unhappy wretches clutching at his arms and legs loosed their grip and vanished beneath the surface.

Other passengers that night were dragged under, not by their dying fellow creatures, but by the dying ship herself. Cedric Gallagher was nineteen, and was travelling to England with his mother. He helped her over the ship's side, and the pair of them went down deep. When Gallagher surfaced, he could see his mother, trapped by the neck in the entangling rigging of the *Empress*'s mast, now down at water level. Gallagher struggled to swim towards her, but before he could reach her, the ship disappeared. He did not see his mother again.

Many strange companionships were formed that night. None was stranger, perhaps, than that of Tiria Townshend and Clayton Burt. They had met briefly at dinner the night before. A few hours later, whether they knew it or not, they had been close together among the First Class passengers heading for the boat deck, for each had witnessed the last moments of the Irvings. From then on, they had their work cut out trying to ensure their own survival.

The task was hardest perhaps for Tiria Townshend, for she had made what turned out to be an almost fatal mistake. After being awakened by the squalling of the liner's siren, she had dressed completely, including her overcoat and lace-up shoes, before making her way on deck. Presumably she was among the many passengers, particularly in First Class, who had gone on deck with no thought of real and immediate danger, for Tiria Townshend had also made a second mistake; she had failed to take her lifebelt. Being an athletic young woman, she had had no great difficulty in climbing the left-hand rail as the deck reared up under her feet like a cliff. She walked down the horizontal side of the ship, over the lines of portholes, and was standing on the side of the liner when the ship vanished under her and left her floundering in the water.

Tiria was carried down deep. She came up half-drowned and nearly exhausted. Already, the weight of her sodden, cumbersome clothing was dragging her down. Nearby were three men wearing life-jackets. Tiria reached out her hand to them, but they pushed her away. That would probably have been the end of Tiria Townshend, but for a curious encounter. Splashing through the river towards her came a man. Not only was he wearing a life-jacket, but he was holding on to a large and buoyant suitcase that was floating serenely beside him. Gasping with cold and fright, Tiria asked him to let her use his extempore life-preserver. 'Most certainly,' he replied from the darkness, as if it were the most normal request in the world.

Whether she realised it or not at that moment, Tiria's knight errant was none other than Mr Clayton Burt. He, too, was lucky to still be alive, for he had slept peacefully through the collision and might have gone on doing so, had he not been awakened by the crash of breaking china as a rackful of cabin plates and glasses fell to the deck. Burt hurried on deck in his pyjamas to see what was happening and then, braver or more foolhardy than he knew, he returned to his cabin to dress.

Burt not only dressed, but carefully pocketed his money – and then made the frightening discovery that he could not find his life-jacket. The ship was listing beneath his feet; there was clearly no time to lose. Burt gave up his frantic search in the darkened cabin, and rushed out into the passageway. Just as he did so, a man hurried by with no fewer than three life-jackets in his arms. At that moment, the man dropped one in his haste, so Burt picked it up and put it on before going on deck again. It must have been at this point that Burt had his brief but memorable encounter with the Irvings. He might have seen more of them, but as Burt climbed the rail, calling to Irving and his wife to follow him, a violent explosion blew Burt clean off the rail and into the water. When he came to the surface, he found himself accompanied by the suitcase. How an empty suitcase came to be floating in the river that night he never knew, but however it came to be there, it saved Tiria Townshend's life. With the girl temporarily buoyed up by her makeshift raft, Burt tried to help her out of her sodden outer clothes. After a long while he managed to get her heavy overcoat off by tugging at the sleeves, and then the two tried to take off Tiria's clumsy lace-up shoes, which she confessed were 'a terrible tie'. They failed, for the sodden laces beat them, but despite that the girl managed to hang on to the suitcase and paddle herself along for about half an hour before the two were picked up.

There were probably a lot of other people, passengers or

crew, who were saved by odd items of flotsam that night. One member of the crew floated to safety while affectionately embracing an empty beer crate.

Alice Bayles, undismayed by the unhappy forebodings of her nameless dinner companion, had gone contentedly to bed in the little Second Class cabin that she was sharing with two other girls, named Willmott and Coult. The three had slept soundly enough until the gentle jolt of the collision awoke them. The other two had been unwilling to get up or indeed to take any other precautions, but Alice jumped from her bunk, grabbed the life-jackets from a rack above her head, and threw one to each of the other girls. They were reluctant to don them, but Alice insisted, and thereby saved their lives. True, Miss Willmott nearly drowned in the passageway before Bandsman Fowler chivalrously towed her to safety on the end of a rope, but like Miss Coult, she was eventually saved.

Alice had a stranger adventure. Struggling in the water, she nearly lost her life, despite her life-jacket, when a big man, badly wounded in the head, clung to her. Alice tried to shake him off, but he began to drag her down. Then his head fell forward in the water, and she knew that he was dead. The man drifted away and disappeared. Although buoyed up by her life-jacket, Alice was unable to propel herself through the water because she had no idea how to swim. Soon, a man swam past her, so Alice grabbed at his arm. 'Don't hold me,' the man gasped. 'I'm exhausted. We shall both drown.' Alice was determined not to be left behind. 'Oh, do show me how to swim,' she implored him. He was unwilling to give a swimming lesson at that particular moment, but as he swam away, Alice watched his movements closely and tried to imitate them. By kicking like a frog, she found she could move forward a little. Happily, before her new-found powers of locomotion could be seriously tested, she was picked up. So was her involuntary swimming instructor.

Not far away, another young woman was also struggling for her life. Mrs Helena Hollis was stewardess in the Third Class quarters, and like many another who went to sea, Mrs Hollis followed her calling, not from choice but from necessity. She was a widow, and had to support herself and her young family.

Mrs Hollis found herself struggling in the water after the ship sank. She recalled later that it was her first swim for ten years. Beside her in the water was a fellow stewardess, Mrs Dunwoodie. The two women swam strongly enough for a while, but Mrs Dunwoodie was wearing two overcoats. The weight of the sodden material relentlessly dragged her down. Helena tried to keep her afloat, but the other girl slipped from her grasp and sank. 'It was a pity,' said Mrs Hollis matter-of-factly afterwards, 'that she put on those two coats.' For a little while, Mrs Hollis thought she was going to join her friend, for she was growing more exhausted. But just as she, too, was about to slip below the surface, a greaser from the *Empress*'s engine-room swam up beside her, reached out a hand, and put it under the girl's chin. He kept her afloat just long enough for a lifeboat to reach them.

Not all the survivors found immediate succour at the hands of the lifeboat crews, who sometimes showed a nicely balanced sense of priorities. A young Swede, supported by a life-jacket, heard a lifeboat near him in the night, and yelled at the top of his powerful lungs: 'Come over here.' The rowers were Norwegians from the *Storstad*, and they were not disposed to be sympathetic to the pleas of their fellow Scandinavian. 'If you can yell as loud as that, you must be all right,' they shouted back, and rowed off into the darkness in search of those in more urgent need of assistance. The young Swede lived to see what at a pinch might just possibly have been described as the funny side of it.

One of the crew survivors was a quiet, matter-of-fact old man with a kindly expression. He was an ex-soldier from County Louth, in Ireland, named William Clarke, and he was described as looking rather toilworn, as well he might. For not only had Clarke escaped alive from the *Empress*'s stokehold with the river water foaming at his heels, but it turned out that two years earlier, he had escaped in rather similar circumstances from the stokehold of the *Titanic*.

FOURTEEN MINUTES

Clarke had been stolidly shovelling coal into the *Empress*'s boilers when the *Storstad* struck. He had scrambled up the tall boiler room ladders with his mates as the St Lawrence thundered into the narrow stokehold, reached the deck, and made his way to boat Number Five. By the time he and his mates had finished clearing it away, it was hardly a matter of lowering it, for the river had risen to meet it in its chocks. 'We swung her down, but the list threw her out from the side, and the hooks of the davits loosened off and she floated away.' The startled Clarke had to dive into the river and swim after the boat to catch up with it. As he scrambled into the boat, the *Empress* sank. Clarke and his shaken colleagues did not have to debate their next move. Clarke reached over the side and started the heavy task of hauling people from the water into the boat.

Later, Clarke was asked to compare the *Empress* disaster with that of the *Titanic*. The latter, he decided after a little reflection, was much more awful. The waiting aboard the *Titanic* had been the terrible thing, he confided to the reporters. 'There was no waiting with the *Empress*. You just saw what you had to to do and did it ... The *Titanic* went down straight, like a baby goes to sleep. The *Empress* rolled over like a hog in a ditch.'

CHAPTER 13

Rescue

The survivors, frozen and exhausted, stumbled or were hauled aboard the *Storstad*. Many had broken limbs. Most were in a state of shock. For many, that shock was too great, and nearly twenty actually died aboard the collier. Over 400 survivors crowded aboard the *Storstad* that night. Their most urgent need was for warm clothing and medical attention. The collier, by nature of her calling, had little enough to offer of either; but what they had, the thirty-six men and one woman of the *Storstad* offered without stint. The crew gave away their clothes, their blankets and their food. Andersen himself produced half a dozen bottles of whisky from a private store, and doled them out among the survivors. The crew's bunks, for which they had little enough use themselves that night, went to those too weak to stand.

The Andersens had started their voyage with ample wardrobes, for Mrs Andersen had all the new clothes that she had made herself, while Captain Andersen, who was inclining to portliness, had recently bought himself a complete new outfit. Both ended with little more than the clothes they stood up in, for they had given the rest away Mrs Andersen later observed ruefully that her complete remaining outfit consisted of two dresses and two blouses. Andersen himself took his coat off, and wrapped it around the shoulders of a woman survivor. Mrs Andersen, hurrying among the survivors with two bottles of whisky under her arm and an urn of coffee in her hands, even gave away her shoes. She later borrowed a pair from an engineer. When the crew's clothes gave out, they used every remaining scrap of fabric that the ship could provide. Women wrapped themselves in tablecloths and curtains. One man spent an hour aboard the *Storstad* with a single pillowcase to cover his nakedness. A Salvation Army officer wrapped himself in sheets of newspaper. Major Frank Morris cheerfully admitted to having commandeered one of Mrs Andersen's treasured chenille drapes as being the only covering he could find. At that, he was not necessarily the most strangely attired survivor of that night. Another man left the *Storstad* clad in one of Mrs Andersen's new petticoats.

The scenes below decks defied description. Drawn by a desperate search for warmth, hundreds of survivors crowded into the engine- and boiler-rooms. Some of them leaned against the cylinders until their flesh blistered. Women, shuddering with cold, tried to dry their scraps of nightdresses. Many of them were so frozen that they could not even remove what little clothing they were wearing. Mrs Andersen had to undress them and put on their numbed bodies whatever garments she could find. Then the women were packed into the Norwegian seamen's narrow bunks two by two, head to toe like herrings in a can, to warm each other back to life.

Many passengers, mostly foreigners, were screaming in terror. Fergus Duncan, the young London solicitor, put it quite simply. Many of the survivors, he said, were raving mad. Into this squalid chaos, one man brought a semblance of order. Dr James Grant had little to offer except the sheer force of his personality. He used it to the full. Frozen, exhausted and half naked as he was, Grant turned to the treatment of the injured and the dying. For some, the little aid and comfort that Grant could bring came too late. At least five women died as the young doctor tried to treat them. The cause, in each case, was a combination of cold, exhaustion and shock.

Some of his other efforts were more rewarding. He set broken limbs, and there were many aboard the collier that night, in rough splints; he set the able-bodied survivors to giving artificial respiration to the apparently dead, with marked success in a number of cases. Where he had no professional aid to offer, he brought comfort and consolation. Single-handed, he quelled a riot among the foreign survivors. To those past any mortal aid, he offered the last decency. Under his direction, the dead were laid out in lines on the deck. Every disaster provides its hero: James Grant, by common consent, had earned that title.

Personality, however, was not the only force at the young doctor's disposal. Samaritan or no, Grant was not a man to interfere with when he was at work. While he was examining Sampson, the *Empress*'s old Chief Engineer who was lying close to death from exhaustion, a hysterical male survivor burst into the little cabin where the old man lay, and started to threaten Grant. The doctor knocked him flat and went on with his examination.

Later the Faculty of McGill University not only set a precedent, but broke its own rules by publicly presenting him with a duplicate diploma in medicine. The original was at the bottom of the St Lawrence.

Even amid the misery, there were flashes of humour. Mrs Andersen, hurrying among the survivors with whatever comforts she could find, came across one woman clad in a nightdress and a pair of corsets. Why, Mrs Andersen inquired, had the lady stopped to don her stays? To be honest, the woman replied, she was quite unable to remember what she had put on, or why.

The crew of the *Storstad* would have much to answer for, justifiably or otherwise, in the days that followed. But that was in the future. There were men and women aboard her that night who were grateful enough to the Norwegians for the mere gift of life. One woman Salvationist put her arms around Mrs Andersen. 'God bless you, my angel,' she said, 'If it had not been for you, we should have gone to the bottom.'

By the time the *Lady Evelyn* arrived on the scene, the *Empress* had long disappeared from sight, and the waves of her passing had died away in the sullen calm of the great river. Behind her she left a litter of empty lifeboats, masses of drifting wreckage, and everywhere, the dark, huddled bodies of the dead. There were a good many boats cruising among the debris of the great ship, for the *Eureka* had already arrived and her boats, together with those of the *Storstad* and the few from the *Empress* were quartering the river in a vain search for any more survivors. But the only living souls that the little mail tender found that night were five of the *Empress*'s crew whom she took from one of the liner's own lifeboats. The *Lady Evelyn* went alongside the *Storstad* and took off 338 survivors and a number of dead. The *Eureka* took most of the rest.

Among the living was Captain Henry Kendall. He had done his best to save his ship and her complement immediately after the disaster, he had survived the numbing battle for life in the river, and he had taken command of one of his ship's boats and saved as many lives as he could. Now, with his ship at the bottom of the river and two thirds of her passengers and crew dead, Kendall was in a state of collapse. Perhaps the most poignant recollection of Kendall's plight was to come, a good deal later, from Mrs Andersen. It was a memory she shared with nobody except Kendall himself, perhaps, for it was Mrs Andersen, bustling among the survivors with the ship's last reserve of comfort, a bottle of Benedictine, who found Kendall alone in the *Storstad*'s chartroom. He was stretched out, his face buried in his hands, on the leather sofa that traditionally served as the captain's couch during long vigils on the bridge. He was still wearing his sodden uniform. As she stood in the doorway, Mrs Andersen heard Kendall sobbing to himself: 'Why didn't they let me drown? Why didn't they let me drown?'

The apocryphal Mr Thomas Smart had a further story to tell about Kendall's return to Rimouski. When he himself got aboard the *Lady Evelyn*, Smart was reported to have told *The Times*, Kendall was stretched out on the deck, and men were giving him brandy to revive him. If it really was brandy, it was the first occasion in his life upon which spirits had passed that determined teetotaller's lips. When he was able to speak, Smart went on, Kendall looked around him and asked: 'where's the ship?' A man who looked like a doctor, and who was almost certainly James Grant himself, told Kendall that the *Empress* had gone. And Henry Kendall, master mariner, pushed his face into a piece of dirty tarpaulin and wept as if his heart would break.

Melodramatic though the account may be, it could have been true. Even though Mr Thomas Smart remains a shadowy figure, the story fits well with the other accounts of events that night. Kendall had certainly collapsed aboard the *Storstad*, and Grant had later done his best to bring him round with spirits. For a while after the disaster, Kendall was reported to be dying of pneumonia, and though he recovered from the shock and exposure from which he was certainly suffering, he was subsequently reported to be in a highly nervous state. He was not fully recovered from the ordeal when he appeared before the public inquiry a little over two weeks later.

The *Storstad* transferred her burden of humanity, living and dead, to the rescue ships, and resumed her voyage upstream, leaving the *Eureka* and the *Lady Evelyn* to land the survivors. As the early summer light spread over the great river, the melancholy little flotilla steamed back to Rimouski. Astern of them they left only a few empty lifeboats bobbing idly on the current. For days afterwards, bodies would be taken from the river but for the present, every human being, living or dead, who had been found was aboard one or other of the steamers.

For the living, huddled frozen and naked aboard the decks of the two little steamers, the voyage to Rimouski was an ordeal beyond description. The temperature at Rimouski that morning was 36 degrees, and there was frost on the ground. For many of them, those last hours out in the river were too much. No fewer than 22 of the survivors died after being taken from the water. A woman died as she was lifted ashore at Rimouski. One man died on the special train that was taking the survivors to Quebec.

Despite the protests of many of her shocked and frozen passengers, whose sole desire was to set foot on solid ground at the earliest possible moment, the *Eureka*'s captain decided not to make for her normal base at Father Point, but for Rimouski several miles further on. It may have seemed to the survivors callous to keep them afloat even minutes longer than absolutely necessary, but it was a wise and humane decision. Rimouski could furnish the clothing, the medical attention and the simple human help that the tiny settlement at Father Point could not hope to provide.

A number of passengers, on the other hand, did not want to be landed at Father Point anyway. They were terrified, it was said later, that they would be shipped straight off to England on the next vessel that passed without being given a chance to search for their missing loved ones. Even as the little steamers swirled alongside the quay at Rimouski Wharf, there was a further drama. A woman, screaming 'Oh, Leonard, my poor Leonard,' tried to hurl herself overboard from the *Lady Evelyn*. She was restrained, and was taken ashore struggling and shouting hysterically. At first it was thought that she was probably the wife of Leonard Palmer, the British financial writer. She was not, for as it later turned out, both Palmer and his wife were dead.

Despite the generous help of the *Storstad*'s crew, who had given away practically everything except the clothes they were wearing, many of the survivors were nearly naked. As they stumbled ashore at Rimouski that morning, they looked to Fergus Duncan like a bunch of Red Indians. The people of Rimouski met them at the quayside. They led down hand-carts piled with food and clothing. They fed the ravenous and warmed the frozen. They opened wardrobes and treasured family clothing chests and clad the naked. When their own wardrobes ran out they opened up the little town's few clothing shops and ransacked them. They carried the injured and the shocked, and there were many of both, into their homes and nursed them.

Every doctor in the district was called to help. The Intercolonial Railway station platform was turned into an emergency hospital. When the people of Rimouski had done all they could, the able-bodied survivors climbed aboard a special train for Quebec. The best that could be said for most of the survivors was that at least they were no longer naked. City gentlemen accustomed it was said to all the refinements of civilised existence, walked to the train in the blue jeans, heavy boots and mackinaw jackets of the farming folk among whom they had descended that morning. The pitifully small number of women were similarly unmodishly clad. As the special train pulled out for Quebec, carrying all the survivors fit to move, it was derailed before it had even left the station. The survivors had to wait for another one to be assembled.

There had been many partings aboard the *Empress* that night. So few had happy endings that they are worth recording. The strangest, perhaps, was that of an Italian couple named Breuga. They escaped alive from the Third Class quarters but became separated, and reached the *Storstad* in different lifeboats, each believing the other to have died. For two days in Rimouski, they were alone and heartbroken, and when they joined the Allan liner *Alsatian*, which was to take many of the survivors to Liverpool, they did not at first meet. They were on board the *Alsatian* for twenty-four hours before they literally fell into each other's arms on a companionway.

The dead remained. The *Eureka* and the *Lady Evelyn* made voyage after voyage to the scene, hoping against fading hope that by some miracle there would be fresh life to be saved from the river. All they brought back were corpses, laid out on their decks in ragged lines. The crews of the two little ships lifted them, head and foot, and laid them out on the quayside in the sunshine. Most of them, like the living, were nearly or completely naked. The men on the quayside arranged their pathetic scraps of clothing as decently as they could. Where there were none, they covered them with pieces of canvas, sacks, anything they could find. As the line grew, the shed on the quayside was turned into a makeshift mortuary, until it could hold no more. When it was full, they requisitioned buildings in the town, and filled them as well. There seemed to be no end to the long files of bodies lifted gently from ship to shore.

A reporter who walked along those silent lines in the gentle sunlight wrote that one of the saddest sights was the number of children. There were babies in arms, there were girls of eight or nine. One little girl, he said, was perhaps ten years old. Her brown hair was quite dry, and blew gently across her face. Beside her lay a young mother, perhaps twenty-five years old. A little baby was clasped to her breast, her arm curved around the baby's body in a grip that not even death could loosen.

A special trainload of coffins was despatched from Quebec to Rimouski. Many of them, a reporter observed disapprovingly, were tawdry articles covered with cheap ornamentation and intended for the use of the peasantry. In such, he observed, great and lowly alike were laid. Even then, there were not enough to go round. Local carpenters hastily manufactured rough wooden boxes for the overflow. On 30 May, the day after the disaster, the white painted Canadian Government revenue cutter *Lady Grey* arrived at Quebec, bearing 188 bodies. The British armoured cruiser *Essex* had arrived in the St Lawrence from the Caribbean. She was too late to aid the living, but she could and did perform a last melancholy service for the dead. One hundred of her crew sailed in the *Lady Grey* to unload her tragic cargo. For over an hour, the gaitered bluejackets carried the long lines of coffins from the little steamer to the quayside.

The big freight shed of Pier 27 on the Quebec waterfront had been turned into a vast mortuary. It had been reverently draped in black and purple, and long benches had been erected to support the dead. They were not long enough; the last few coffins had to stand on the floor. Hour after hour, the friends and relatives filed past the rows of bodies. The identification of the dead was nearly always difficult, because so many were naked. Among the Third Class passengers, it proved in many cases quite impossible. Not only was there no article upon the body that might identify it, but there was no grieving man or woman, as in the case of the First and Second Class passengers, to walk along the line of the dead, pause for a moment beside an open coffin and whisper; that is my husband, my father, my son. The Third Class passengers, in many cases, were drawn from that great army of foreign workers, Russian, Ukranian, Polish, Italian, who had wandered to Canada or the USA to labour on farm or railroad, make a little money, and move on. In many cases, there was a tragically simple reason why the bodies remained unidentified. It was because every single soul who could have identified them was also dead. The CPR had the utmost difficulty in even establishing how many of them there had been aboard the ship, let alone who they were. Many, in consequence, went to their graves as anonymously as they had lived.

One man, a splendid, big fellow the reporters said, lay in a rough pine coffin. His name was Martin Siecrinyk. The only reason anybody knew that was because around his neck he wore a little wallet, and in it the patient searchers found a sodden bundle of postal order counterfoils, bearing his name and sent from the settlement of Fernie, British Columbia to his mother in an obscure village in Central Europe. To which village, presumably he had been intending to return.

Even when the victims were claimed at all, there was often disagreement as to who they were. Painful scenes occurred as rival relatives brawled over the bodies of the disputed dead. Two fathers argued over the body of a small boy until the mayor of Quebec had to be called in to adjudicate. Five separate families claimed the remains of a baby. Typical of the confusion was that over the body of an elderly woman. Tiria Townshend claimed it was that of her aunt, Mrs Wynn Price. A group of crew survivors insisted it was that of a stewardess, Mrs Leader. Miss Townshend won. So difficult was the task that one body, confidently identified as that of a male member of the crew, subsequently turned out to be that of a woman. A considerable number of the dead were almost certainly buried under the wrong names.

Sometimes there was a clue to the identity of a particular body, but it did not always prove helpful. One corpse, that of a young man, had a yellow telegraph form clutched tightly in its outstretched hand. Only one word of the sodden, smeared writing was identifiable: 'marriage'. The problem of identification sometimes plumbed depths of macabre humour. An office boy, bearing a telegram, entered the dockside mortuary and inquired timidly for a Mr Frank Hamilton, of St John, New Brunswick. A British bluejacket pointed grimly to an open coffin. The youth dropped the telegram into the coffin, and fled. It made little difference, for the body turned out not to be that of Mr Hamilton anyway.

One woman, uncertain whether a body was that of her Finnish husband, asked the undertakers to unpick the lapels of his jacket. They did so, and found the 2000 dollars she had sewn there herself. In addition, about 1,400 dollars in unclaimed money was found by the searchers, including an unidentifiable wallet containing 430 dollars. Altogether there was a good deal of money lying around, and not all of it was handed in. To add to Andersen's discomfiture, two of his crew were arrested and charged with stealing £200 in traveller's cheques belonging to Mr Lionel Kent, who had actually swum to safety with them in his dressing gown pocket and then lost them in the lifeboat. Neither man was Norwegian; one was Maltese, the other Hawaiian. Both had signed on in Algiers as able seamen, a rank to which they had proved so manifestly unentitled that Andersen had kept them scrubbing decks and polishing brasswork. He handed them over to the authorities with undisguised relief.

CHAPTER 14

The Mathematics of Disaster

In the hours and days that followed the sinking, the CPR patiently totted up the mathematics of disaster. They were shocking. Of 1477 men, women and children who had left Quebec the previous afternoon, 1012 were dead. Of these, 840 were passengers. The other 172 were crew. One statistic was so astonishing, perhaps, that in all the acres of newsprint devoted to the disaster around the world, nobody commented on it. The number of passengers who had lost their lives in the *Empress* was actually greater than that in the *Titanic*. The total deathroll aboard the *Titanic* – 1503 – was nearly half as great again as in the *Empress*. But only 807 of those were passengers. The other 696 were crew.

Of the 465 people aboard the *Empress* who survived, a little under one third of the total aboard, 248 were crew, and only 217 were passengers. Almost exactly 80 per cent of the passengers had perished, against 41 per cent of the crew. Although there were good reasons for the disproportion, it was hardly surprising that eyebrows were raised at the fact.

There was, on the face of it, an almost equally suspicious imbalance in the proportion of passengers saved from each class. Of the 87 First Class passengers, 36, or almost exactly 41 per cent, had escaped with their lives. Of 253 in Second Class, only 48, or 19 percent, had survived. Those in Third Class, who made up almost exactly half the total of souls on board, had fared equally disastrously. Of 717 Third Class passengers, 133 were still alive. That again was almost exactly one in five.

Not surprisingly, women fared worse than men. Whereas 172 out of 609 adult male passengers had survived, in itself an appallingly small proportion, exactly 41 adult women had lived out of 310. Again, class of travel had had a considerable bearing on the chances of survival. One third of the women in First Class reached safety. Among their 169 sisters in Third Class, just 17 lived.

The most shocking statistic of all was the death toll among the children. Of 138 children – 65 boys and 73 girls – aboard the *Empress* three girls and a boy lived. Of the four children in First Class, one had been taken alive from the water. In the Second Class, it was two out of 32. In Third Class one child, a boy, lived out of 102 children aboard.

Among the crew, death was less discriminating. The deck officers suffered worst, for of the seven who sailed from Quebec, just two – Kendall and First Officer Jones – lived to testify at the inquiry. But overall, 36 of the 59 deck staff survived. So did 92 of the 130 engineering staff. One hundred and thirteen of the 212 catering staff also survived. So did three of the five musicians. Three of four supernumerary engineers from the liner *Empress of Asia* who were taking passage to Liverpool came through the ordeal alive. But among the crew, as among the passengers, death dealt cruelly with the women. Matron Jones and nine stewardesses had sailed from Quebec. Mrs Helena Hollis was the only one who survived.

The disaster fell with appalling force upon the people of Toronto. Of an estimated 200 from that city who had boarded the *Empress*, about thirty escaped with their lives. Other Canadian communities suffered equally savagely. The town of Galt, Ontario, contributed ten passengers to the *Empress*'s passenger list. Two survived. Many families were simply wiped out.

At the age of sixty-seven, William Russell had had his fill of Canada and was returning to his native town of Newmains, near Glasgow, where for many years he had worked as an engineman in an iron foundry. With him went his daughters Sarah and Minnie plus Minnie's husband and their five children, aged between two and thirteen. Not one of them survived. Four young sisters named Farr had been orphaned by the death in London, Ontario of both their parents. The girls, whose ages ranged from three to eight, were on their way back to the care of relatives in England. Father Point was as far as they were to go. The Jay family had emigrated to Canada some four years earlier from the respectable North London suburb of Leyton. John Jay was a carpenter by trade, and his little jobbing builder's business in Toronto had flourished, so much so that by the spring of 1914, he could afford to send Mrs Jay and their four children off to England to spend a summer with her parents in Leyton. There had been a little confusion about their travelling arrangements, for at the last minute, Mrs Jay for some unexplained reason had become nervous about the White Star liner *Teutonic* in which they were due to sail. Mr Jay had gone down to the shipping office himself and changed their tickets for berths aboard the *Empress*. He was on the quayside to wave them farewell when they sailed. He never saw his family again.

A generous Toronto employer had rewarded his English coachman's faithful service with tickets aboard the *Empress* for himself, his wife, and their two children. None survived. William Davies was taking his young wife to England so that their first child might be born in their native land. George Hedgewe was escorting telephone operator Nellie Jones to Brierly Hill in Staffordshire so that they might be married among her family. Both men found themselves alone. Frank Fraser was so homesick for his native glens that he withdrew 250 dollars of his savings and boarded the *Empress* without telling his family, whose disapproval he feared. They were not to see him again.

Of all those who had boarded the *Empress* in Quebec, none had come further than the Byrne family of Brisbane, Australia. Edward Byrne had saved for ten years to take his wife and daughter on the journey of a lifetime around the world. The reporters who stood vigil over the mortuary found a lonely old man crying bitterly in the corner of a shed. His lament was not only that his wife and daughter were dead; it was that he himself was still alive.

Mrs Amelia Mott, of Woodstock, Ontario was travelling

under her maiden name, for she had run away from her husband, a Chinese laundryman named Chou, and was heading home to England. Her flight ended in death. Harry Yudin was a Russian who worked in a Toronto factory. Word had reached him that his wife in Russia was dying, and was asking for him. Yudin had no money for the fare. His workmates passed the hat to buy him a ticket aboard the *Empress*. A week later, they turned out in force for his funeral.

The first rumours of disaster reached the great cities of Canada at about 3.10 a.m. Montreal time. The Toronto and Montreal morning newspapers, nearing the end of their normal night's work, hastily put back their front pages as the ticker tapes chattered into life with the first ominous reports from Father Point. There was time to launch hurried extra editions upon the streets of Canada's principal cities, bearing the grim reports that 800 people were feared to have lost their lives. All that day, the afternoon papers followed up with extras as the story broke.

Tragically, the crowds who gathered at the CPR offices as the news spread were buoyed up by a cruelly false hope. Around midday, the news spread that the reports of heavy loss of life were untrue; although the *Empress* herself had been lost, the rumours ran, the passengers and crew had been saved. The CPR officials, in perfect good faith, seem to have believed the story themselves and to have encouraged the public to believe it too. Then, about 2.30 p.m. the blow fell. The first reports, it seemed, had been all too appallingly accurate. Sir Thomas Shaughnessy, the CPR's president, put his company's *imprimatur* upon the reports of the disaster with a statement which, considering that he still had no first hand report from the captain of the *Empress*, was reasonably accurate.

From the facts available, he said, it seemed that the *Empress*, when stopped in a dense fog off Rimouski, had been rammed by the collier *Storstad* 'in such a manner as to tear the ship from the middle to the screw, this rendering the watertight bulkheads with which she was equipped, useless'. The accident, he went on, occurred at a time when the passengers were in bed, and there was insufficient time before the ship went down for the officers to rouse the passengers and lead them to the boats, of which there were sufficient to hold a very much larger number of people than those on board. After that, there was nothing for the relatives to do except gather once more in silent crowds around the doors of the steamship offices and wait to learn who had lived and who had died.

Although Sir Thomas's statement was reasonably accurate, it contained one curious error that was to be repeated many times in the first hours and days after the disaster. He claimed that the ship had been rammed on the left-hand side. Whether Sir Thomas himself created that misconception, or whether he had been misled by the early reports is impossible to say, but virtually all the early press reports, and many of the survivors' stories, repeated the error.

Sir Thomas's dramatic statement that the ship was 'torn from the middle to the screw' was widely believed for a time, possibly because nobody could conceive of a large, strong and well sub-divided vessel sinking within minutes unless she had been so torn. The memory of the *Titanic*, slashed open for a hundred yards of her length, seemed consciously or otherwise to have influenced what people genuinely believed had happened. Whether they were right or wrong we shall probably never know. The evidence lies many feet down in the silt at the bottom of the St Lawrence, but it seems doubtful if the damage, appalling as it was, was remotely akin to the early descriptions.

So sudden had been the disaster that one Canadian newspaper still had an advertisement for the *Empress* in the edition that announced her loss. Even after that, there were odd lapses. Nearly two weeks after the sinking, the London *Daily Telegraph* carried a CPR advertisement with a drawing of the *Empress*, labelled with her name.

In London, the first word of calamity came at about nine in the morning, when the two men who were to be most heavily involved in the London office were just reaching their desks in the CPR's headquarters in Cockspur Street. They were G.M. Bosworth, CPR's vice-president in charge of the company's shipping interests, and George McLaren Brown, the company's European manager. By an irony of fate Bosworth was in Britain, where he was arranging a merger between the catering activities of the CPR and Allan lines, at precisely the time when his employers must most badly have needed his services in Canada.

The two men sent telegrams to their head office, asking for more details, but details were precisely what nobody could give them. The early editions of the London evening papers contained much the same starkly disquieting news as the Canadian and and American papers. Predictably, the reports sent crowds of the anxious, the interested and the purely curious hurrying to Cockspur Street to crowd around the CPR's office windows. The crowd, the reporters said, was 'greatly concerned and agitated'. Many were in tears.

John Burns, President of the Board of Trade in Mr Asquith's Liberal Government, was already at his desk. He was responsible for all matters concerning British shipping, particularly safety. Considering the cudgelling his department had received over the manifestly inadequate safety regulations under which the *Titanic* had been permitted to put to sea, Mr Burns's lively interest in the fate of the *Empress* was entirely proper.

Nonetheless, Mr Burns's first recorded action that morning was perhaps a little odd. He sent a telegram to Ottawa, requesting the Canadian Minister of Marine to render all assistance. That gentleman's private reactions have not been preserved, which is perhaps as well. Then, for good measure, Mr Burns despatched a similar message to Washington, asking the United States authorities to send the Coastguard ice patrol cutter *Seneca* at once to help in the rescue efforts. Washington responded swiftly, promising every assistance in its power, but pointed out that the *Seneca* was three days' steaming from Rimouski. The Canadian press remarked tartly that the Board of Trade did not seem to be quite sure where the St Lawrence was. Perhaps Mr Burns simply felt that to do absolutely anything was better than to do absolutely nothing.

Then Mr Burns set out for Cockspur Street to interview Mr Brown. He did not stay long, for Mr Brown had little to tell him. However, Cockspur Street had not seen the last of Mr Burns that day.

For the relatives outside the office, more concerned with their private terrors than with the comings and goings of statesmen, the first tidings of interest came at 11.20 a.m. Those close enough to the notice board to read the hastily typed sheet learned that at 2.30 that morning – incorrect, but near enough – the *Empress*, homeward-bound for Liverpool, had sunk after a collision with the collier *Storstad*. Two steamers were at once on the scene, and 'a large number of passengers' had been picked up and landed at Rimouski. A later announcement said that there had been 1181 souls on board, and that it was rumoured that of these, 337 had been saved.

That afternoon, the same cruel delusion that had deceived Canada ran around the waiting crowds in London. A Reuter report quoted the Rimouski correspondent of the French language newspaper *La Patrie* as saying that the *Lady Evelyn* and the *Eureka* had docked at Rimouski, and that their captains had reported that the balance of the passengers and crew were in lifeboats from the *Empress* and from the two rescue steamers. As soon as the steamers had landed the 400 passengers they had aboard, they would return to the scene of the wreck to take up the balance who were reported as being saved.

Given the confusion, the uncertainty that prevailed about how many people had been aboard in the first place, and the pitfalls of hurried translation from the French, it is easy to understand how such a message, sent in good faith, was 'joyfully received'. Two people fainted. Mr Burns returned. After another brief consultation, he hurried off again to stir the Admiralty into taking suitable action to rescue or assist the passengers. As he left Cockspur Street, he spoke words of reassurance to the waiting crowds, and told reporters that the news, 'if true', was excellent. But the news was not true. The cruel illusion of hope vanished at 8.40 p.m. with a bleak message that said simply: 'the best available information gives 400 only saved'. The flag over the CPR office was at half-mast. It was to stay there for a considerable time.

In 1914 Liverpool was still to a large extent the principal British terminus of the transatlantic shipping business, and the citizens, from merchant princes to dock labourers, were deeply involved with ships and the sea. Certainly, they were no strangers to disaster. Nonetheless, Liverpool was shocked by the news of the disaster. The loss of the *Empress* was a far worse blow to the city than the loss of the *Titanic*, for the *Empress* was to a far greater extent a Liverpool ship. Not only was Liverpool the port from which she began her Atlantic voyages, and to which she returned, but it was also the city from which she drew her crew. Ninety per cent of them, it was estimated, came from Merseyside. Accordingly, the tragedy struck with appalling force among the mean back streets from which so many of her crew, particularly her firemen, were drawn. There, poverty was never more than a meal away. The Liverpool Irish families that dwelled there knew the bitter hardship of unemployment. They knew, too, that the death of a breadwinner could mean something close to actual physical starvation for his family. A job, any job, was a privilege. One man, out of work for nearly three months, had hurried home not long before with the good news that he had found a fireman's berth aboard the *Empress of Ireland*. He did not return. Accordingly, few among the crowds who gathered at the CPR offices on the Liverpool waterfront were seeking news of passengers. The great majority were waiting anxiously for tidings of a father, a husband or a son among the crew. As in London, as in Canada, the office staff did what they could to inform and comfort, but there was initially little to tell.

As the news trickled in, the company tried to pass it on by posting typewritten notices in their office windows, a practice that probably compounded the anxiety and confusion as the crowd jostled forward to read the sparse announcements. A police inspector, struggling with his men to control the crowds, stood the office commissionaire on a stool and bade him read the announcements in a loud voice. The commissionaire did so, and a hush fell on the crowd. It was broken only by a woman's scream: 'Oh my God, there's no news of my boy.' She spoke for hundreds.

Chief Officer Steede's wife, described as being 'of delicate constitution', was taken home in hysterics. She had three children, one of them in hospital, and she did not yet know that she was a widow. As in Canada and London, the ordeal was made immeasurably worse by the cruel and baseless report that all aboard had been saved. As it spread, many hurried home to offer a prayer of gratitude, only to have their illusions shattered a few hours later. Even when there was good news, it was not always easy to take in. One woman, distraught with worry, heard her son's name read out from a list of those saved, assumed it was a list of the dead, and became hysterical. Her friends had great difficulty in persuading her that she had not been bereaved.

At Lloyd's, the first rumours of the sinking were treated with something close to disbelief. The *Empress*'s hull was said to be insured for £400,000, and her cargo, excluding bullion, for another £150,000 or so. About half the risk was covered by Lloyd's, the rest being shared out among some fourteen or fifteen German insurance companies. Accordingly, the ship's safety was a matter of the most direct and material concern to many members of Lloyd's.

Marine underwriting, however, is an occupation that calls for strong nerves, for disasters and rumours of disaster are its stock in trade. The first reports to reach London spoke of a collision with ice, no doubt yet another echo of the *Titanic* disaster. Since the gentlemen of Lloyds knew that ice was unlikely to be a menace to large ships in that part of the St Lawrence at that time of year, the report seems to have been largely discounted, so much so that those cautious souls who had underwritten a portion of the risk on the *Empress* and who felt like hedging their bet had no difficulty reinsuring their liability for two, three or four per cent. A few hours later, they would have been hard put to it to cover themselves at ten times the premium.

There was a curious reason for the scepticism. Since the general adoption of wireless, insurers had been plagued by supposed reports of marine disasters which subsequently turned out to be misunderstandings or even complete hoaxes, so much so that there was serious talk of including secret passwords in distress calls in order to establish their authenticity. Only weeks before, there had been a highly circumstantial report of the stranding of the Pacific Mail liner *Siberia* off the coast of Formosa while on passage from Hong Kong to Yokohama. It had cost the underwriters upwards of £20,000 in reinsurance before it was established that the *Siberia* was still snug in harbour, and that the report was due to a garbled wireless message. In another case, a garbled transmission had sent the reinsurance rate on the German liner *Wildenfels* soaring to 80 per cent before it came to light that she was the rescuer, not the rescued. The early reports of the sinking of the *Empress* were suspected of being just such a *canard*.

Nonetheless, as the morning wore on, the reinsurance rate on the ship gradually rose to 10 per cent as the conviction spread that something, serious or otherwise, had happened to the liner. Then confirmed reports came in of a collision with another vessel. Some said she was the German liner *Hannover*, known to be somewhere near Rimouski on her way upriver. The rate leaped to 30 per cent, and thousands of pounds' worth of risk were covered at that price. The market was thoroughly alarmed now, and the rate climbed higher still, to 35, 40 and finally 50 per cent. Whether it would have risen further is a matter for speculation, for at that figure the reinsurance market on the *Empress* collapsed. The bleakest fears were confirmed. The *Empress* had sunk.

Ironically, exactly the same happened to the insurance market on the *Storstad*, which was insured almost entirely on the Continental European market. Reinsurance rates upon her rose to 50 and 60 per cent on the erroneous assumption that she, too, had probably been sunk.

Shortly thereafter, the *Empress*'s British underwriters paid out the sum of £250,000. They were probably thankful that it was no worse. One unnamed passenger was reported to have insured his life on that particular voyage for 'a very substantial sum.' To the underwriters' relief, as well as his own, he survived.

The world's press was in no doubt about the magnitude of the story. Most English-speaking newspapers cleared their main news pages of almost every other topic for the first day or two. The *Daily Mail* got things into perspective the day after the accident with a streamer headline across the entire page which read simply: *ANOTHER TITANIC DISASTER*.

Some curious misconceptions surfaced briefly among the early reports. One Britsh newpaper, reporting that the great majority of the survivors were from the Third Class, drew certain odd conclusions from the fact. The First Class passengers, it explained solemnly, had mostly perished because their cabins were so large and ornate that the occupants had been unable to find their way out of them.

Almost every British and Canadian newspaper of note ran a leading article upon the disaster. Through them all there ran, convincingly and movingly, a single immensely human theme; a cry of agonised outrage at the sheer brutality of fate. Two years before, the worst maritime accident in history had snatched 1500 to their deaths. Since then the best brains in the industry had laboured to devise ways of ensuring that such a calamity as that of the *Titanic* could never happen again. Legislation, belated but competent, had been enacted to try to ensure that never again should human life be put in such jeopardy. And now, as if to mock all men's efforts, the world had awakened to yet another appalling tragedy. There were some sober reflections upon a social system that could devote an infinity of resources to building ships ever larger, ever more luxurious, ever faster, but which could not or would not build a ship that could stay afloat for fifteen minutes after a collision in calm waters within sight of shore.

The *Glasgow Herald*, which spoke for the greatest shipbuilding city in the world, expressed the hope that the imminent entry into service of the new 45,000 ton Cunarder *Aquitania* might mark the end of the fashion for building ships so large that to a single hull was entrusted the equivalent of the entire population of a fair-sized town.

CHAPTER 15

Homecoming

Battered but navigable, the *Storstad* swam her way upstream on her interrupted journey to Montreal, watched by curious eyes, her progress reported from bend to bend of the wide river. Her bulkheads were holding well, and she had been brought back to an even keel by flooding her aft-ballast tanks to compensate for the weight of water in her crushed flooded forepeak. Just before 1.30 p.m. on the afternoon of Sunday 31 May, the *Storstad*, her Norwegian ensign fluttering at half-mast, nosed gently alongside the Hochelaga Wharf at Montreal. A silent crowd of spectators had gathered at the dockside to watch her arrival. Their demeanour, an observer noted, was mildly curious rather than hostile. Andersen, gazing down from the bridge-wing, megaphone in hand, studiously ignored them. Beside him, bareheaded, stood Mrs Andersen. As the big collier nudged the wharf, she turned, rested her hand for a moment on her husband's sleeve, and went below.

A crowd of about forty reporters was waiting to meet the *Storstad*. They learned little. The men of the *Storstad* had no wish at that moment to share their inmost thoughts, or anything else very much, with the world's press. Their captain was taciturn, and the crew themselves were totally uncommunicative. To the questions shouted from quayside to ship, they replied with shrugs or shook their heads.

The first man aboard was the Norwegian Consul General, Finn Koren. He had matters of importance to impart, including the fact that the CPR's lawyers had issued a writ against the *Storstad* for two million dollars for the loss of the *Empress*. However, while the attorneys might have acted with despatch in issuing the writ, they had a certain difficulty in serving it. The High Court's Admiralty Marshal, who tried to follow the Consul General aboard, was unceremoniously shoved ashore again. It took some little while to convey to Captain Andersen that whether he liked it or not, he was going to have to permit the Admiralty Court's officers to perform their duties without being thrown overboard.

Even when the Admiralty Marshal, a Mr Marston, finally got aboard to arrest the *Storstad*, Andersen hotly demanded to know by whose authority his ship was being detained. Mr Marston was by now in no mood to be trifled with. 'By authority of the British Empire,' he replied majestically. Eventually, a writ was nailed to the *Storstad*'s chart-room door, together with a summons requiring Andersen to answer to the writ. It took a little time, because the representatives of the law had neglected to bring a hammer. They had to use a shoe instead. Andersen looked at the summons, and walked away. A little later a seaman came along and pulled it down.

Meanwhile, the reporters, unable to get anything worth writing about out of Andersen, were casting appraising eyes over the *Storstad* herself. Although it was Sunday afternoon, the big dockside grabs were already biting into the 11,000 tons of coal in her holds. As her hull rose steadily higher in the water, it could be seen that her stem had been twisted so violently that it had been bent almost into a semi-circle. Some of her lower plates had been torn from their rivets and twisted to the right. Wedged in the torn plating were splinters of white enamelled woodwork from the *Empress*'s cabins.

Later, with a battery of lawyers on hand, Andersen let the reporters look aboard his ship. Mrs Andersen sadly showed them the living-quarters over which she had laboured so lovingly. They were a ruin. The trunks that Captain Andersen had grumbled about were empty, so was the wardrobe where Andersen's gargantuan blue serge suits had hung. Of the bright new chenille curtains, a single drape dangled drunkenly from the rail around the Andersens' bunk. Every other scrap of material aboard the collier had gone. So had her food supplies, Andersen's little private store of spirits, and every other creature comfort that the *Storstad* had had to offer.

All the right things were done. King George V sent condolences, so did President Woodrow Wilson. Prince Henry of Prussia sent a most amiable expression of regret, adding how much he had always admired the Company's ships in Hong Kong. George McLaren Brown, who had other things on his mind, found time to send gracious and suitable appreciative acknowledgements. An astringent note was added by Mr William Holman, Premier of New South Wales, who sent his commiserations but added that shipping company directors whose vessels could be sunk in fifteen minutes ought to be jailed for manslaughter.

A memorial service for the Irvings was held in St Margaret's, Westminster. The list of mourners read like a Who's Who of the theatre. *The Stage*, in a moving obituary of the couple, said that the Irvings' fate, 'engulfed suddenly in the night in a vortex of icy waters', was symbolic of the professional uncertainties of an actor's life.

The Lord Mayor of London opened a relief fund; the Lord Mayor of Liverpool opened another. A sum of £180,000, it was estimated, would be needed to relieve suffering in Liverpool alone; £100,000 for the relatives of the passengers and £80,000 for those of the crew. The City Fathers of Toronto voted an immediate 25,000 dollars for the relief of suffering. Those of Montreal voted 30,000 dollars. The list of donors to the various funds ran into many hundreds. Among the donations was a unobtrusive £100 from a certain Mr A.F. Klavenes, of Christiania, Norway. He was the owner of the *Storstad*. Mr Herbert Towers opened his own relief fund in Dewsbury, Yorkshire. The audience at the Palace of Varieties gave him two pounds, thirteen shillings and tenpence. The magistrates gave him three months in jail.

Mr Herbert Tree gave a benefit matinee of 'Pygmalion' in aid of the distress fund. Mrs Patrick Campbell and Mr

George Bernard Shaw donated their services. The Boston Grand Opera Company gave a benefit performance in Paris. A lady named Felice Lyne insisted in taking part as a gesture of thanksgiving. It was by pure chance that she had not been a passenger aboard the *Empress*. In the Albert Hall in London, 400 musicians from six British orchestras united in a concert in aid of the stricken. Their seven conductors included Sir Henry Wood and Mr Thomas Beecham. The programme was of a melancholy nature.

As after any great disaster, there were those ready to claim that they had been visited by portents. Mr Tatting, the stage manager of the Kingsway Theatre, recounted a most complicated and highly allegorical dream, the burden of which was to lead him to a conviction that some ill must have befallen his friend Irving. The wife of one of the *Empress*'s stewards said that her husband had three times dreamed that the ship was sinking, and had hesitated to sail in her again. Since her name has not been preserved, we do not know if the unfortunate man benefited by the portent. A woman passenger was reported to have cancelled her passage because a gypsy fortune-teller had counselled her against a journey in May. Her companion boarded the ship, and died.

Strange stories multiplied. None was stranger than that of Mr Charles Hirxheimer, who despite his name was an Englishman. Shortly before sailing, it was said, Mr Hirxheimer had attended a small farewell party at which sundry other passengers and some officers were present. When glasses were raised to a pleasant voyage, Mr Hirxheimer, who seems to have been a regular First Class passenger, refused to join the toast. The ship, he said glumly, was going to the bottom. The sailors, traditionally sensitive where matters of luck were concerned, rebuked him sharply. His joke, in their view, was in very bad taste. It was no joke, Hirxheimer maintained stoutly. They were all going to drown. The little party ended on a sour note. The story, as such stories do, grew stranger. After sailing, it was said, Mr Hirxheimer roamed the ship, trying to give away 500 dollars on the grounds that he would soon have no use for it. He tried to throw in his small change for good measure. Although the strange tale of Mr Hirxheimer was recounted by more than one source, it can hardly be regarded as authenticated beyond reasonable doubt. One thing, however, is quite certain. There was a passenger aboard named Hirxheimer. And he drowned.

There was also the strange tragic story of Mrs Wilde, a nurse from Liverpool, whom the London reporters found waiting patiently outside the CPR offices in Cockspur Street. Her story was heart-breaking, and it duly rent the hearts of readers all over the world as surely as it had sparked the professional interest of the reporters themselves. For Mrs Wilde explained with moving simplicity that she was the widow of the late Chief Officer Wilde of the *Titanic*, as well as being also the bereaved sister of the late Sixth Officer George Evans also of the Titanic. Now she was waiting, hoping against hope, for news of her younger brother, Third Officer Cedric Evans of the *Empress of Ireland*. Oh, and it was worth adding that her uncle was Captain Henry Kendall. Nor was this the end of her tragic story. Seventeen years before, Mrs Wilde was said to have added, her father, himself a master mariner, had perished in the loss of the liner *Britannic*.

It was an undoubted fact that Chief Officer Wilde of the *Titanic* had died with his ship two years earlier. It should simply be placed on record that there was no officer named Evans aboard the *Empress* on her last voyage. Moreover, while a White Star liner named the *Britannic* had indeed figured in a nasty collision in the Atlantic, it had happened in 1887, not 1897, the ship did not sink, and there is no record that her captain was even hurt, let alone killed. Which is certainly not to say that Mrs Wilde's tragic story was untrue in all particulars. It simply remains a mystery, one of the many that flourished during the first confused days after the disaster.

The inventors had a wonderful time. Their proposals varied from the eminently sensible to the bizarre. They included double-sided rafts that could be boarded no matter which way up they floated, a device widely adopted during World War II; uncapsizable lifeboats; and entire detachable decks that would float away if the ship sank. One writer simply wanted an inflatable air cushion attached to each deckchair, so that it might become an *extempore* life-preserver. The *Daily Graphic* wanted ships to have buffers, just like a railway engine, and produced a workmanlike sketch to show how they would appear. The writer seemed confident that with their aid, 17,000 tons of coal and steel moving at the speed, perhaps, of a running man would have rebounded with the ease of a carelessly-shunted goods wagon.

The Gaskin-Hart double-sided lifeboat was actually launched into the West India dock in London before the eyes of a not-very-interested national press. Since it consisted essentially of two lifeboats fastened keel to keel like Siamese twins, so that one was always submerged and upside down, it was not perhaps the handiest of craft. Mr William MacDonald of Portland, Oregon demonstrated his waterproof, rubberised survival suit with built-in inflatable life-jacket. It appeared to have possibilities. The inventor splashed about happily in the chill waters of the Fraser River for eight hours without either drowning or catching pneumonia.

The anti-collision, or prevention-is-better-than-cure school, had much larger ideas. One system involved detecting the whereabouts of a vessel in fog with the aid of hisses of steam that would be detected with the aid of sound reflectors and earphones. The rival Kelway system involved explosive charges, stopwatches, a mechanical computer on the bridge for solving problems in trigonometry, and the use of 'Hertzian waves'. It was not to be widely heard of again. One gentleman said that four years before, he had invented a system for rendering ships watertight. However, he added grumpily, since it was practically impossible to get any kind of professional in Britain to listen to a layman, his invention had remained in the chrysalis stage. Joseph Conrad said the disaster would never have occurred if the *Storstad* had hung a strong fender over her bows when she saw the Empress ahead of her.

The survivors came home. A special train steamed into Toronto's Union Station, bearing the pathetic handful of Salvationists and other Toronto passengers. A crowd of 4000 people broke into the 'Old Hundredth' 'Praise God from Whom All Blessings Flow'. Then the survivors were taken off to Eaton's famous department store to receive a speech of welcome, a lunch, and a new outfit of clothes, with the compliments of the store.

Most of the surviving Third Class passengers, together with the crew survivors, were hastened aboard Allan liners bound for Liverpool or the Clyde. Most arrived in Britain penniless and clad in whatever clothes had been found for them on the spot in Canada. They included Swedes, Poles, Italians, French, Russians, Irish and English. The CPR's British representatives assembled a vast array of clothing of all kinds and sizes, and invited the survivors to help themselves. But many of the Third Class passengers refused to sail for Greenock aboard the liner *Corsican*, and demanded to be returned to their various starting places in Canada and the United States.

Much the same happened when other survivors were offered passage aboard the liner *Alsatian* to Liverpool. A group of Russians and Finns booked to sail aboard her found themselves contemplating a vessel remarkably similar in their eyes to that from which they had so recently and so narrowly escaped with their lives. The Finns marched stolidly up the gangway; the Russians staged a sit-down strike on the trunks and boxes in the embarkation shed, and flatly refused to budge.

On 1 June, three days after the disaster, a woman was found in Rimouski. She was stark naked and quite mad. From her incoherent ravings it at first appeared that she was probably Swedish, and had drifted ashore from the *Empress* upon a piece of wreckage. Later it was decided that she was Norwegian, and that while she had come ashore in more orthodox fashion aboard one of the rescue ships, she had immediately fled into the neighbouring woods where she was found. For a time it seemed that she might be Mrs Magnus Luren, the wife of the Norwegian who had so gallantly befriended young Mrs Greenaway. She was not; but if her true identity was ever discovered, there appears to be no surviving record of the fact.

HOMECOMING

A Mrs Willets of Toronto, having left her husband and four children, was believed to have sailed aboard the *Empress* and to have perished miserably. Several weeks later she was arrested in California in company with two gentlemen, and accused under the Mann Act of crossing the state line with immoral intent.

The dead, too, came home. Seventeen Salvationists were buried in Toronto. Over 1,600 people walked in the funeral procession. An estimated 150,000 lined the route. Three thousand people jammed into St James's Methodist Church in Montreal for a memorial service to the dead; an apocalyptic thunderstorm broke over the city, and plunged the overwrought congregation into pitch darkness. A panic was narrowly averted.

In Quebec, nine crewmen and three passengers were carried to their graves escorted by fifty constables, a party of sailors from the *Essex*, and the band of the Garrison Artillery playing the Dead March. It poured with rain all the way. Kendall, wearing a gold-braided uniform frock coat and cap, attended the funeral. The upright, firm-jawed young captain would no longer have been recognised by most of his passengers. He was a stooped and haggard-faced figure who walked with a stick, leaning heavily on the arm of John Walsh of the CPR. The strain was too much; at the end of the melancholy ceremony he broke down and wept. Later, they stopped preparing individual plots and opened a mass grave in Mount Hermon cemetery. In it, they buried another fifty-three bodies, most of them unidentified.

In London, the Salvation Army Convention went ahead. There, the men and women of the Salvation Army from all over the world remembered their fellow soldiers. Every seat in the Albert Hall was filled, save for 148 chairs that stood empty, one for every Salvationist who had died. Across them was thrown the white mourning badge of the Corps. A Salvation Army band marched past the CPR offices in Cockspur Street, playing: 'For those in peril on the Sea.'

CHAPTER 16

Attempt at Salvage

For days, the bubbles rose in lazy streams to glitter and burst upon the surface of the river. Over the wreck, a great cloud of yellowish mud marked the liner's grave. A little later, a green painted wreck buoy was laid to mark the spot.

The CPR swore in special constables to patrol the river bank for miles below the scene of the disaster and watch for bodies drifting ashore. The people of Rimouski, wise in the ways of the river, prayed for a thunderstorm, presumably in furtherance of the old belief that the reverberations of the thunderclaps would break the river's grip upon the dead and bring them to the surface. The curé of Rimouski led his choir out upon the river in a boat to conduct a memorial mass over the grave of the men and women who had met so violent an end upon the very shore of his parish.

In the days that followed the sinking, it was said, no fewer than fourteen of the liner's lifeboats were recovered from the St Lawrence. Many of them would appear to have been collapsibles that had broken free from the wreck long after the sinking, and they must have added materially to the confusion over how many boats were actually launched at the time of the disaster. The *Empress*'s bridge log was found floating on the surface of the river amid vast quantities of flotsam. Its sodden pages were eagerly examined, but proved to contain nothing of substance for it was complete only up to midnight, when the previous watch had handed over to their reliefs and gone below. The ship's scrap log, in which the events of two final, fatal hours of her career should have been jotted down in pencil as they occurred, was never recovered.

There was talk of salvage. Almost at once, a crack American salvage team arrived upon the scene. Their leader, William Wotherspoon, had made his reputation recovering the bodies of drowned seamen from the American battleship *Maine*, whose sinking in Havana harbour had started the Spanish-American war. Wotherspoon's role was a little ambiguous; he had been engaged, it was said, by the CPR to recover the bodies of the dead from the liner's hull. Since this was patently impossible, even to the lay eye, it might have been surmised that the real purpose of his mission was less to recover bodies than to demonstrate to distraught relatives that if the remains of their loved ones were not restored to them it was not due to any callous disregard on the part of the liner's owners. Then there was the mail. The Canadian Post Office would have liked to see that restored to them, if only because the sodden mailbags contained very substantial sums of money.

Finally, of course, there was the bullion. Mr Wotherspoon had little to say about that. Gentlemen who earn their dangerous living diving on wrecks for bullion are inclined to be reticent upon the subject.

Wotherspoon's efforts came to nothing much, largely because almost immediately the *Empress* claimed yet another victim. Wotherspoon's chief diver, an expert salvage man named Edward Cossaboom, recovered two bodies from the wreck but almost immediately afterwards lost his own life, apparently by falling from the hull of the wrecked ship while exploring far beneath the surface.

Wotherspoon's explorations were shared by the men from the cruiser *Essex*, which had an expert diving team aboard. Their task was simply to establish precisely the position of the sunken ship and the direction in which she was lying, a task that was most adequately accomplished by the simple process of taking a compass bearing on the lines of bubbles that rose from her divers' helmets as they walked along the sunken hull.

The divers themselves might have described their task a little differently. Leading Seaman Wilfred Whitehead of HMS *Essex* had inched his way along the steel plates of the liner's left-hand side, feeling rather than seeing his way in the murk and bitter cold of the river bed as the wayward currents of the St Lawrence tugged at his clumsy canvas diving suit and copper helmet. It was not an easy journey, even for an expert diver like Whitehead. Already, a thin layer of slime covered the steel plates, so that Whitehead left a pattern of fingermarks behind him as he groped his way along them. He found little enough to report, for he came across no portholes open on that part of the left-hand side that he was able to examine. Instead, he found a piece of blue cotton cloth nipped in the brass frame of a closed porthole. He pulled out his diver's knife, hacked it off and brought it to the surface. Apart from its curiosity value, it contributed nothing in particular to the debate about the causes of the disaster. What might have been found if Whitehead and his fellow divers had approached the other side of the ship remains a matter for speculation.

So far from attempting to enter the sunken hull, the *Essex*'s divers were wisely forbidden even to venture beneath the menacing overhang of her right hand side, for fear the liner should turn in her grave and roll upon them. It was not for lack of incentive. Captain Hugh Watson, RN, was offered substantial sums of money if his men would attempt to enter the ship and recover the bullion from her strong room. The offers were declined.

The St Lawrence stayed open. Of necessity, the big ships passing up and down the river sailed almost directly over the spot where the *Empress* had gone to the bottom. One after another, they paid their respects to the ship and her complement. The White Star liner *Teutonic* with the Irvings' fellow actors and actresses aboard, called her crew to attention by bugle. Aboard her sister, the *Megantic*, the passengers gathered on deck to sing 'Abide with me' as they sailed past the green wreck buoy bobbing and turning on the broad flood of the river. The Cunarder *Alaunia*, eastbound to Liverpool on the return leg of her maiden voyage, carried another contingent of Salvationists. As they sailed past the scene of the wreck, the Salvation Army band played 'Nearer my God to Thee', and Bandmaster Perry stepped forward and dropped a wreath over the side in memory of their dead colleagues. They included his mother.

The *Empress of Britain* arrived in Quebec, having sailed over her sister's grave. It had not been a happy voyage, for even as they sailed from Liverpool, the newspaper headlines had been shouting the first tidings of disaster. The facts that came in over the liner's wireless were carefully kept from the passengers and crew. Rumour flourished. Many of the crew, and a number of passengers, had had friends or relatives aboard the lost liner. They had to wait until the papers came aboard at Rimouski to learn the truth. To add to the air of gloom, the ship had battled with almost continuous fog from one side of the ocean to the other.

The passengers aboard the Allan liner *Victorian* crossed the Atlantic ignorant of the disaster. Captain Cook had picked up the news by wireless three days out from Britain, but had kept it to himself. The Canadian newspaper headlines that greeted the passengers at Rimouski brought them the first news. No doubt Captain Cook was wise to be discreet; soon afterwards, the Allan liner *Calgarian* came up river in a typical North Atlantic fog. Many of her passengers, their nerves already strained by news of the calamity, had refused to go to bed for two days and nights. The passengers aboard yet a third Allan liner, the *Grampian*, had perhaps the most shocking introduction to the tragedy. The first they knew of the disaster was when the liner, inbound to Montreal, stopped to pick up an empty, abandoned lifeboat drifting lazily down the broad river. In bold black letters upon its bows it bore the legend: EMPRESS OF IRELAND.

A malevolent fate seemed to dog the Atlantic seaway that summer. Barely two weeks after the *Empress* had gone down, the American liner *New York* collided with the Hamburg

America liner *Pretoria* in a fog off the American coast. Both ships survived; the *New York's* passengers held an impromptu thanksgiving service on deck. Less than a week later, the Norddeutscher Lloyd liner *Kaiser Wilhelm II* collided with a British freighter off the Isle of Wight. Again both ships survived, though the German liner wound up in a British dry dock. Again, the drama was played out in dense fog.

There was a good deal of debate as to what effect, if any, the disaster had had upon the North Atlantic passenger trade. Many people, it was claimed, had hastily switched their bookings from the St Lawrence route to the rival New York route, but other reports said that even the enormous new Cunard liner *Aquitania*, which sailed on her maiden voyage to New York on 30 May had lost a lot of custom through last-minute cancellations arising from the news of the *Empress* disaster. Cunard's *Aquitania's* maiden voyage would have been a relatively low-keyed affair anyway, for she was the first major new British liner on the New York route since the *Titanic*, and nobody felt like tempting providence with the fanfares hitherto accorded to a new Ocean Greyhound. Despite the diverting efforts of Mr George Robey, Miss Vesta Tilley and other great names of the music hall engaged to entertain the guests, the principal topic of conversation at the pre-departure press visit was the news from the St Lawrence. The big ship sailed from Liverpool with her passengers and crew in a notably sober frame of mind.

A score of American Salvationists, due to sail for the Albert Hall gathering aboard the White Star liner *Olympic* at the last minute cancelled their passages. A Montreal shipping reporter wrote gloomily that just about everything that could have happened that summer had contrived to do so. Most commentators were agreed that it was a bad year for business on the North Atlantic anyway.

Even if the passengers stayed ashore that year, the men who earned their living aboard the big ships had less choice in the matter. Within a few weeks, many of the *Empress*'s surviving crew were back at work on the North Atlantic. In July, a score of her stewards arrived back in Montreal as

ATTEMPT AT SALVAGE

members of the crew of the Allan liner *Virginian*, having sailed phlegmatically across the waters where so shortly before they had struggled for their lives. Others displayed less equanimity. In Glasgow, a survivor named Boyle was put in the workhouse for committing 'wild excesses'. Their precise nature is unknown.

CHAPTER 17

Inquest

The unpleasantness began almost before the last ripple had died away over the *Empress*'s grave. A disaster of these proportions could not be misfortune pure and simple, ascribable solely to the workings of providence. Somebody, somewhere, must be to blame. There was room for every shade of disapproval, from innuendo to outright accusation. For one thing, there was the unfortunate contrast between the proportion of passengers who survived and the proportion of crew. Not surprisingly, the figures gave rise to unhappy memories of the *Titanic* disaster, where there had been clear evidence that some at least of the crew had abandoned any sense of responsibility or duty towards the passengers in a determined scramble to save themselves.

Mr L.P. Godson, an Englishman who was studying mining at Queen's University in Kingston, Ontario, was reported to have claimed that Second and Third Class passengers had been unable to reach the upper decks because doors from their quarters were locked; that there were only three lifebuoys on the left-hand side of the ship, and that they were so tightly tied to the rails that they could not be released; and that even when lifeboats did reach the water, there was no means of freeing them from the falls that tethered them to the ship. He had never seen the captain or any of the ship's officers while the boats were being lowered, he claimed, adding that the boat that took him to the *Storstad* was half empty. Most of his charges, albeit they sounded as if they had been made in good faith, were never seriously corroborated by other passengers. Moreover, it is possible that Mr Godson was a slightly nervous passenger anyway. Before leaving the university for the summer vacation, he was reported to have told fellow students that he would be back in the fall – 'if I don't get drowned.'

However, there was one account that rather disturbingly echoed Godson's account of passengers trapped behind locked doors. A Second Class passenger named Langley, who hailed from Tipperary, claimed that as he struggled to the deck, he found the doors to the open air were jammed, and a group of passengers was vainly trying to force them open. Langley, who must have been a fairly slender young man, thereupon went out through a porthole feet first in order to get to the deck and try to open the door from the outside. For a few horrifying seconds, Langley stuck halfway. But by dint of much wriggling he forced his way free, and began trying to drag the jammed doors open from the outside. But again, he failed to shift them. He had had time, he said later, to do no more than shout to the wretched passengers inside that he must leave them. He had just enough time left himself to climb the tottering rails and plunge into the sea as the great ship rolled over.

There were plenty of voices ready to defend the crew. It was quickly pointed out that they had in large measure survived because many of them were awake and at their posts at the time of the collision, because they knew their way around the ship blindfold after months and years of service aboard her, and because they had been exhaustively trained in just those emergency procedures that had saved their lives. After those repeated drills under Captain Staunton's critical eye, they could hardly be blamed for being adept at finding their way to their lifeboat stations. Moreover, the crew found a stalwart champion in Captain Murray, the Quebec Harbour-master. As a former master of the *Empress*, Captain Murray was clearly jealous for the reputation of the men who had served under his command. The crew, he said, had standing orders to go to their boat stations in any emergency. The

FOURTEEN MINUTES

Empress had as fine a crew as had ever stepped upon the deck of a ship.

Nor did there seem to be any very convincing grounds for implying that the First and Second Class passengers had received preferential treatment over those in Third Class. But again, the suspicion was easily and understandably aroused. It was hard to forget the allegations, made on very good grounds, that Steerage passengers aboard the *Titanic* had virtually been denied any chance to save their lives, while First Class passengers were escaping in half empty boats.

In the *Empress*'s case, the reason for the imbalance seems to have been tragically simple. The First Class passengers were housed high in the superstructure, where they had a relatively long time – a matter of minutes – in which to collect their life-jackets and escape, through uncluttered exits close at hand, to the nearby lifeboats. By contrast, the far larger number of Third Class passengers, housed in crowded quarters far below, had perhaps seconds in which to seek to escape, through unfamiliar passageways and up staircases crowded with people, from the mighty flood of water that poured into their quarters on the heels of the collision. Bearing in mind the speed of the disaster, the wonder is not that so few survived, but that any survived at all.

No details of selfishness or cowardly panic had come to light, *The Times* assured its readers. There had been no violation of traditional British heroism by the sailors. Many had sacrificed their lives after putting passengers into the boats. It was clear that *The Times* was speaking of the Anglo-Saxons aboard the ship. The wretched foreigners, by contrast, had a terrible time of it. Any survivor who spoke disparagingly of his fellow passengers invariably did so in terms of the foreigners. It was the foreigners who had forced their way on deck clutching their baggage; it was the foreigners who had jostled around the boats and swarmed into them as fast as they could be filled; it was the foreigners who rioted; it was the foreigners who screamed and struggled uncontrollably aboard the *Storstad*. No doubt some of them

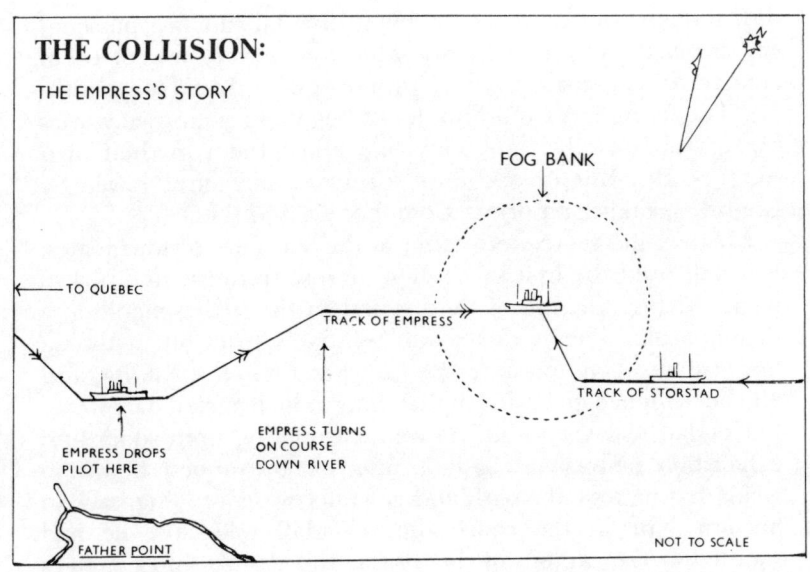

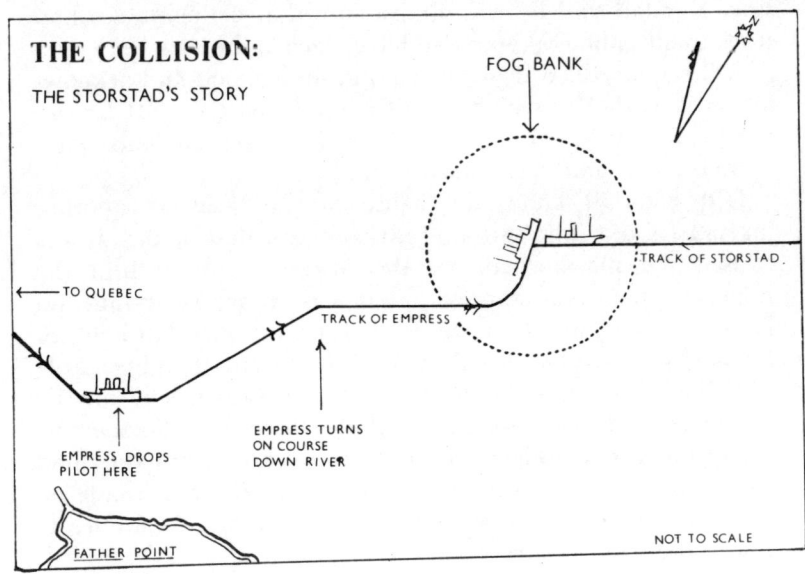

did, though considering how few of the Third Class passengers survived, it is at least arguable that a very few of them created an impression out of proportion to their true numbers. The foreigners would no doubt have had their own stories of heroism to tell, if anybody had asked them in their own tongues. But English-speaking survivors were interviewed by English-speaking reporters. So nobody asked them.

Meanwhile, there were other and even more serious issues. Kendall fired the first shot when he rose from his sick bed to testify at the opening of the inquest in the little schoolhouse in Rimouski. The evidence was relatively brief but it took a long time to give, because the jury was French-speaking, and all the evidence given in English had to be translated.

Kendall was visibly ill. As well as suffering from shock and exhaustion, he was very badly bruised. At the inquest, he was so weak that he took the oath and gave his evidence lying back in an armchair in the courtroom. Kendall told how he had shouted at the captain of the *Storstad* to keep his ship's engines going ahead to fill up the gash the collier had made, but the Norwegian had backed away, and the *Empress* began to fill and sink. Kendall said he was almost sure that if the *Storstad* had stuck to him, the *Empress* could have reached the shore.

A juryman asked if Andersen had understood and acknowledged Kendall's plea. Kendall's reply was terse: 'If he did not hear that, he should have done that,' Kendall said. 'As a seaman, he should have known that.'

Did Kendall know the cause of the disaster? another juryman asked. The captain had no doubt that he did. It was caused, he maintained, by the *Storstad* running into the *Empress*, which was stopped. That was an article of faith on Kendall's part, and he never varied from it. Kendall had not finished with the *Storstad*. Although the *Empress* had been able to launch only four boats, Kendall claimed, nearly all the survivors had been saved by those four. The *Storstad*, he maintained, had indeed lowered several boats, but they had each only 'three or four people' in them. Kendall made no secret of his feelings about the *Storstad*'s supposed failure to rescue more of the survivors.

James Rankin said in evidence that he believed most of the survivors had been picked up by the Norwegians' boats. Kendall objected strongly to his evidence. The survivors had been saved by the *Empress*'s boats, he insisted, not by the *Storstad*'s.

It was not true, but there is no reason to doubt that Kendall genuinely thought it was. At that, he was more generous than Mr Gosselin, the gentleman who had claimd to have escaped from the *Empress* without even getting his feet wet. He told reporters who interviewed him after his rescue that the *Storstad* had never lowered any boats at all, and had taken no part in the rescue operation. He accused the Norwegians of 'odious insouciance', and of brutal indifference towards the 'important people' who had escaped from the *Empress*. He did not actually say whether or not he regarded himself as being among their number. Perhaps that was going a little far. Nonetheless, the correspondent of *The Times* reported that there were other ugly reports and rumours abroad, supported by survivors of 'the best reputation' to the effect that the crew of the *Storstad* were indifferent to the fate of the *Empress*; that Andersen had failed to act properly in coming to the rescue of the passengers; and that practically no boats were lowered from the *Storstad* until some time after the collision. Some witnesses were said to have asserted that no boats left the *Storstad* at all until after daylight, when two small boats were launched.

Mr Gosselin may have been one of the survivors of 'the best reputation'. If so, he was answered by a survivor of even better reputation at that moment. Dr James Grant staunchly defended the Norwegians. The collier's men, he said, had done everything they could to save life. Their boats had been quickly on the scene and none had left until it was well loaded.

Nonetheless there was a strong public feeling in Canada, *The Times* reported, that the collier had been badly handled. The day after the sinking, *The Times* delivered itself of a leading article upon the tragedy. The Thunderer strove not very convincingly to maintain a high judicial tone, for while

The Times might have a reputation for impartiality, the writer had already made up his mind on which side he was going to be impartial. The *Storstad*, he declared, must have been steaming 'pretty fast'. The usual practice of vessels in fog was to slow down or stop altogether, he explained. 'The *Empress of Ireland* did so, and we have no doubt that she signified her whereabouts in the usual manner. What, then, was the *Storstad* doing to run into her so suddenly and with so much violence? That is the question to which the public will expect an answer.' Reassuming the mantle of Olympian detachment, he concluded: 'Speculation on the precise causation of the disaster is perhaps premature, but the strictest investigation of the circumstances will be demanded.'

Considering his implicit assumption of the *Storstad*'s guilt, this was shutting the stable door of surmise long after the horse of prejudice had bolted. It was not surprising that the *Storstad*'s representatives were to protest over the next few days at what they felt, with reason, was the English-speaking world's determination to hang them from the yardarm of public opinion before the court martial had even convened. *The Times* was not alone in its assumption of the *Storstad*'s guilt. On the other side of the Atlantic, the *Independent*, an American magazine whose trenchant outlook lived up to its title, demanded to know: 'Why was the collier hastening to reach port to make swift profit on her cargo with no regard for what she might meet or whom she might smite as she was running amok on the highway of commerce? It was her duty to heave to and stop until the heavy mist was blown away. The weight of a thousand needlessly slaughtered men and women just started on their happy return to the old homeland seems now to rest on the head of the captain of the *Storstad*.'

The *Liverpool Daily Post*, greatest newspaper of one of the world's greatest seaports, was more circumspect. Its staff were perhaps a little better versed in the endless perils of the sea and therefore less ready to deliver thunderbolts against fallible men contending with the hazards of their calling. Nonetheless, its leader-writer could not resist the observation that the *Storstad* 'must have been making light of the hazards of the fog'. But he did go on to make one remark of extraordinary prescience. He speculated upon that possibility of one day transmitting images by wireless that was exercising the mind of Dr A.M. Low. 'It remains to be seen,' he remarked, 'if this strange addition to our vision will enable us to penetrate fog and follow the movements of shipping.' He was writing roughly a quarter of a century before the advent of marine radar.

The Canadian press was every bit as ready to assume the *Storstad*'s guilt. The *Toronto Globe*, in a leading article typical of comment throughout the Dominion, spoke of the *Storstad* 'driving through the dangerous night, reckless of the consequences'. It was in no sense an accusation. It was merely mentioned in passing, and as if it was an established and incontrovertible fact. Underlying much of the Canadians' implied criticism of the *Storstad* was clearly a thinly-disguised resentment of the dominant role of the Norwegians in the country's most important waterborne traffic, the carriage of coal and iron ore upon the St Lawrence. Two million tons of coal a year moved up the river; the Dominion Coal Company alone despatched an average of two colliers a day from Nova Scotia. In a single day, they had shipped 25,000 tons of coal from Sydney, much of it in Norwegian vessels chartered at rates so low that there must be a temptation, it was hinted, to cut corners, both metaphorically and literally. Although the Norwegians were specifically permitted by law to engage in a domestic traffic that in most nations would have been closed to them, Canadian law had no power over their officers' certificates of competence. It was high time, the critics grumbled, that Canada's raw materials were carried by Canadian ships in home waters. Reports from Ottawa hinted that legislation was on the way to bring Norwegian seafarers under the jurisdiction of Canadian law.

By 2 June, the *Storstad* party had clearly had enough of being blamed indiscriminately for the disaster, and they called a kind of press conference in Montreal. It opened with a statement by Captain Ove Lange, as agent for the *Storstad*'s managers, the Maritime S.S. Company. It was read for him by Mr J.W. Griffin of Haight, Griffin, Deming and Gardner, a New York law firm of which more was to be heard. The statement sounded as if it were written by Griffin, as well. The public, the statement said, was entitled to know the facts. The two ships had sighted each other while still far apart, and those aboard the collier had seen the liner's green light. In those particular circumstances that gave the *Storstad* the right of way, and the *Empress* had changed her heading in such a way as to permit the two vessels to pass safely.

Shortly afterwards, the statement went on, fog had enveloped the two vessels. The collier's engines were first slowed and then stopped but her heading remained unaltered. Whistles from the *Empress* were heard and answered. The *Empress* was then seen through the fog close on the bow, showing a green light and making considerable headway. The *Storstad*'s engines were put full astern, and her forward motion was nearly checked when the two vessels came together. It had been said, Captain Lange's statement went on, that the *Storstad* should not have backed out of the hole made by the collision. In fact she had done nothing of the kind. When the ships struck, Andersen had ordered his engines full ahead in order to hold his bows against the *Empress's* side and prevent entry of water. But the *Empress*'s headway had been great enough to swing the *Storstad* round and twist her bow out of the hole, bending it to the left in the process.

After the collision, Lange went on, the *Empress* had disappeared in the fog. The *Storstad* had repeatedly sounded her whistle in the hope of getting an answering blast she might make for, but she had received no clue to the *Empress*'s whereabouts in the fog until the cries of the survivors were heard. Then she moved in as close as she dared, bearing in mind that there were survivors in the water, and had lowered all her boats, despite the fact that she herself was in serious danger of sinking. Not only had the collier's boats made several rescue trips, but when two of the *Empress*'s boats had reached the *Storstad*, the collier's own crew had promptly manned them and rowed back to the scene to help in the rescue work. Not only had 350 people been taken aboard the *Storstad*, but everything in the ship's stores that could contribute to their comfort had been freely given. Captain Lange, or perhaps it was really Mr Griffin, was in full cry by now. Press reports imputing the slightest delay in rendering efficient aid did 'cruel injustice' to Captain Andersen. The *Storstad*'s owners asked the public, in fairness to both ships and their captains, to suspend judgement as to where the blame should rest until an impartial tribunal heard the evidence.

Having launched this entirely reasonable appeal for impartiality, Mr Griffin and the officers of the *Storstad* proceeded to give their own case full rein. Had Andersen heard Kendall shouting to him to keep going ahead?' Certainly, Griffin replied; Andersen had shouted back: 'I'm going ahead.' He would have done it anyway, for the sake of his own ship's survival. The *Storstad*'s owners accepted neither that the *Empress* was motionless in the water, nor that the *Storstad* was going too fast. Had the collier had any real way on her, Griffin maintained, she would have gone through the liner like paper. Andersen, breaking the silence of days, said he had kept his hand on the engine-room telegraph as the two ships came together, and as soon as they touched he had rung down for full ahead. But it was impossible to keep his ship wedged in the hole because of the speed the *Empress* was making. Kendall himself had said he had called for full speed ahead from his own engines in order to try to beach the liner, Andersen pointed out. That was why he himself could not keep the *Storstad* wedged in the gash. She was twisted out by the bigger ship's forward motion.

More than that, Andersen suggested, the decision to put the liner full ahead had made matters worse, because the *Storstad*'s anchor was imbedded in the liner's right side and when the *Empress* began to move forward, the anchor had torn the plates off her, causing the liner to founder. On this last point, there is no reason to doubt that Andersen was stating what he genuinely believed to be a fact. If he had any evidence to support his claim, it was never produced.

More wounding than the charge of incompetence had been that of inhumanity. Andersen was reported to be 'almost speechless' at reports that most of the survivors had been saved by the liner's own boats, and that he and his crew had been indifferent to the fate of those aboard the *Empress*. 'It is beyond all reason, it is without an atom of truth,' he protested. Far from having backed off, as so many of the survivors had claimed, Andersen insisted that he had taken his ship right in among the survivors as close as he had dared, so close indeed that from the collier's bridge, Andersen had watched some survivors swim right up to her stern.

Ault, the pilot who had brought the collier up on the final leg of her journey from Quebec to Montreal, was called to testify that he had several times found Andersen on the verge of tears. In particular, he had actually wept from sheer indignation when he had read the papers in Quebec, and seen for the first time the allegations that were being levelled at his crew and himself. The press reported that the captain had appeared before them red-eyed. Later still, Andersen was reported to be in a very nervous condition, and to have required special care for several days. Possibly he did. The Canadian press, which was emphatically not well-disposed towards Andersen and his men, had earlier reported that the captain had been smiling broadly when he brought his ship alongside the wharf at Montreal.

Mr Griffin clearly felt that in view of the kind of charges that had been levelled against the *Storstad*, the best form of defence was attack. Mrs Andersen was quoted as saying that when Kendall came aboard the *Storstad* after his ship was sunk, he was under the influence of liquor. Considering that the captain of the *Empress* was frozen, half drowned and badly shocked, as well as severely bruised, it might have been expected to take a rather more leisurely and professional examination to determine whether he was or not. In any event, the charge was not pursued. John Walsh, the CPR's chief marine superintendent, later roundly denied that Kendall had ever taken a drink in his life. Dr Grant went further and said that after the sinking, Kendall's state of mental and physical exhaustion was so dangerous that Grant had forced him to swallow a mouthful of brandy. But after that, even though he was literally out on his feet, Kendall had resolutely refused to take any further stimulants. The charge of drunkenness against Kendall was hastily dropped. Later, Mrs Andersen denied ever having made it anyway. Her English was not good, she explained; she had been misunderstood. Even if that particular shot had misfired, the *Storstad* had plenty more in her locker. Two of the *Empress*'s officers, the Norwegians roundly declared, had reached the *Storstad* safely, but had then refused to take their boat back to look for other survivors, claiming that the boat was too heavy to row. So three of the *Storstad*'s own firemen had taken the boat over, and rowed it back to rescue a further fifty survivors.

Kendall, it was alleged, was not really a hero at all. In his indecent haste to board the *Storstad*, he had clambered over half-dead survivors with broken limbs lying in the bottom of his boat. Far from having spent three hours out in the river searching for survivors, Mrs Andersen was further quoted as saying, Kendall had actually been one of the first survivors aboard.

Then Griffin called a Captain Holtung, of the Norwegian collier *Alden*. Captain Holtung weighed in on behalf of his compatriots by alleging that when his ship had passed the *Empress* some thirty miles upstream from the scene of the collision, she was zigzagging down river so erratically that both the pilot and the officer of the watch aboard the *Alden* were greatly concerned. This was the first time the *Empress*'s steering qualities had been called into question. It was not to be the last.

To all these allegations, Captain Kendall himself made no reply. He was said to be in a highly nervous condition, and unable to give any further account of the accident. John Walsh said he was convinced that Kendall had meant to go down with his ship. It was only the providential force of an underwater explosion as she sank that had broken his grip on the bridge rail and blown the captain to the surface again.

FOURTEEN MINUTES

The *Storstad* press conference served only to fuel the flames. The 'bitterest feelings' existed between Kendall and Andersen. Some of the *Empress*'s surviving crew, it was said, were so incensed by the *Storstad*'s supposed failure to come to their aid that they planned a physical attack on Andersen. A police guard was placed over the *Storstad* as she lay alongside the Hochelaga wharf.

The Times delivered itself of a further judgment. It was a matter for profound regret, the newspaper declared, that before the bodies of the victims had even been decently buried, a heated quarrel had broken out over their graves which threatened to be taken up all round. It did no credit to human nature. It was all most confusing and unfortunate. The two captains' stories were irreconcilable, *The Times* reporter said, and yet both had given an impression of sincerity. The charges and counter-charges must be received with caution, especially since many passengers had paid tribute to the work done by members of both crews in rescuing and caring for survivors. The truth could only be established by a court of inquiry.

Meanwhile, as if the story of the sinking were not already sufficiently macabre, the *Toronto World* weighed in with a piece of pure Grand Guignol, spiced with xenophobia. It reported 'very devilish work by steerage passengers' and told with relish how, as the ship settled, 'fear-crazed demons, armed with murderous dirks, slashed their way through the crowd, stabbing and maiming'. Undertakers in Quebec, the *World* reported in shocked tones, had declared that many of the dead had been slashed in a way that no accident could have caused. The suggestion was being made, the report continued, that when the crash came, foreigners – those fearful foreigners again – had tumbled from their bunks in terror and made a desperate flight for safety. The *World*, which tended to wallow in purple prose, really let itself go. There had been 'an inferno of human passions' aboard the sinking liner, it assured its readers. Worse, there had been 'a carnival of butchery'. It added, for good measure, that many of the dead had been robbed of their money and valuables.

INQUEST

Later, the 'ghoulish story' was officially discredited. What was not denied was that a very high proportion of those whose bodies were recovered – one report said nine-tenths – had been killed, usually instantly, rather than drowned. The report, said to have medical corroboration, suggested that death in these cases was due either to the collision or to the subsequent rain of wreckage from the decks of the listing ship. Those medical authorities might have added, had they known, that persons jumping into water from any height in a Board of Trade pattern cork life-jacket stood an excellent chance of having their necks broken as neatly as by a hangman's noose when the jacket rode up and hit them under the chin. Whatever the cause, it was a curious fact that although the life-jackets were intended to keep the wearer floating upright, a great many bodies were found slumped forward in their life-jackets with their heads under water. Mr Burns, the President of the Board of Trade, was to have quite a knotty time answering awkward questions on the subject from Members of Parliament.

The argument moved from the merely macabre to the sublimely supernatural. There had been a report current in 1910 that when Dr Crippen had been arrested aboard Kendall's ship at Rimouski, he had fallen to his knees and pronounced a curse upon the man whose alertness had unmasked him. Was it possible, the *Montreal Daily Star* inquired, that Kendall had fallen victim to the Curse of Crippen?

CHAPTER 18

Public Inquiry

The Canadian Government, shocked by the scale of the worst disaster ever to occur within the boundaries of the Dominion, decided on a public inquiry. There was no legislation to cover such a procedure under the current Merchant Shipping Act, so additional legislation was hurried through the Canadian Parliament in three days. Faced with a catastrophe quite outside their experience, the Canadians turned to the United Kingdom Government for help. The gentlemen in Whitehall had no hesitation in recommending their choice of Chairman. They sent for Lord Mersey.

John Charles Bigham, first Baron Mersey, had become something of an international celebrity in curious circumstances. After a prodigiously successful career at the commercial bar, and a brief and undistinguished spell as a Member of Parliament, he had become a High Court judge and finally, for a short time, President of the Probate, Divorce and Admiralty Division, a role that had brought him quite briefly into contact with the judicial aspects of affairs nautical. His career had been a distinguished one, but no more so than those of a dozen other High Court judges of his time, and there was no very obvious reason why he should ever have attained particular prominence in the public eye. However, at the very end of his career, and at an age when he might have expected to retire, Lord Mersey was called to the most memorable role of his entire life. In 1912, largely on the strength of his brief Admiralty Court experience, he was named as Chairman of the Court of Inquiry into the sinking of the *Titanic*. Almost overnight, as the dramatic story unfolded, he was catapulted into a measure of international fame.

Despite having been born and bred in Liverpool, his lordship's knowledge of nautical matters was something less than encyclopaedic, and he never pretended otherwise. Nonetheless, he was regarded at the time as a very Nelson of the legal profession. In appearance, Mersey was exactly what a distinguished English judge of his time ought to have looked like. A short, slight figure, cleanshaven but for prominent sidewhiskers, his avuncular features contrasted sharply with a piercing and quizzical eye. A pair of pince-nez spectacles on a black silk ribbon was perched judicially upon the end of his nose. At seventy-three, Lord Mersey had the bearing and alertness of a man twenty years younger. He was famous, or notorious, within his profession for an impatience with legal niceties and a robust determination to brush aside fine points of argument and get down to brass tacks. Moreover, while he could display great personal charm, learned counsel did not always share the public gallery's appreciation of his sardonic and deflating wit. His lordship also suffered intermittently from the upper-middle-class occupational disease of gout.

Time has not dealt kindly with Lord Mersey. A suspicion, to put it no higher, has arisen that he was guilty of a bitter injustice towards the unfortunate Captain Stanley Lord, master of the liner *Californian*, who was virtually condemned without trial, and upon suspect evidence, for his supposed failure to steam his ship a few miles to the succour of the sinking *Titanic*. There were no such misgivings in 1914. His appointment was received with 'great gratification' upon both sides of the Atlantic.

Lord Mersey, undeterred by a sharp attack of gout, hobbled aboard the *Mauretania* with his left foot gingerly encased in a brown felt slipper. His journey to Quebec by way of New York was to be his lordship's first visit to the New World. At his age, he observed philosophically to the reporters who met him on arrival, it was likely also to be his last. He might well have remarked, but did not, upon the irony that the only reason why he had boarded a transatlantic liner in the first place was to inquire into the circumstances in which just such another vessel had been lost. The sinking of the *Empress* was to be the second great nautical disaster into which his lordship had inquired in the past two years. Had he known that just twelve months later he would complete an unenviable judicial hat trick by inquiring into the loss of the *Mauretania*'s sister ship, the *Lusitania*, he might reasonably have decided that it was rather safer to stay on dry land.

To sit with Lord Mersey, the Canadian Government named two distinguished Canadian judges. They were Sir Adolph Routhier, a former Chief Justice of Quebec, and Mr Ezekiel McLeod, Chief Justice of New Brunswick. To advise them, a panel of four professional assessors was appointed. Two were seamen, one a marine engineer, and one a naval architect. Mr Newcombe, KC, Canada's Deputy Minister of Justice, would lead for the Crown before the learned judges.

Lord Mersey was not the only lawyer of note to pack his bag for Quebec. A legal sea battle on the scale of Trafalgar was in prospect, and both parties were bent upon securing the best talent on the market. The CPR turned to Butler Aspinall, KC, a London barrister with a first-class reputation and a substantial Admiralty Court practice. Predictably, he and Mersey were far from strangers; indeed, Aspinall had appeared before his lordship in not entirely dissimilar circumstances in the *Titanic* inquiry two years before. Aspinall was urbane and ingratiating, with a kindly and sympathetic manner. He was straight out of the pages of Dickens, said one reporter; he learned the inmost secrets of a witness, not by forcing the facts out of him, but by pure friendliness. It was not like being questioned by a lawyer at all, said the reporter, warming to his theme: it was like a pleasant talk with a nice, chatty person. He could have added that the trouble with friendly chats with Mr Aspinall was that those who enjoyed them were likely subsequently to realise, a little late in the day, that the conversation had not been entirely to their advantage.

The *Storstad* team was nominally to be led by Claude

Duclos, KC, a distinguished Canadian barrister. But the real cutting edge in the Norwegians' armoury was to be the sparely elegant figure of Charles Sherman Haight. Haight had been bred to the practice of maritime law. The family firm in New York that bore his name was one of the most distinguished in the field, and at forty-three Haight himself was firmly established as one of the acknowledged leaders of the United States Admiralty Bar. A tall, slim figure with a lined face and a neat imperial beard, he was keen and quick in manner, said one observer; direct and ruthless, said another. He was recognised as a cross-examiner of formidable talent. If Haight was flint, Aspinall was mild steel. The two men were professionals of a high order, and they paid each other the supreme compliment of their trade. They watched one another like hawks.

In addition there were counsel to represent the master and officers of the *Empress*, there was another to guard the interests of the *Storstad*'s charterers, and there was the slightly forlorn figure of Mr George Gibsone, who represented the interests of the National Seamen's and Firemen's Association, a forerunner of the National Union of Seamen.

The inquiry opened in the King's Bench Courtroom in Quebec on 16 June, less than three weeks after the disaster. Kendall, pale and limping badly, shared a table in the courtroom with Captain Andersen. What, if anything, the two men said to each other has not been recorded. Above them, their wives watched from the crowded public gallery. For Kendall, the scene had an added poignancy. It was the same courtroom where, four years earlier, he had described from the witness-box the arrest of Crippen.

The court swiftly found that Lord Mersey's reputation for going after the salient facts and casting lesser issues to the winds was not misplaced. His lordship was an old man in a hurry, and there would be no dawdling, nor fishing trips after red herring. The celerity of his lordship's methods, *The Times* reported, set the legal representatives gasping. He swept aside all obstacles to an immediate commencement. Except one. Mersey began on a note of high comedy. The law said that members of an inquiry must be sworn, did it not? Very well then, they were going to be sworn, and that right swiftly. He was absolutely right, but there were difficulties. Nobody knew what form the attestation had to take, and then they could not find the relevant legislation. They had to send out for a copy of the appropriate Act. When they had found one, and located the right page, it transpired that among all those legal luminaries from three nations, not one was qualified to administer an oath. The legal gentlemen waited uneasily under Lord Mersey's lowering eye until an obliging High Court judge was shanghaied into performing the office.

Lord Mersey had a most curious effect upon the court. Not only did the speed of his opening leave the distinguished lawyers breathless, but according to a Quebec reporter, who was watching fascinated from the Press gallery, they seemed to be suffering from an extreme nervousness that grew into a general confusion. The lawyers, the reporter, wrote, seemed to be stage-struck by his lordship's august presence.

Mr Newcombe opened the proceedings for the Crown. Since the inquiry was not a trial as such, and since nobody stood accused of anything, not formally at any rate, his role was that not of prosecutor but of narrator, interlocutor and stage manager. It was a difficult role, and he filled it with distinction. It might seem, said Mr Newcombe as he outlined the facts, that it was a situation in which one ship or the other must have been at fault, and possibly both. One element that was not at fault, he hastily added, was the St Lawrence. Mindful of his countrymen's sensitivity towards the river's dubious reputation, he expressed confidence that those wishing to disparage the St Lawrence route could suggest no reason for attributing the disaster to the river or its facilities. Having poured a little oil upon those troubled waters, Mr Newcombe went on to assure the inquiry that counsel for the various interests had met the night before, and he was happy to report that all the parties had displayed the utmost harmony. No doubt it was true at the time, and it was no fault of Mr Newcombe's if that relationship became markedly less harmonious in the days that followed.

Newcombe sat down. The first witness was called. Captain Henry Kendall, still pale-faced and leaning on a cane, limped into the witness-box. His manner struck one Canadian reporter as very defensive; he replied to Aspinall's questioning in terse and rapid sentences, his replies emphasised by the descent of his clenched fist on to the ledge of the witness-box as if to hammer his points home. The two ships, Kendall maintained, had been steaming green to green; he had himself checked the bearings of the *Storstad*'s lights. He had no doubt at all that the two ships could and should have passed safely, right-hand to right-hand. The only possible action that could have caused the collision had been that of the *Storstad* in putting her wheel over in the fog, and making a right-hand turn that brought her into the *Empress*'s side. Lord Mersey interrupted Aspinall to ask the question that must have been in the minds of everybody in the room. Why, his Lordship asked, did Aspinall think the *Storstad* had turned to the right? Had Aspinall a theory? Mr Aspinall had indeed a theory. The explanation, he suggested, was that the *Storstad*'s third mate had believed he would thereby avoid the *Empress*, and give himself more room to pass.

Mr Aspinall had no further questions for Kendall. Mr Haight, by contrast, was to have a great many. Haight's case was startlingly simple. The *Empress*, far from passing green to green down the *Storstad*'s right-hand side, had set out to do precisely the opposite. When her lights first came clearly visible from the *Storstad*, Haight maintained, she had indeed been showing her green light. But then the watchers on the collier's bridge had seen her swing until her range-lights came into line, her green light disappeared, and her red light came into sight. She had gone on showing her red light to the Norwegians for between two and five minutes, and she had still been showing it when she disappeared into the fog.

The *Storstad* had stopped her engines, confident that the liner was passing, red light to red light, down the collier's *left* side. Later, the *Storstad*'s chief officer had indeed ordered the wheel over to the right, not because of any idea of danger, but because with the engines stopped and the ship losing way, he did not want the ship's head to sheer away to the left in the current. If there was going to be any danger of a change of course in the fog he wanted it to be to the right, away from the liner. But the gentle wheel movement had no effect, so the Chief Officer had ordered the wheel put hard over to the right, but still the collier would not swing, because by then she had lost steering way. So Toftenes had ordered the engines slow ahead, and called the captain.

It was with this proposition in mind that Haight set out to test Kendall's story, seeking for the weak points, the hidden inconsistencies in the captain's account. How long had the ships been in contact after the collision, Haight inquired? and what speed did Captain Kendall suggest the *Storstad* had been going? A matter of moments, Kendall replied. Perhaps three or four seconds, before the collier had backed off. Her speed at impact had been perhaps 10 knots. Ten knots? said Mr Haight. And in contact after the collision for only three or four seconds? Did Kendall really think that a ship moving at 10 knots, laden with nearly 11,000 tons of coal, could back away in three or four seconds? Captain Kendall did indeed think so. The *Storstad*, he believed, had rebounded off the *Empress*.

Now, about the stopping of the *Empress*. Why had Captain Kendall thought it necessary to stop his ship if he was so satisfied that the two vessels would pass green to green? And why did the captain suppose that the *Storstad* should have changed course so radically in the fog, as he had suggested? What explanation could he offer for such a singular action? It would sound almost as if the *Storstad* was *trying* to run the *Empress* down, would it not? Kendall was not prepared to go quite that far. But he, too, had his theory. The Norwegians, he believed, had seen the Cock Point gas-buoy close under their left bow, and had altered course to seaward to avoid running dangerously close to the shoal that the buoy was guarding.

Mr Haight changed his point of attack. About those whistles from the *Storstad* that Kendall had heard moving down his right-hand side. Supposing it had been the *Empress*, not the *Storstad*, that had turned in the fog? Supposing the liner had put her wheel over and swung leftward? That would have put the *Storstad*'s whistles on precisely the bearings that Kendall had described, would it not? Yes, Kendall admitted, it would.

Mr Haight was interested in the *Empress*'s command system. Was it customary for the captain to remain on the bridge during his first officer's watch, when everything, at least up to the advent of the fog, would have appeared to be normal? It was in the CPR service, Kendall replied shortly. He always stayed on the bridge when the ship was near land, and on that occasion he had intended to stay there until he handed over to his chief officer at daylight.

If there was any doubt in Kendall's mind about where Haight's questioning was leading, it was dispelled when Lord Mersey interposed to ask exactly what Haight had in mind. The *Storstad*, Haight replied, had never altered course to the right as Kendall had suggested. On the contrary, it was Haight's hypothesis that it was the *Empress*, not the *Storstad*, that had first turned right; that would explain why the men on the collier's bridge had seen her red light, not her green. And then, Haight suggested, somebody else – it might have been the first officer– had ordered the wheel back to the left again, and had taken the *Empress* across the *Storstad*'s bows in the fog, thinking there was time to do so safely. Haight made no claim that it was a rational action. 'It is very hard to explain, I admit,' he said.

Lord Mersey relapsed into a judicial silence, and Haight chose a fresh rapier for the question of the *Storstad* backing away until she was a mile off. Supposing it had been the *Empress*, not the *Storstad*, that had been doing 10 knots in the fog? And supposing it had been the *Storstad*, not the *Empress*, that had been virtually stopped in fog? Would that not have produced the same effect of leaving the *Storstad* some considerable distance away in the fog from the point where the *Empress* actually sank? Mr Haight was very interested in that thought. Was it true that aboard the *Storstad*, Kendall had dropped on to a bench in the chart-room, saying: 'I wish to God I had gone faster?' No, Kendall retorted. What had happened was that on the *Storstad*'s bridge, Andersen had accused him of going full speed, to which Kendall had replied: 'I wish I was. If I had been, you would never have hit me.' Very well, had Kendall accused Andersen of deliberately trying to run him down, or of deliberately backing off half a mile and leaving the *Empress* to sink? No, and no again.

Haight had stopped feinting. He had marked his target, and for the rest of the inquiry he never stopped thrusting at it. His first tentative thrust was innocuous enough. Did the *Empress* steer easily? Very easily. Had there been any recent change of rudder on the ship? Not that Kendall knew of. Had Kendall, in his CPR service, ever heard a story to the effect that it had been necessary to fit a new rudder to the *Empress* to improve her steering? Kendall had not.

Haight had no further questions for the present. Aspinall re-examined. It had been suggested that somebody else had contradicted Kendall's orders. Was Kendall the class of officer to allow that sort of thing? He was not. 'What,' inquired Mr Aspinall, 'would you have said to a man that did that?' 'I do not say what I would have said,' the captain replied ominously. 'It is what I would have done.'

There was a good deal of debate about why the *Empress* had sunk so swiftly. Kendall, it seemed, had his own thoery. He spoke of a 'sheet of fire' that had sprung from the liner's side as the *Storstad* struck, a sheet of fire that he believed indicated that a boiler had been torn from its seating by the 'terrible shock' of the collision. The displaced boiler, Kendall believed, had rolled over to one side of the ship, holding her down as the water rushed in through her wounded side until she sank. In this respect, if in no other, Kendall's theory was something of an oddity, if only because it seemed to have been almost completely lacking in corroboration. To be sure, a few other survivors spoke of seeing a ragged flame, or a shower of sparks, as the steel plates of the two ships ground together, but that was all. Nobody else talked about a sheet of fire or displaced boilers rolling about the bilges. There were men who had emerged alive from both boiler-rooms, which in itself was probably convincing testimony that nothing of the sort had happened. Above all, nobody but Kendall taalked about the collision as a terrible shock. Scores of survivors described the collision at one time or another. With unanimity well-nigh unique in eye-witness accounts of a great disaster, they all spoke of the gentleness of the impact. A nudge; a jolt; one man had even thought that they were making fast to a jetty in the middle of the night. Henry Kendall was about the only man who ever talked of a terrible impact. True or not, Kendall's views did not pass unremarked. Charles Haight diligently noted what the captain had to say.

Kendall's first innings was over. It was the Norwegians' turn to face the bowling. Alfred Toftenes was everybody's idea of a Norwegian; a tall, phlegmatic, blue-eyed young man with fair hair. He was completely self-possessed, leaning comfortably over the rail of the witness-box as he spoke slow, deliberate sentences in excellent English. From time to time, he stroked his neat blond moustache.

Toftenes bore out Haight's opening account. When he first saw the lights of the *Empress*, he claimed, she was clearly going to pass green to green down the collier's right-hand side. Then he had seen the liner change course until, about a mile and a half or two miles away, her red light replaced her green. He was sure then that the liner was going to make a left-hand passage, and indeed there was ample room for her to do so. What is more, Toftenes told Haight, as the fog came down he heard the *Empress* blow *one* blast, the 'passing' signal. And all the blasts he heard had been on his left-hand side, not his right.

Toftenes was a very tough young man indeed. Few witnesses among the three score called before the court faced a more gruelling ordeal than he; none survived it better. Assailed by hours of technical questioning about courses, speeds, navigation lights and helm orders, Toftenes navigated his way deftly through the minefields that Aspinall sought to sow around him. The hours of questioning yielded remarkably little grist to Aspinall's mill, for Toftenes would concede nothing. Calmly and logically, he defended his decision to put the collier's wheel over. Equally calmly and logically, he defended his decision not to call Andersen to the bridge sooner. He had called his captain, he insisted, just as soon as he thought it necessary to do so. There had been no apparent danger. He sometimes waited a few minutes in such cases, he added, to see if the fog would clear of its own accord. The impression that his testimony left, rightly or wrongly, must have been of a very self-confident young man who had felt himself perfectly capable of handling the situation on his own.

Thomas Andersen followed his first mate into the witness-box. Andersen, like most of the *Storstad* witnesses, was completely at ease as he gave evidence. Mrs Andersen, wearing a black hat with a white feather, sat in the public gallery, nodding approvingly as her husband gave evidence in fluent English. From time to time she caught his eye and smiled. Nevertheless, none of the *Storstad*'s men can have enjoyed the inquiry and Captain Andersen least of all. For days after the collision he had practically needed police protection, so high was feeling running against him and his men. After his appearance in the witness-box, he probably felt he needed it again.

It must have been extremely difficult for Andersen to sort out in his mind any coherent impression of what happened in those few seconds between his arrival on deck and his first hair-raising sight of the *Empress*'s masthead lights through the fog. He was insistent that his first action, as always on mounting the bridge, was to check his ship's course. And that course, he stoutly maintained, was what it should have been – west by south. After that, there was just about time to throw his engines astern, and they had been running astern for about thirty seconds before the crash. By that time, his ship was going very slowly indeed.

Lord Mersey took up the questioning in what sounded like a mood of heavy irony. Captain Andersen's understanding of the matter, his lordship gathered, was that the *Empress* had come up crabwise against the *Storstad* and poked a hole in her side against the collier's bow? Andersen was not the man to be ruffled by judicial sarcasm. That was indeed just about it, as nearly as he could say. And what explanation could Andersen offer for such extraordinary conduct on the part of the other ship? He could only think that the liner was trying to cross his bows at full speed in order to get further out to sea, where the weather was clearer.

Haight tried to put a salvage line aboard his client. If the fully laden *Storstad* had really been doing ten knots at the time of the collision, as Kendall had suggested, would she really have been able to disengage and back out of the hole three or four seconds later? 'I think,' said Andersen simply, 'that we would have gone straight through her, pretty near.'

Aspinall rose. Did Andersen's officers have standing orders to call their captain in a fog? Yes. Should Toftenes, then, not have called him ten or fifteen minutes earlier? Well, the fog hadn't been that bad, Andersen protested loyally. Aspinall turned the screw. Did Andersen feel that his standing orders had been adequately obeyed? 'I should have wished,' Andersen replied sadly, 'to have been called earlier.' Although, he added, he did not think that it would have made any difference.

Aspinall pressed his attack. Andersen claimed that his ship was stopped. But then, it was very important to his case that his ship should be stopped, was it not? He claimed that she was still on her proper and original heading. That also was very important to his case, was it not? And now, about Toftenes's order to put the wheel over. Had the *Storstad*'s officers standing orders not to alter course in a fog unless absolutely necessary? Andersen could only agree. They had.

Aspinall invited Andersen to explain why, having shown her red light for a left-hand passage, the *Empress* should have taken the highly dangerous course of crossing the *Storstad*'s bows in the fog? Why should she signal that she was stopped, if she was not? Why should she indicate that she was going astern if she was really forging through the fog at about 10 knots? There was a note of weariness in Andersen's reply. He had no explanation to offer.

Poor Mr Gibsone, mindful of his professional obligations towards his Liverpool seamen and firemen, tried to quiz

Andersen about the state of the *Storstad*'s boilers, and received short shrift from Lord Mersey. His lordship emphatically did not wish to know about the *Storstad*'s boilers. Mr Gibsone retired hurt.

The batting changed again. First Officer Edward Jones told his story. It bore out Kendall's testimony almost to the letter. However, neither Haight nor the court itself was disposed to let Jones go as easily as that. Haight worried away at Kendall's conduct in remaining on the bridge for so long. Jones had testified that masters usually left the bridge at Cock Point when the ship was safely settled on course for her long run towards the distant sea. Would it not, then have been the ordinary, proper course for the captain to have left the bridge earlier than Kendall had done? Jones stonewalled. That was up to the captain.

Haight was not satisfied. If the *Empress*'s officers had seen another ship three or four miles away, her lights clearly visible, and bearing a safe 20 or 30 degrees off the bow, was it not a most unusual manoeuvre to put the engines astern? Not at all, Jones maintained stoutly. Kendall had done it to take way off the ship and navigate with caution. In clear weather, with no other ship in sight? In all his seagoing experience, had Jones ever known it done before? 'I have never been before in that predicament,' Jones confessed.

Both Mersey and Sir Adolph Routhier were after him now. Why had the liner stopped her engines, when the Rules of the Road did not call for her to do anything of the sort? If the *Empress* was well clear of the *Storstad*'s path did Jones still think it ordinary navigational procedure to do so? Jones would not be shifted; it was done to moderate the ship's speed in a fog. Mersey did not pursue the topic. But the learned judges were clearly puzzled as to why the big ship had been brought to a halt in the fogbound seaway when the normal rules of navigation did not require any such thing.

It was left to Mr Newcombe to give Jones the chance to make his most telling and emphatic point. If Jones was right, the *Storstad* could never have seen the *Empress*'s red light at all, could she? Jones agreed. 'Absolutely never?' Newcombe inquired again. 'No, sir,' Jones replied. Amid the burgeoning confusion of technicalities, Newcombe had put his finger on the fundamental point. Had the light the *Storstad* saw been red or green?

The issue was very simple. If the collier's officers had really seen a red light, then the liner was set to pass south of the collier, left-hand to left-hand, and only a highly dangerous left turn in the fog could have taken the liner across the collier's bows to disaster. But if, by contrast, the liner was really on the course her officers had insisted she was on, then the *Storstad* could not have seen a red light, and the liner must have been planning to pass the collier to the north, right-hand to right-hand. In which case, only an equally dangerous right-turn by the collier in the fog could have swung her off her safe parallel course and sent her plunging at a tangent through the fog to hit the liner amidships on her right-hand side.

The two accounts, in short, were totally irreconcilable. One Canadian newspaper observed sardonically that if the evidence of their captains was to be believed, the ships had collided violently while lying motionless two miles apart.

Mr Haight was still preoccupied with the *Empress*'s steering gear. The device that most particularly engaged his attention was called a telemotor, a hydraulic mechanism used to transmit the movement of a ship's steering wheel to the rudder far away at the stern. The telemotor was an essentially simple device, in which the movement of the wheel forced a piston through a cylinder filled with a slushy concoction of glycerine and water. According as the piston moved, the pressure upon the glycerine would vary, and the pressure, transmitted along 500 feet of copper piping, moved a similar piston at the other end, which in turn was linked to the valves of the steam engine which operated the rudder.

It seemed, judging from the evidence of many of the witnesses, a simple and reliable device which had served the liner well since she was built. Haight, however, would have none of it. He devoted considerable effort to seeking to demonstrate the device as installed in the *Empress* was totally unreliable, negligently maintained and incompetently supervised. His efforts were bent towards showing that the telemotor could have leaked without anyone noticing, and that if it did, the liner's steering might have gone berserk witthout warning. His argument was possibly aided by thefact that none of the witnesses seemed in truth to be quite sure what *would* happen if the telemotor developed a serious leak in its glutinous entrails.

Mr Haight quizzed Sampson, the Chief Engineer, about the state of the steering gear. Had it been overhauled while the ship was berthed in Quebec? Had the engineers not been actually working on the steering system during that last fatal voyage down the river to Father Point? Sampson, who had known the ship throughout her working life, scouted the suggestion that there was anything wrong with the steering. He had never heard complaints that she was hard to steer, and as for anything being wrong with the mechanism itself, he could not remember when it had needed even minor repair.

Mr Haight was not to be shrugged off. Had Sampson not heard that a quartermaster with the unforgettable name of Cadwallader had threatened to sue the CPR because he had strained himself trying to turn the ship's wheel? Sampson could not conceal his scorn. 'He must be either a very weak man, or a baby,' he retorted. Lord Mersey chose to intervene. 'Are you suggesting the steering gear was not in proper order?' he asked Haight. That was exactly what he was suggesting, Haight replied, and went on to tell a remarkable tale.

The previous night, Haight said, a man named James Galway, a quartermaster in the *Empress*, had come to see him and had claimed that for several minutes while the liner was on her way down river to her fatal meeting with the *Storstad*, the steering gear was out of action. Moreover, when Galway had tried to tell his story to CPR officials, they had endeavoured to return him to England on the next boat. Galway had even shown Haight a letter from John Walsh, the Company's chief marine superintendent, asking the captain of another CPR ship to take Galway to Liverpool as supernumerary crew.

Haight's story produced a sensation in the crowded courtroom. Lord Mersey was visibly perturbed by the implications of Haight's tale. Was it Haight's suggestion that the CPR was deliberately trying to get Galway out of the way of the court of inquiry? 'I regret to say, my lord,' replied Haight, 'that I can think of no other suggestion.'

Mersey took a grave view. 'That,' he said, 'is a very serious suggestion to make, Mr Haight.' Haight had no intention of being overawed. 'I fully realise it, my lord,' he replied. And where, Lord Mersey inquired, was Quartermaster Galway to be found? Haight knew the answer to that. Galway, he replied, was in the Neptune Inn, a colourfully named Quebec hostelry where the CPR had lodged the surviving crew members pending their repatriation to Britain. Lord Mersey turned his quizzical gaze upon Haight. 'I think,' said his lordship simply, 'it will be wise for you not to leave him too long at the inn.'

While Galway was being fetched, Haight called Kendall back to the stand. On the *Empress*'s last voyage up river to Quebec, had the ship sheered so violently in the narrows called the Traverse that the wheel had been put hard over to correct her, just before she hit something? Had they missed a schooner by about 10 feet? No, said Kendall, he couldn't remember her ever steering badly. As for the schooner, they had passed at least half a dozen in the Traverse, possibly more. The river at that point was so narrow that they always passed close to other vessels there. It was impossible to do otherwise.

Then how about that last voyage downstream, Haight asked. Had the *Empress* sheered so badly that she had alternately shown approaching vessels first her green light and then her red? Not through any fault of the ship, Kendall replied. Moreover, he had been on the bridge continuously all the way from Quebec, except when he went to his adjoining cabin for a cup of coffee. Nor had he received a report from anybody about trouble with the steering gear.

Kendall left the witness box. Quartermaster James Galway took his place. Galway was a heavy-featured, curly-haired man in his mid-twenties. Like many of the witnesses before the inquiry, he was notably self-possessed, at least when he began his evidence. He was to become noticeably less so in the minutes that followed.

Quartermaster Galway did not make a good impression. He entered the witness-box chewing gum. Lord Mersey inquired sardonically if he had not had time to finish his dinner. Galway obligingly parked his gum on the floor of the witness-box. From then on, Mersey clearly regarded him with a jaundiced judicial eye. The Press reported that his evidence was often unintelligible. Aspinall nearly lost his temper with him for his dull-witted habit of repeating back to his interlocutor every question that was asked him, and ended by accusing Galway of being a sea lawyer. This, in Mr Aspinall's estimation, was clearly quite different from being a land lawyer.

The Inquiry's attitude to Galway was little short of contemptuous, the Press observed. He incurred the lawyers' antagonism, and Lord Mersey's undisguised scorn. Galway, the reporters added, had made his lordship lose that urbanity which up to then had been such a marked feature of the Inquiry.

Asked why he had not told his alarming tale to CPR lawyers and officials who had questioned the survivors, Galway retreated into a series of rambling and inarticulate replies that seemed to boil down to a plea that he had not told anyone about the recalcitrant steering gear because he had not been asked. Nonetheless his testimony about the steering of the *Empress*, true or false, was intelligible enough. In the Traverse narrows, he maintained, the liner had behaved 'extraordinarily', swinging from side to side and refusing to answer her helm. Nor was that all. On the final passage down river the steering had actually jammed for some minutes, before Galway had wrenched it back into operation again. Had Galway experienced this kind of problem before? Indeed he had. On this last outbound voyage from the Mersey, she had again been difficult to manage. Then had Galway not reported this alarming state of affairs?

Certainly he had. On two occasions he had told the officer of the watch. He had also told Murphy, the quartermaster who relieved him on the last voyage down river to Father Point. And who was the officer of the watch on these occasions? Why, Mr Williams, the second officer, on each occasion. Perhaps Galway really had complained to Williams about the *Empress*'s steering. Nobody would ever know now, for Williams was dead.

Quartermaster Murphy, by contrast, was very much alive, and he denied Galway's story completely. The *Empress*, he maintained stoutly, had steered as well as any ship he had ever sailed in.

Pilot Bernier, who had sailed in the *Empress* on and off for the last seven years up and down the St Lawrence, also denied the truth of Galway's story. John Walsh, the CPR's marine superintendent, was very put out indeed. Not only had he emphatically not tried to smuggle Galway out of Canada, but he went on to allege that Galway was the only man in the disaster who had failed in his duty. Instead of making straight for his boat station when the alarm sounded, he had gone to his quarters to collect his lifebelt.

The appearance of Quartermaster Galway had severely strained the harmony of which Mr Newcombe had spoken so highly. Lord Mersey was visibly angry. Relations between learned counsel were at a low ebb. The next morning, Mr Haight rose to tender a suitable olive branch. In answer to certain definite questions from Lord Mersey, he had made answers that he would not like to stand upon the record unexplained. While he felt that the CPR should have taken more care to hold Galway as a witness, he did not for one moment wish to suggest that counsel for the company had had any part in a manoeuvre to spirit away a witness or suppress evidence. Nothing could be further from his thoughts than that the eminent gentlemen, ... Lord Mersey had also had time to sleep upon it. It might be, his Lordship replied condescendingly, that he himself had become a little heated. He went out of his way to praise Haight's handling of the case. He had been acting in the best interests of those he represented. Professional amity had been restored. Quartermaster Galway's evidence was debated again, but there were no further dark aspersions upon the conduct of his employers.

Jakob Saxe, third mate of the *Storstad*, earned 100 krone a month, or about 27 dollars. For a sum of rather under two dollars in salary, he spent nearly two days on the witness stand in Quebec, and during that time, he answered as best he might a total of 497 questions about his conduct, and that of his shipmates, during perhaps fifteen minutes in a small patch of fog. Trying to comprehend the questions aimed at him hour after hour by Aspinall and Lord Mersey, struggling to phrase his replies in a tongue that he spoke imperfectly, Saxe faced the unremitting attack. Once or twice, his English broke down under the effort. Lord Mersey questioned him in German. The court stenographers laid down their pens in despair.

Hour after hour, Aspinall probed Saxe's story, seeking to break him down on the two main issues. On which side had Saxe really seen the *Empress*? And why had the collier's wheel been put over in the fog? On the first point, Saxe could not be shaken. The liner, he insisted, had first shown her green light. But even as Saxe watched, she had swung steadily over until both red and green lights were showing. Then the green light had disappeared, and the red light alone was visible from the *Storstad*'s bridge. Saxe insisted that the big steamer was still on the collier's left-hand side, and that the two ships were set to pass red to red, left-hand to left-hand. And they were still showing red to red, he stoutly maintained, when fog blanketed the *Empress* from his sight. At that time, the liner was perhaps two or three miles away.

Haight, leading Saxe through his story, did his best to force the point home. The siren blasts that Saxe had heard from the *Empress*. Was Saxe sure which side they had come from? Saxe was very sure indeed. They had come from the *Storstad*'s left-hand side, not her right.

Aspinall, in cross-examination, was merciless with Saxe's convictions. Why was he so sure that the *Empress* was on his left, not his right? Whatever the truth, Saxe's reply at least had the ring of honest conviction. 'I *knew* she was there,' he replied earnestly. Aspinall was not impressed. It was difficult, was it not, to tell the whereabouts of a ship in a fog by her siren alone? Saxe agreed. Aspinall pressed his point home. In fog, you could never be sure, could you? 'But we had seen the ship only a few minutes before,' Saxe protested. Lord Mersey repeated Aspinall's question: You could never be certain of a ship's location by her siren blasts? 'You cannot always be sure,' the third mate admitted at last.

'That is all I want,' said Aspinall simply. 'You cannot always be sure.'

Aspinall swung his sights on to the second crucial issue. Why had Toftenes ordered the wheel over? Saxe didn't know; nobody had told him. Perhaps it was to offset any tendency by the current to carry the ship's bows to the left. No, it hadn't thrown the ship's bows off to the right at all. Yes, Saxe knew it was wrong and dangerous to alter course in a fog, but not in this case. Aspinall would not give up. After that initial order from Toftenes to put the wheel a little to the right, it had been put hard over to the right. Aspinall found that puzzling. 'Did that surprise you?' he asked. 'No,' Saxe replied simply, 'I did it myself.' Aspinall was incredulous. 'Without orders?'

'Yes, sir.'

Poor Saxe. He had stood off Aspinall's attack as long as he could; he answered Lord Mersey, in English and in German, as well as he knew how. Now he had the pair of them after him in full cry. Mersey and Aspinall went after Saxe like one lawyer. Had he really put the wheel over by himself? Yes. And without orders? Yes. Did he think that had been the right thing to do? Yes. Did he think that action had caused the collision? No.

Haight did his best to throw Saxe a lifebelt. Why was he so sure the first officer had been right to put the wheel over in the first place? Because that strong current could have carried the ship's head over leftwards, where Saxe was convinced that the *Empress* was bearing down on them in the fog. The *Storstad* would not answer, Saxe insisted, and he feared she was dropping off to the left, so, without asking the first officer he,

Jakob Saxe, had personally taken the wheel in his hands and put it over hard to the right. Mersey was not going to let Saxe's story pass without further investigation. Surely, all his past testimony had been to the effect that the *Storstad*'s course had *not* altered? Now he was saying, was he not, that it *did* alter to the left, and that was why Saxe had put the wheel over? Well, Saxe was saying, the course had not exactly altered, but he had been sure that it was about to. 'Just before the ship is coming,' he explained in his disintegrating English, 'I could see as if she started to move.'

There was nothing left to say. After two days of questioning, Aspinall had got what he wanted.

The rest of the *Storstad*'s watch stood shoulder to shoulder with Saxe and Toftenes about what they had seen as the big CPR liner came steaming down upon them. Ludwig Fremmerlid, the lookout, told almost word for word the same story as Saxe. He had seen the *Empress* over the *Storstad*'s left bow, showing her red side light. Moreover, she had gone on showing it for five minutes or more before the fog had spirited her away. True or not, it was one aspect of the story to which the *Storstad*'s men struck steadfastly, and no amount of questioning could shift them in the slightest.

Only once did the Norwegian crew's solidarity waver, and that was when Alfred Toftenes was called back to the witness-stand after Saxe's remarkable story of how he had put the wheel over. Aspinall wanted to know why the *Storstad*'s fair copy log – the official version, written up after the event from thorough notes made at the time – contained no reference to the wheel having been put hard over by Saxe. Toftenes was quite frank about it. He hadn't logged it, he said, because he hadn't even known that it had happened. Nobody had told him what Saxe had done.

Ludwig Fremmerlid, the lookout, had one curious and important contribution to make to the debate about exactly where the *Storstad* had struck the liner. It was a small metal plate, bearing the figures '328' and Fremmerlid had found it some hours after the collision, lying on the collier's fo'c's'le, some feet behind the crumpled stem. It had come from one of the *Empress*'s outside cabins on the upper deck, and it established more or less exactly where, and how deeply, the *Storstad*'s bow had penetrated the liner's side.

Haight called the men from the collier *Alden* to tell their story of their late-night encounter with the *Empress*. The second mate, the helmsman and the lookout all told much the same story of how the big liner had borne down on them, swinging so erratically that the side-light they could see kept changing from red to green. They differed only on how many times the *Empress* had swung. Three times, said one; the others said five times, or seven.

Whether that is what they meant to say is open to some question, because the inquiry was in dire trouble again with languages. One sailor's English broke down, so the court called on a Norwegian interpreter. He gave up after a few sentences. The man wasn't Norwegian at all, he complained; he was a Russian Finn who was trying to talk to the Norwegian in Swedish. The court went back to piecing together his story in English. There was no doubt, however, about what the *Alden's* Canadian pilot Lapierre was trying to say. The *Empress*, he claimed, had come twisting down upon the collier, so that Lapierre had to keep ordering the wheel further and further over to avoid her. She had finally cleared the collier with about 200 yards to spare. Certainly he had been frightened, he told Aspinall. Anybody would have been frightened with a big ship bearing down on him like that.

Between them, Kendall and Gaade disposed of a macabre report, which had apparently reached Mersey in a letter, that 300 passengers had died, trapped in the ladies' second class lounge, because they had been unable to force open the doors that led to the deck. To start with, the captain and the chief steward replied, the lounge would not have held more than 50 people, 'even if you had packed them in'. Moreover, Gaade said shortly, even if there had been anybody in the lounge, they would have had no difficulty reaching the deck; the door was never locked, and like every door in the ship, it opened outward on to the deck. No more was heard about the 300 passengers.

FOURTEEN MINUTES

Haight, meanwhile, was running into troubles of his own in his efforts to prove that the *Empress* had still been moving ahead fast at the time of the collision. To this end, he had called Ensign Pugmire to testify that the ship had had way on her when the *Storstad* struck her. Oh yes, Mr Pugmire agreed, the ship had certainly been moving through the water when he went on deck after the collision. But she hadn't been moving ahead; she had been moving astern. Yes, he was quite sure. He had looked over the left-hand side of the ship, and seen the water moving past from left to right. Haight exploded. He accused Pugmire of telling a story which was the precise opposite of that which he had related in an interview with a Detroit newspaper. Aspinall leapt to his feet in protest. He objected strongly to Haight asking questions of a witness and then attempting to supply his own answers. Lord Mersey upheld Aspinall's protest. Haight, he pointed out, had called the witness in the first place, and now he was annoyed because he hadn't got the answer he wanted. Haight hastily dropped his line of questioning. No more was heard from Ensign Pugmire, of whom it might in justice have been said that he was not the only man who had not been quite sure that night if he was coming or going.

Lord Mersey turned the court's attention to another issue. Why had a modern, well-equipped liner, with a thoroughly trained crew, gone to the bottom in calm water in less than fifteen minutes? The *Empress* was supposedly designed to float with at least any two compartments open to the sea, and there had been no evidence that more than two compartments had been flooded. His lordship confessed to having expressed a hasty conviction that the *Storstad*'s stem had destroyed a bulkhead, flooding two compartments, and had then torn its way along the ship's side, opening further compartments as it went. Now he was not so sure.

Percy Hillhouse, naval architect from the Fairfield yards at Govan, was in no doubt about the *Empress*'s reserves of buoyancy, and he was in the best position to know, for he had helped to design her. Hillhouse explained that the *Empress* would theoretically stay afloat even if both boiler-rooms,

208

175 feet in total length, were completely flooded. But that assumed that the water would come in evenly from some central point, so that the ship did not list. It also assumed that all the *Empress*'s portholes were closed, for with both boiler-rooms flooded, the *Empress* would sink 9 feet 3 inches deeper into the water – and the lowest row of portholes amidships was only 5 feet above the normal waterline anyway.

Moreover, even if the boiler-rooms were not flooded, it would take a list of only 9 degrees from the vertical to submerge that lowest row of portholes. A list of 18 degrees would put two rows of portholes under water. So long as the ship kept her inherent stability, it did not greatly matter how much she rolled, for her natural buoyancy would right her. But if any loose weight, be it water, coal or grain, settled to one side, it would hold her down, progressively destroying her stability. While Hillhouse was certain that the *Empress* could have survived with flooded boiler-rooms, any further water coming aboard through portholes or windows would pull her down until she capsized.

Nobody ever settled the question of what portholes were open on the *Empress*'s right-hand side, any more than they settled which bulkhead doors were left open. Theoretically, all the cabin portholes were closed at night. In practice, it was admitted, if a passenger objected vigorously enough the steward would simply leave the porthole open and report the fact to the night watchman. In any event, not all the portholes were in individual cabins. Each of the cross-alleyways giving access to the cabins had its own porthole in the ship's side. Some at least of these were quite definitely open. James Rankin actually saw water starting to lap through a passageway porthole as he scrambled out of his cabin, only seconds after the collision. Nobody could ever be sure about the portholes, but it seemed extremely likely, to put it no higher, that a large number of portholes were open, officially or otherwise, on that calm summer night.

Neatly and professionally, Mr Hillhouse unrolled his blueprints before the learned judges and spelled out the mathematics of disaster. The *Storstad*, he believed, had penetrated about 18 feet into the *Empress*'s side, her stem coming to rest momentarily at or very close to cabin 328, which was almost exactly amidships. Cabin 328 was just under 16 feet astern of Number Five bulkhead, the one that separated the two boiler-rooms. That being so, as Hillhouse pointed out, there was a very good chance that the collier's bows, shouldering their way into the liner's interior, had damaged the bulkhead as well. Since the *Storstad* had gone in at an angle of about 80 degrees, Hillhouse believed, the damage to the collier's bows extended a little further on the right-hand side than on the left. If he was right, the *Storstad* had forced her way in to the liner to a width of about 28 feet. He could not be quite sure about the damage to the collier, Mr Hillhouse added mildly, because when he had tried to inspect her in Quebec the *Storstad*'s watchman had refused to let him aboard, having apparently taken him for a reporter.

Hillhouse calculated that the *Storstad* had cut a hole in the *Empress*'s side of at least 350 square feet, in which case the ship would have been flooding initially at a rate of about 265 tons of water – 60,000 gallons – a second. That made no allowance for the flood increasing as the gash sank deeper and deeper into the water, and it made no allowance for those neglected portholes. Mr Hillhouse's arithmetic may well have been conservative. If the *Storstad*'s bows went in to their full draught of 25 feet, and if the hole they made was 28 feet wide, that would have left a gash of about 700 square feet, and the initial inrush of water would have been nearer 500 tons a second. Even at Hillhouse's figure, the two boiler-rooms would have flooded in about a minute and a half. It was in the face of this Niagara that men had struggled in the darkness with the watertight doors. Mr Hillhouse proved very knowledgeable about the layout of these doors but he displayed a curious ignorance about the practicalities of operating them. He had simply no idea how long one of the doors he had designed would take to close. 'I have never had to close a watertight door personally,' he admitted cheerfully.

Of the *Empress*'s 24 watertight doors, there were four that

Hillhouse believed could have been of critical importance because they led from the forward-boiler-room to the rest of the ship. Two were probably shut because they were bunker access-doors that would normally have been kept closed anyway. The other two were the doors that Hayes and Harrison had tried in vain to close against the list of the ship. There were almost certainly many other doors that were not closed, but they only became important in that once the water had filled and overflowed from the boiler-rooms, they had a bearing on how fast the water spread to other parts of the ship, and therefore on how fast or slowly the *Empress* sank. Once the water was out of the confines of the boiler-rooms, they could not in themselves have kept her afloat.

The learned judges listened respectfully to Mr Hillhouse's evidence. Now he had to deal with Mr Haight, who was not at all respectful. Mr Haight was still out to prove that there was something radically wrong with the *Empress*'s steering, and Mr Hillhouse, after all, was the man who had designed her. Haight's case was that the *Empress* had been designed with an unusually full stern, likely to set up eddies that would affect the efficiency of the rudder. In pursuing it, he elicited from Hillhouse the interesting fact that about two years after the liner was built, her rudder had been changed for a larger one. Hillhouse conceded reluctantly that the *Empress*'s stern was indeed a little fuller than that of some other ships, and that this could have affected her steering to some extent. But he maintained stoutly that during her trials, everybody had been very satisfied with the way the ship handled. It was true that in about 1908, the rudder had been damaged and the opportunity had been taken to enlarge it, apparently because the CPR wanted to improve further the ship's steering qualities. What Mr Hillhouse could not explain was why a similar modification had been made to the sister ship, the *Empress of Britain*, which had never been damaged at all.

As the Inquiry drew towards its close, Haight and Aspinall clashed, inevitably and indecisively, over the vexed question of the *Empress*'s heading. The wrecked ship, the court was told, was lying with her bows pointing almost exactly north-east. It was a gift to Haight, and he seized it with both hands. The *Empress*'s men had claimed she had been sailing east-north-east – yet here she was lying on a course over 20 degrees more northerly. The *Storstad* witnesses had always claimed that the *Empress* had turned left across their bows; was this not proof positive that she had indeed been sailing north-eastwards when the collision occurred? Not at all, said Aspinall, dismissing the point as of minimal importance. The sunken ship's heading proved nothing whatever; a listing, dying ship, her screws performing erratically if at all, her helm unattended in her last moments, could have been pointing in almost any direction as she went down.

CHAPTER 19

Closing Addresses

The Inquiry was nearly over. The last witness had left the stand, the last blueprint had been rolled up. There was nothing left now except the closing addresses.

Aspinall was generous where he could afford to be. All the passengers had praised the conduct of the officers and crew, he said. There was no suggestion – and Aspinall went out of his way to stress the point – that the officers and men of either ship had failed in their duty in trying to save life. To be sure, there had been confusion aboard the *Empress* but no panic. The engineers, like the wireless operators had stuck to their posts to the last. Aspinall was as vague as everybody else about how many boats were launched. He made it five, plus a few Englehardts. One boat, he believed, had reached the water full of people, but was apparently lost. Perhaps, Aspinall opined, it had been hit by the funnel as the ship fell over. Nobody produced any evidence to support that particular explanation but it was as likely as any other.

Aspinall turned to the heart of the case; who was to blame? He had no doubt about the answer to that. It was 'a very remarkable fact', he said, that precisely the story he himself had outlined in his initial statement had been borne out in evidence by the men of the *Storstad* themselves. His case had always been that the collier must have put her wheel over in the fog and lo, it had emerged that not only had she done so, but that one of her officers had put it hard over without orders. Not only had her men admitted that the wheel had been put over, but they had gone further, and admitted that they had actually heard the *Empress* signalling that she was going astern.

Aspinall turned aside in his argument to dispose fastidiously of Quartermaster Galway, a man who had not even told his strange story to his own employers' legal representative after the accident because they didn't ask him about it. Quartermaster Galway was best ignored. Then Aspinall hurried back to the fatal helm order.

We should probably never know what really happened on the bridge on the *Storstad* that night, said Aspinall. But he did know that Andersen, the man who should have been there, was not; that the wheel had been put over without orders; and that the ship, despite everything that had been said to the contrary, had *not* been stopped. The engines had been halted, true enough; but the ship had been steaming for hours at 10 knots, and she was still moving smartly when the wheel was put over. Irony was Aspinall's long suit, and he played it effectively. It was odd, was it not, that everybody aboard the *Storstad* was so certain that the ship had not altered course, because they had happened to notice the compass? How strange that they had all spent so much time looking at it, when they might have been expected to have been staring out into the fog, straining their eyes for a first glimpse of the big ship so close at hand?

Aspinall clearly thought he could afford to be magnanimous towards the men of the *Storstad*. The real culprit, he said, was Saxe, the man who had put the wheel over without orders, not because of that ambiguous current, but for a far simpler reason. The wheel had been put over because the men on the bridge quite genuinely believed that the liner was on their left-hand side.

Mr Aspinall sat down. He had had a good deal to say. The transcript of his closing remarks ran to thirty-four pages.

The next morning, Mr Haight rose like a giant refreshed to make his own closing remarks. Like Aspinall, Haight would admit of no division of guilt. The accident, he argued, was 'absolutely inexcusable'. The vessels had been on safe passing course, and the position of each had been known to the other. Moreover, it was the elementary duty of any vessel to hold its course in a fog. No ship could inadvertently change course eighty degrees without somebody knowing about it at the time, he insisted.

Mr Haight had been building up his case, question by question, for the last ten days. The accident had happened because the *Empress* had changed course in the fog. And she had changed course because there was something radically wrong with her steering gear. After all, he submitted, it had already broken down once before that night, when the liner was passing the *Alden*. Quartermaster Murphy himself had testified that sometimes the wheel would not 'catch', and although the court had treated the wretched Quartermaster Galway as a deliberate perjuror, Haight believed the man was genuinely trying to tell the truth. With the two ships still a couple of miles or more away, and set to pass safely green to green, as he claimed, why had Kendall suddenly put his engines from full ahead to full astern and, by doing so, risked wrecking them into the bargain? Mr Haight had no doubt at all why. It was because something had gone desperately wrong with his ship's steering gear.

Haight thought that Kendall's conduct that night had proved the point. His reactions had not been those of a cool, deliberate master mariner. His order to go full ahead had been worse than futile, for if Kendall had been right in saying that the *Storstad* was pointing directly at the liner's bridge, then putting his ship's engines ahead had merely moved the point of impact from the relatively invulnerable area below the bridge to the far more dangerous area of the boiler-room. Something, Haight argued, had led the normally efficient Kendall to lose his head in those fatal seconds in the fog, and that something, Haight argued, was the appalling knowledge that even as the collier's bows bore down upon him, there were men on the liner's bridge wrestling to free the jammed wheel. That was what had confused and distracted Kendall.

Mr Haight was singularly unimpressed by Kendall's

evidence. It contained extravagances. There was that story about the 'sheet of fire' as the ships collided, the 'terrible impact' that nobody else had even noticed, the story that the *Storstad* had stopped a mile away, the suggestion that the *Storstad* had rebounded like a rubber ball. Haight even scouted Kendall's story that he had personally thrown off the gripes of the lifeboats.

By contrast, Haight could find nothing odd at all in the testimony of the men who had been on the *Storstad*'s bridge. The order to put the wheel over, he insisted, had had absolutely no significance. It had never been denied that the *Storstad* had been moving ahead at the time of the impact, but as the engines had only been going ahead for 20 or 30 seconds, they had not had time to influence the collier's course.

Haight was unimpressed by the claim that the *Empress* had signalled that she was going astern before she ever entered the fog. She might have done so while she was actually in it, when that disastrous fault developed in the steering gear. But far from going astern when Kendall said she had, the liner, he claimed, had actually sounded several single blasts to indicate that she was holding her course in the fog.

Haight was not kind to Kendall. Must the unhappy captain be believed simply because he had faced death, lost his ship and had been connected with a disaster that had meant the loss of 1000 lives? Was it not more likely that for those very reasons, he would not dare face the world with a frank admission that he had been at fault? It would take heroic courage for any man to stand up and say that within 4 miles from land, he had so manoeuvred his ship that she had come across the bows of another vessel that had not changed her course. 'Is it not likely, my Lords, that the fearful experience through which Captain Kendall went has left its mark, and that his testimony bears its mark inevitably? I submit, my Lords, that the heading of the wreck of the *Empress* was the heading of the *Empress* at the time of collision, and because of that, the *Empress* alone is to blame.'

Mr Haight sat down. He had appeared late upon the scene, for he had been briefed only shortly before the Inquiry opened. For nearly two weeks, he had argued skilfully and forcefully through the long days of question and answer, and had then retired to his hotel room for more long hours of work upon the next day's case. He had fought with Mersey, he had fought with Aspinall, and at times he had fought with his own witnesses. Whatever skill and determination could do for the men of the *Storstad*, Charles Haight had provided. He had borne Lord Mersey's interruptions and animadversions with shrewdness and patience, and in the end, he had won Mersey's crotchety respect.

Mr Aspinall was permitted to reply to Haight. If the *Empress*'s steering gear really had failed, why should Kendal have come before the inquiry and sacrificed himself to save the pockets of the Canadian Pacific Railway? Why did he not say at once, it was not I that failed, it was the instrument entrusted to me by the Company? Since the *Empress*'s controversial rudder had been altered some six years earlier, the vessel had sailed thousands upon thousands of miles. Was it conceivable that for many voyages past, there had been a steering defect that had never been brought to the notice of the company? If there was really a radical defect, surely Kendall would have brought it to the notice of his employers, if only for the safety of his own life? He, after all, was the man who had to navigate the ship through narrow waters. Nor would Aspinall accept the doubts that Haight had cast upon the wisdom of Kendall's actions. Considering that the two ships were closing upon each other at nearly 30 miles an hour, what Kendall had done showed a high standard of care.

Mr Newcombe rose to make his closing address. As leader for the Crown, Newcombe had had little to say during the ten days. Now, he had in effect to sum up for the civil power to whom the learned and distinguished judges would shortly have to present their findings. Newcombe represented no interest other than the public good, and he could afford to seek the common ground that both Aspinall and Haight had refused to take. He would not accept that one side or the other must be lying.

The case, he conceded, was 'a very peculiar' one. One ship or the other must have made a mistake about the position of the other. Newcombe believed that the testimony of the men of the *Storstad* was honest. If it had not been, they would never have mentioned the putting over of the wheel at all, since it could only harm their case. 'They may have been mistaken about many things, but I submit that they were not intending to mislead,' said Newcombe. Moreover, he added, the same assumption could be made about the testimony by the men from the *Empress*.

Newcombe had an interesting argument to advance about the real course of events in the fog. He believed that the two ships had been a great deal closer to each other when they disappeared into the fog than the men on the bridge of either ship had believed. If those men had been right in their assumptions, the two ships would have passed a half a mile apart. And it was absolutely certain, Newcombe maintained, that the *Storstad* had not steered, or drifted, anything like that far off course in the brief time that her rudder had been over to the right. The fatal fog, 'the most unfortunate thing that ever happened', had not lasted longer than the time it took the two ships to cover the distance between them; yet, when it lifted, the *Empress* was gone. It followed, as Newcombe saw it, that the two ships must have been very close together indeed in the fog.

Newcombe thought he knew why the accident occurred. When the *Empress* swung her bows from 47 East to 73 East, and settled on her course down river, she had exposed her red light to the *Storstad*; and in that fatal moment, the collier's officers had decided that the ships were going to pass red to red. Probably their lookout was not very good anyway, and when the fog came down, they were convinced that the liner was on their left-hand side. No doubt they had convinced themselves that that was the direction from which the *Empress*'s signals were coming – because that was the side from which they expected to hear them. It was to give the liner a slightly wider berth that the *Storstad*'s men had put the wheel over, but even so, Newcombe doubted if Saxe had been guilty of any breach of duty. He and the helmsman had an order from the officer of the watch to put the helm over, and that was what they did, believing they were turning away from the liner.

Newcombe could hardly have been more lenient with the *Storstad*'s men. By contrast, there was no leniency at all in his views about Kendall's conduct. He clearly found it completely indefensible. Kendall had already encountered two fog patches on his passage down the river, said Newcombe, and had responded correctly by slackening speed. Yet on the third occasion, with the *Storstad* ahead of him and on a fine bearing off his bow, he had responded by reversing his engines and bringing the ship to a dead halt. Was that not an inconsequential and unexpected course for him to take, considering that the rules of the road required him to proceed at a moderate speed? It was a grave question, said Newcombe, warming to his theme, whether any rule would have justified the action of the *Empress* in stopping or reversing, an action that might well have been embarrassing to the *Storstad*.

There had been negligence on both sides, in Newcombe's view, for there had been an improper use of helm by the *Storstad*, and an improper action in reversing and stopping engines on the part of the *Empress*. But there was no possible doubt about who, in Newcombe's view, bore the greater share of the blame. If the liner had not taken 'this extraordinary course' almost in the track of the approaching *Storstad*, the accident would never have happened. Why, he asked again, did Kendall stop his ship and lie there, so close to the collier's track? Was that good seamanship? Was that the sort of conduct to be expected of a ship carrying so many passengers? With a ship close at hand on one side, and with 30 miles of open water on the other, why had Kendall invited an accident?

Newcombe was not very much more charitable about the reasons why the *Empress* had foundered so suddenly. The CPR's rules said that in the event of fog or snow in the St Lawrence, hands were to be stationed at the watertight doors, ready to close them instantly. Despite that, Kendall had not thought it necessary to have men standing by the doors. As a result, the ship had gone down in very much the condition she had been in before the fog, with doors unclosed. If there had been men at the doors, and if the emergency signal had been sounded before the collision, not after it, there would have been ample time to close the doors. Though whether that would have saved the ship or not, Newcombe added cautiously, it was impossible to say.

But in any event, it was most desirable that doors below the waterline should be under control from the bridge. Newcombe speculated that the ship might in any case have sunk because of the quantity of water that had poured in through open portholes. There should be a rule, he suggested, that on a signal from the bridge, the stewards should at once close all portholes and watertight doors, and not wait until after an accident. By then, he concluded sagely, it was inclined to be too late.

Mr George Gibsone had a rather touching plea to make on behalf of his national seamen and firemen – or more precisely, on behalf of his firemen. Their recommendation, he said, was that ships should be equipped with detachable life-rafts, because by the time the stokers got on deck from a sinking ship (he was tactful enough to say when, not if) they were inclined to find that all the seamen had rowed away and left them to swim for it. It was a sound enough point technically, even if it left the impression that true fraternalism between the firemen and seamen still had a certain way to go. Although he did not actually suggest that his criticisms applied to the *Empress,* Mr Gibsone also had some cogent observations to make about boat drills on big liners. All too often, he suggested, they were formalities designed to impress the passengers, with the crew dressed in their best uniforms and more concerned about not spoiling their clothes than with the efficiency with which they went through the motions of lowering a couple of boats. Gibsone wanted real emergency drills in working clothes, so that the crew got used to putting all the boats into the water at once.

CHAPTER 20

The Findings

The inquiry had sat for eleven days. It had listened to sixty-one witnesseses; and between them, the distinguished judges and learned counsel had asked something like 9,000 questions. Whether all the witnesses had understood all the questions is doubtful. Whether the court had understood all the answers is even more so. Now Lord Mersey and his colleagues retired to begin what Mersey resignedly described as the heavy task of preparing their report.

On Saturday, 11 July, on a morning of blinding heat, Lord Mersey and his colleagues filed back into the courtroom to deliver their findings. Kendall was not present. Andersen was; he leaned forward eagerly in his seat, his hand cupped over his ear to catch Mersey's softly spoken words in the crowded court. The findings covered sixty-five typed pages, and they took Lord Mersey over an hour to read.

The report was long, detailed and extremely well written. In measured phrases it reviewed the tangled and conflicting claims of the two captains. Those stories, Mersey found, were irreconcilable, and the issue of who was to blame depended largely on which story was accepted. Even so, many of the details of times, distances, bearings and so on varied so much that it was impossible to draw conclusions from them.

The main difference in those stories, the report went on, was in the issue of whether the two ships were set to pass left to left or right to right. After carefully weighing the evidence, the court had concluded that Toftenes was mistaken in thinking that the *Empress* had ever had any intention of passing on the *Storstad*'s left, or that her lights had ever indicated any such intention. But then it hardly mattered. Toftenes' mistake would have been of no consequence if both ships had thereafter kept to their courses. And so the question of which ship was to blame resolved itself to a very simple issue; which ship had altered course in the fog?

The *Empress*'s officers had strongly denied that the liner had ever changed course. Why should they have done so anyway? What object could such a change have served? The court could find no ground for saying that the liner's wheel had been moved wilfully. Haight had argued for a fault in the steering gear, but Quartermaster Galway was so unsatisfactory a witness that he could not be relied upon and in any event, his story completely contradicted the evidence of the *Alden*'s men. A jammed wheel would drive a ship off course; it would not make her oscillate wildly from side to side. The court's advisors concurred in the finding that no real complaint could be laid against the steering of the *Empress*.

Kendall did not wholly escape. While the court did not believe that he had put his engines astern because his ship was unmanageable, they did believe that his action in stopping the ship was evidence of his uneasy consciousness that the ship was probably too close to the *Storstad*. 'We think,' Lord Mersey went on in terms of mild reproof, 'that he would have been better advised if he had given the *Storstad* a wider berth, and had navigated his ship so as to pass the *Storstad* at a greater distance on his beam than he originally intended. We do not think, however, that his stopping, which was really done for greater caution, can be said to have been an unseamanlike act, nor do we consider his failure to give a wider berth as a contributory cause of the disaster.'

Lord Mersey turned to the conduct of the *Storstad*. It had been admitted that her wheel had been put hard over. If it had been kept there, and if the ship had way on her, then the effect must have been to have put the ship on a collision course with the *Empress*. True, it had been said that the order had been given to counteract the effect of the current, and that it had not changed the ship's course because she had had no way upon her. The court could not accept that view. They had seen the damage to the *Storstad*'s bow, and they were satisfied that she must have had considerable way on her when she hit the *Empress*. Granted, Kendall might have been mistaken in thinking that his ship was completely stopped in the fog. Perhaps the liner herself had to some extent added to the force of the blow.

Those were the last crumbs of comfort for Andersen and his crew. The scales of Lord Mersey's findings tipped inexorably against them. The fact remained, his Lordship went on, that the *Storstad* had put her wheel over, and changed her course. And in doing so, she had brought about the collision. Lord Mersey had no doubt about why. Toftenes and Saxe had believed, quite wrongly, that the liner was passing them red to red, and they wanted to make sure that the two ships had ample room to pass. Instead, they had brought the two ships into collision.

'We are further of opinion,' Mersey went on, 'that Mr Toftenes, the officer in charge of the *Storstad*, was negligent in omitting to call the captain when the fog was coming on.' At that time, the captain was asleep in his room; but he had left orders that in the event of fog coming on, he should be called to the deck, and there was a standing order on his ship to this effect. 'It is of the last importance,' Mersey wrote, 'that when a ship encounters a fog, her navigation should be in the control of a man of experience and of judgement. In this case, no step was taken to bring the captain to the deck until too late. The captain is the man who ought to have been there ... Mr Toftenes says he thought there was no danger and therefore that it did not matter. He was wrong; there was danger, and anyway it was his duty to obey the order which he had received to call the captain when the fog came on ... We regret to have to impute blame to anyone in connection with this lamentable disaster, and we should not do so if we felt that any reasonable alternative was left to us. We can, however, come to no other conclusion than that Mr Toftenes was wrong and negligent in keeping the navigation of the vessel in his own hands and in failing to call the captain when he saw the fog coming on.'

And that was that. The river itself was exculpated. In similar circumstances the court found, the disaster could as easily have happened in the Thames, the Clyde, or even the Mersey itself.

Blame for the disaster had been duly apportioned. Lord Mersey turned to the question that he regarded as being of much greater public interest and importance. Why had the *Empress* sunk so quickly, and what steps could be taken to avert so terrible a disaster in the future?

Lord Mersey turned his attention to the watertight doors. There had been evidence to show that the door between the after-boiler-room and the engine-room was closed, and some of the doors on the left-hand side of the ship had been closed, because they were on the upper side as the ship listed, and the closing mechanism had been close to the stewards' quarters. But efforts to close the right-hand door leading to the Third Class dining-room area had failed. Worse, the vital door in Number Six bulkhead, which closed off the end of the boiler-room from the Second Class accommodation, had stayed open. Practically all the doors between the main and upper decks were normally open, and it seemed almost certain that they had stayed open as the ship rolled over. It was equally certain that some portholes at the same level had been open as they dipped below the waterline.

Theoretically, Mersey said, the ship would have stayed afloat, even with both boiler-rooms flooded, if the doors in the bulkheads bordering the damaged area above main deck level had been closed. But with the side of the ship slashed open above maindeck level, and the bulkhead doors on that side of the ship still open, the water was free to find its way along the ship, carrying her relentlessly over until she capsized. What had happened in practice, the report surmised, was that the right-hand side coal bunkers had flooded first, and the water trapped in the bunkers, unable to spread rapidly enough across the ship, had pulled the ship over into a fifteen or twenty-degree list. Had all the portholes higher up

THE FINDINGS

in the side of the ship been closed, and had the watertight doors also been shut, the ship, would slowly have righted herself as the water spread evenly across the boiler-rooms and into the left-hand bunkers. But those portholes and doors had not been closed. And once they had dipped below the waterline, there could have been only one end. Mersey was kind where he could be. The *Empress*'s crew had responded readily to the emergency call, and had worked well. Nor could the *Storstad*'s crew be faulted in their conduct after the collision. They had done everything in their power to save life.

The court ended its report, as perhaps it was bound to do, with a trio of mild recommendations. Not only should all portholes and watertight doors be closed as a matter of routine in foggy weather, but whenever practical, all those doors and portholes should also be closed between sunset and sunrise. Wisely, perhaps, their lordships did not speculate on how such a rule might be enforced in a ship full of passengers. The *Empress* had sunk so fast, Lord Mersey went on, that most of the lifesaving gear had been useless. It might be worth considering placing rafts on the upper deck that would automatically float free as a ship sank. And finally, the Canadian Government might want to arrange the embarkation and disembarkation of river pilots in such a way that ships passing up and down river did not have to cross each other's paths to reach the pilot station. The report did not attempt to lay down how this desirable objective might be attained either.

There was nothing further to say. Lord Mersey handed over the findings, and caught the next boat home. Andersen's reaction to the Inquiry's findings was both prompt and bitter. He could not understand how what he regarded as Kendall's unsupported testimony had been preferred to that of three or four Norwegians. Toftenes, he maintained, had been completely in the right, and he would never be blamed by Norway for what had happened. Andersen made no secret of his animosity towards the CPR. 'Just because we do not wear gold braid and brass buttons,' he said sardonically, 'does not mean we are not good sailors.' Andersen was even ruder about Lord Mersey, whom he accused of deliberately seeking to find in favour of the CPR. The case, he said, would be pursued through the Admiralty Court in London, where his Lordship could not interfere.

Kendall was not in court to hear the findings, for he and his wife had already returned to England. His position was one of considerable difficulty. He had been completely exonerated by the inquiry, and the CPR had expressed every confidence in him. The fact remained that he was no longer 'the man who caught Crippen'. Instead, he was now unforgettably associated with one of the worst maritime disasters in history. Kendall, it was gently hinted in the Press, was unlikely to go to sea again. He would be given long leave to recuperate, and would then be found a shore job suitable to a man of his energy and talents.

The Norwegians held their own inquiry. In accordance with Norwegian maritime law, it was held in the Consulate at Montreal, and conducted by Mr Johannesen, the Secretary of the Norwegian Legation in Washington. Andersen and his officers gave evidence in private; the evidence was forwarded to the Norwegian Maritime Court for their consideration. As Andersen had predicted, the Maritime Court later absolved the officers of the *Storstad* from all responsibility for the accident.

Strange things happened to the *Storstad*'s legal status. With the consent of the Canadian Admiralty Court and the CPR, she was put up for auction, and fetched 175,000 dollars. Considering that she had cost rather less than twice that amount to build four years earlier, and was facing a 60,000 dollar repair bill, she may or may not have been cheap at the price. The money was paid into court as security for the ship against the CPR's claim. A Mr Wickborg, of Dramma in Norway bought her on behalf of 'foreign clients'. They were reported to be gentlemen with interests in marine insurance. The *Storstad*'s Canadian lawyers strongly denied that Klavenes had anything to do with it. The shipping Press was disinclined to believe them. The *Storstad*, it was assumed,

THE FINDINGS

was being ostensibly sold off and would later be quietly repurchased on behalf of her original owners in a complicated legal manoeuvre. The new owners graciously invited Captain Andersen to retain his post. He accepted. So did Toftenes and Saxe. The *Storstad*, escorted by a Government steamer, sailed off to dry dock in Quebec for repairs to her bows, and to make good the ravages caused by invading hordes of souvenir hunters. Not content with ripping pieces off the lifeboats, they had stolen the brass mouthpiece of the speaking tube from the bridge to the Andersens' cabin. They had even garnered the scraps of woodwork from the *Empress*'s cabins that had lodged in the *Storstad*'s crumpled bow plating.

Six days after Lord Mersey and his colleagues delivered their findings, the CPR lodged suit in the Canadian Admiralty Court against the *Storstad* for two million dollars, alleging among other things improper lookout, improperly failing to maintain course, navigating at improper speed and failing to have competent officers on duty. The subsequent legal proceedings were of great length and almost theological complexity. In 1915, a Canadian court found the *Storstad* to have been solely responsible for the accident. By then, the total claims arising from the disaster amounted to 300,069,483 dollars and 94 cents.

In 1918, the Canadian Supreme Court ruled that claims relating to loss of life had priority over claims relating to the value of the ship herself in the distribution of the modest 175,000 dollars that the *Storstad* had fetched at auction. The CPR appealed to the Privy Council in London. By now, the *Storstad* and her owners had completely vanished from the case, and the legal point at issue had been honed so needle-fine that while a thousand lawyers might dance upon it with ease, the layman might have been forgiven for failing to detect it at all. No doubt there were excellent reasons within the esoteric world of marine insurance for pursuing a case that had lasted for over five years and that must have swallowed in legal costs many times the ostensible sum at issue.

On a grey December day in 1919, the highest legal tribunal

FOURTEEN MINUTES

in all His Majesty's wide dominions allowed the CPR's claim to be admitted to a share of the proceeds of the sale of the *Storstad*. His Majesty would be humbly so advised. There was no further court of appeal. The case was settled.

CHAPTER 21

The End of the Story

The *Storstad*, her bows rebuilt, went back to her workaday existence, much as if that fatal encounter in the St Lawrence had never happened.

By now, however, half the world was at war, and there were deadlier perils afloat than river fog. In the spring of 1917 the *Storstad*, once again flying the Klavenes house flag, was crossing the Atlantic with a cargo of war relief stores for Belgium. Thomas Andersen was still her master, though Alfred Toftenes had moved on; his place had been taken by a new first mate named Hansen. The German Navy's campaign of unrestricted submarine warfare had started, and the neutral flag of Norway was little protection. On 8 March 1917, the *Storstad* was torpedoed off the south-west coast of Ireland. This time, the great Isherwood frames could not save her. The *Storstad* joined the *Empress* in the great company of lost ships. Thomas Andersen and his thirty-eight men took to the boats. Andersen steered his crew to safety.

Kendall went to Antwerp, a major port of call for the CPR's migrant traffic, as marine superintendent. He was still a sick man, and the intention, presumably, was to let him recuperate in a quiet berth ashore. By August, Antwerp was a city at war, and the German Army, eager for the rich prize, was footslogging across Belgium towards the great seaport. Two CPR liners were in Antwerp. The *Montrose*, Kendall's old command of Crippen fame, was seaworthy but her bunkers were empty. Her near-sister, the *Montreal*, had coal in plenty, but her engines were out of action. Kendall hastily transferred coal from the *Montreal* to her consort, and then, with the German Army almost at the dock gates, he filled both ships with Belgian refugees and sailed off down the Scheldt, the *Montreal* towing astern of the *Montrose*. Both ships reached England safely. There, Kendall's old command came to an inglorious end. The ship broke her moorings in a gale, drifted crewless up Channel, and was swallowed by the devouring Goodwin Sands. For 50 years, her rusting masts served as a grim seamark to passing mariners.

Kendall served throughout World War I in the Royal Navy, was torpedoed, survived, and went back to the CPR after the Armistice. The prediction that he would not again serve the company at sea proved correct. Kendall served for some twenty years as the company's marine superintendent in London, and retired shortly before the outbreak of World War II. He lived on, as he had done for many years past, in Burnt Ash Hill, in the pleasant, old-fashioned South London suburb of Lee, almost within sight and sound of the great ships that moved up and down river. A widower for a quarter of a century, he remained a familiar figure in the neighbourhood, a genial old gentleman with a sailor's gift for a good yarn. In November 1965, Henry Kendall died in a London nursing home. He was ninety-one years old, and a great-grandfather.

His death was briefly reported as that of 'the man who caught Crippen'. The British news agency story was published in a number of Canadian metropolitan newspapers. They did not mention the *Empress of Ireland*; perhaps they had never heard of her. Kendall had survived his ship by over half a century, and it was all a very long time ago.

Lord Mersey continued in his role as the world's leading investigator of nautical disasters. In June 1915 he conducted the inquiry into the torpedoing of the Cunard liner *Lusitania*, with the loss of 1,198 of her passengers and crew. He was created a Viscount for his services, and died in 1929 in his ninetieth year.

Butler Aspinall, who had already appeared before Mersey in both the *Titanic* and *Empress* inquiries, did so yet again in the *Lusitania* inquiry, this time as counsel for the Cunard Line. He became a Commissioner of Wrecks, conducted a couple of major inquiries himself, and died in 1935.

Charles S. Haight died in February 1938, at the age of sixty-seven. He was by then one of the world's top authorities upon the international aspects of maritime law, and had been honoured by half a dozen nations for his work in the field.

The law firm that bore his name lived on. On a calm night in July 1956, the Swedish liner *Stockholm* and the Italian liner *Andrea Doria* were approaching each other on roughly parallel courses some 19 miles from the Nantucket Light, which guards the crowded sea lanes on the approaches to New York. Shortly after 11 p.m., in patchy fog, the Scandinavian struck the Italian on her right-hand side. The *Andrea Doria* sank the following day. Fifty lives were lost.

The legal proceedings, which lasted for some five months before the case was settled out of court, turned largely upon the issue of whether the two vessels were set to pass each other right-hand to right-hand or left-hand to left-hand. Each maintained trenchantly that the other had improperly altered course. The fact that both had been using radar served merely to obfuscate the issue. The Swedes were represented by a distinguished New York admiralty lawyer named Charles S. Haight. He was the son of the man who had represented the *Storstad*.

Percy Hillhouse became a practical authority on maritime disasters in odd circumstances. In January 1917 he sailed from the Fairfield yard aboard the newly-completed steam submarine K13. She sank upon her trials in one of the most celebrated and dramatic of all submarine disasters. Hillhouse was one of those rescued from the sunken vessel. He went on to become Professor of Naval Architecture at Glasgow University.

The *Empress of Ireland* sank from history so completely that after a while, even her precise position became uncertain. Only the tiniest symbolic striation survived upon the chart to tell the passing mariner that there was anything down there at all, let alone what it was. Not until the advent of the skin diver was the *Empress*'s position re-established exactly, and the wreck surveyed. Some relics were recovered in the early 1960s; her wheel, bell and compass are in a Quebec maritime museum. Other items are in private hands. In 1968, a Canadian salvage expert named Erbs succeeded in salvaging one of the massive, 20-foot diameter phosphor bronze propellors, the largest single item yet to be recovered.

From time to time, there has been talk of salvaging the ship. More than one plan has been proposed, but none has ever been translated into action.

The *Empress* lies where she sank, some four miles from shore in nearly 150 feet of water, about seven miles north-east of Father Point. She remains the last resting place of the 800-odd men, women and children who went down with her. Near Father Point, a further 88 victims lie buried, their bodies either unidentified or simply unclaimed, in a little roadside cemetery. A simple stone cenotaph marks the spot where their last voyage came to so untimely an end.

The St Lawrence itself is still a great highway of shipping, for the Seaway carries ocean-going vessels into the inland ports of the Great Lakes, in the very heart of the North American continent. But apart from the odd cruise liner, the great passenger vessels no longer ply the broad river. Instead, the big jets murmur overhead on their way to Montreal and Toronto.

In a sense, the stone obelisk at Father Point marks the end of the story of the *Empress of Ireland*. For days after the disaster, a river of printing ink as broad and dark as the St Lawrence itself swirled and eddied about the liner and her tragic complement. For the next few weeks it flowed on intermittently as the story of the inquiry unfolded. But the span of human grief is mercifully short; by the end of that sunlit summer, the story would no doubt have died of its own accord, trickling further and further back into the inside news pages. In the event, the story was pushed into oblivion by other events. A month after the disaster, the sub-editors of the world were poring afresh over their atlases, trying to locate an obscure Balkan market town in Southern Bosnia. It was called Sarajevo.

Conclusion

Disasters, they say, always come in threes; perhaps they do. It is a fact that the three worst ocean-going liner tragedies in history occurred within three years of each other in the second decade of the twentieth century. Each befell a large, modern vessel of British registry flying the colours of a major shipping company; each occurred during a Spring crossing of the North Atlantic; and each claimed over one thousand lives.

The first and last of these three disasters befell the White Star Line's *Titanic* and the Cunard Line's *Lusitania*. Their sad stories have been told many times, and in great detail, in some instances to the verge of obsession. The loss of the *Empress of Ireland*, by contrast, is an almost completely forgotten story, so much so that to the best of my knowledge, this book is the first new work on the subject to have appeared since 1914. And yet the *Empress of Ireland* not only drowned more passengers than either of her famous contemporaries; she actually took the lives of more passengers than any other ocean-going liner in peacetime history. We may reasonably ask ourselves why for two-thirds of a century the story has lain almost as completely submerged as the ship herself.

There are possibly two main reasons. The first concerned the ship herself, and her passengers; the second related to the unique historical context of the accident.

As Atlantic liners went in 1914, the *Empress* was neither an outstandingly large nor an outstandingly fashionable vessel. Nor, for that matter, was the St Lawrence route between Liverpool and Quebec or Montreal a particularly fashionable as distinct from comfortable or convenient way to cross the Atlantic. The routes from Southampton and Cherbourg to New York were the glittering sea paths trodden by the rich, the beautiful and the famous. Compared with the Leviathans that berthed in the Hudson River, the ships that plied the St Lawrence were workaday vessels, and their passengers, rich or poor, were for the most part workaday people. Of those who died in the *Empress*, a very high proportion were from those ranks of society whose members, however bitterly they might be mourned by their loved ones, were unlikely to distract the world for very long by their passing. To be sure, the world was shocked, and rightly so, by the sheer scale of the calamity.

But human nature being what it is, the world was unlikely to pay the same attention to the deaths of a shipload of Eastern European migrant workers that it had paid two years before to the snuffing out of a substantial part of the New York social register. Even where the blow fell upon a more affluent section of the travelling community, as it did in the case of middle-class Canada, the impact was largely restricted to a relatively small section of a sparsely-populated country. The sinking, however heartbreaking its impact upon hundreds and perhaps thousands of individual homes across the world, lacked either the immediate human drama of the *Titanic* or the immense political repercussions of the loss of the *Lusitania*.

In any case, barely two months after the sinking, a world war of hitherto unparalleled destructiveness had broken out. By the time it was over, the violent death of a thousand people in less than a quarter of an hour was an event of no great moment, particularly as the long catalogue of horrors during those four years included the torpedoing of the *Lusitania*, which went to the bottom in about twenty minutes with the loss of 1200 lives, of whom 785 were passengers. After all that it was not easy, perhaps, to remember the *Empress of Ireland*.

CONCLUSION

Even so, there is something faintly indecent about the speed with which the story vanished from the pages of the English language press, not merely before the outbreak of World War I itself, but almost before the court of inquiry had finished its deliberations. By July 1914, nobody had a mind for anything very much except the portents of the coming Armageddon.

I have sought in this book simply to tell a long-forgotten story, without intruding personal opinions or theories. Nonetheless, at least two aspects of the story are so strange that they deserve a second glance.

The essential unanswered question of the sinking of the *Empress of Ireland* is this: When every allowance has been made for that fatal patch of river fog, and for an extraordinarily high element of bad luck, assuming that the men on the bridge of the *Storstad* were indeed in error, how did a team of competent and experienced seamen – and nobody has ever seriously suggested that they were other than that – come to believe that the liner was approaching on their left-hand side?

However wrong they may have been, the Norwegians never concealed that belief. Moreover, their actions supported their arguments. If they had not genuinely believed it then why, short of sheer homicidal recklessness, should they have turned their wheel to the right? So far as I know, only one man has ever attempted to offer a rational explanation of the inexplicable. He was a British nautical writer named Bennet Copplestone, and in 1926, writing in *Blackwood's Magazine*, he offered his own theory.

It was common ground that when the two ships first sighted each other, the *Empress* was crossing the *Storstad*'s bows, several miles off and at a shallow angle. Then, while the two ships were still some miles away, the *Empress* swung on to the course that should have taken her past the *Storstad* on a more or less parallel track. Theoretically, the *Empress* should never at any time have shown her red light to the *Storstad*. But as Copplestone pointed out, long narrow liners like the *Empress* were never particularly easy to steer. Suppose that while the *Empress* was swinging on to her parallel course, the quartermaster had let her swing a little too far to the right? Supposing that for a brief while – moments, perhaps – the *Empress was* showing her left-hand side to the *Storstad* at a fine angle before the quartermaster corrected her swing and brought the ship on to a parallel course? Supposing that for a few brief, fatal seconds Toftenes and his shipmates had seen that red light twinkling in the darkness and thereby convinced themselves that the liner was going to cross them left-hand to left-hand? It is a thin enough theory, to be sure. But it is about the only one, and it may just possibly have been true.

A further possibility exists which was not voiced at the court of inquiry, and which so far as I know has never been advanced before, but which nevertheless occurred at once to a professional master mariner of wide experience who read this book. Passenger liners, he pointed out, can represent a real problem at night to an approaching vessel, simply because their decks and portholes are so brilliantly lit that their relatively feeble red and green sidelights can be very hard to pick out against the general glare. At a very fine angle on the bow, with her range-lights almost in line anyway, and with that insidious mist thickening about her, the *Empress* might well have presented precisely this problem. The Norwegians might well have lost sight of her sidelights altogether, while still believing in complete good faith that they knew which side she was going to pass. Again, it may be an improbable theory. But there is no explanation of the events of that night that will wholly pass a simple test of probability.

One other major discrepancy remains completely unresolved. It relates to the position of the two ships while the *Empress* was sinking, and in the minutes thereafter. Andersen maintained stoutly, angrily, that he took his ship in so close to the sinking liner that some survivors had no difficulty swimming alongside the collier. From his account of the matter he was little more than yards away from the spot, so close that he was afraid that if he went any nearer, he would have added a fresh peril by possibly sucking the wretched

CONCLUSION

survivors into the fatal arc of his propeller. Reinertz, the *Storstad*'s Second Officer, claimed that the collier was not more than two lengths, about 300 yards, away from the sinking *Empress*, and it took him only a couple of minutes or so to row to the survivors in the water. Yet almost every survivor who referred to the *Storstad* at all spoke of her being a very considerable distance away. A mile, or a mile and a half, most of them said. Two miles, said others.

Now anybody could have been wrong in those circumstances. It was dark; Andersen did not know exactly where the liner had been; his estimate of being a length or two away could easily have been wrong. There was a current running, and his ship could well have drifted a little. The survivors could equally well have been wrong in their estimation of distance. Men struggling for their lives in icy water, their eyes an inch or two above the surface, are not likely to be the best judges of distance on a dark and foggy night. But when every possible allowance has been made for honest error, there remains, literally as well as metaphorically, a gap that simply cannot be explained away by saying that one side or the other had slightly misjudged the distance. In a sense, the fatal fog that enshrouded the *Empress* and the *Storstad* hangs over them to this day.

One of the minor complexities of the story of the *Empress of Ireland* is that a large number of different casualty figures circulated at the time and many of them are still to be found in works of reference, in fact there are at least seven different tallies of the dead. The figure of 1,012 that I have used is the one that Lord Mersey's Commission finally settled upon. Whether it was right or not is quite impossible to say. The eastbound passenger was still free to cross the Atlantic with remarkably few documents. The CPR, struggling to produce an accurate list, had an extremely difficult task in trying to establish who had lived and who had died. Lord Mersey's total represented no more than their best-considered effort to get at the truth. It may or may not be entirely accurate.

This book is based almost entirely upon contemporary published sources, and these fall into two kinds. The story of

FOURTEEN MINUTES

what happened before Lord Mersey's Commission of Inquiry is drawn almost entirely from the transcript of the evidence and findings, published by the Canadian Government in 1915. This work is indispensable to any study of the disaster, because in addition to the account of the proceedings themselves, it contains a mass of detailed information about the liner, and also an analysis of the casualty figures. It contains over 600 pages, and runs to upwards of 250,000 words. Much of the evidence was contentious; some of it was incomprehensible. The court spent hours in wrangles over technicalities. I have sought only to present a reasonably balanced account of the main evidence and arguments without bogging the reader down in a morass of technical detail. Nonetheless, much of the evidence was quite genuinely dramatic in character. The account of what happened in the *Empress*'s engine and boiler-rooms, for instance, is drawn straight from the survivors' evidence.

The rest of the story with minor exceptions, is drawn from contemporary newspaper reports, mostly British and Canadian. There are hundreds of these, scattered through newspapers and magazines published all over the world. The principal Canadian sources that I have used are the *Montreal Daily Telegraph*, the *Montreal Daily Mail*, the *Montreal Daily Star*, the *Montreal Gazette*, *The Toronto Daily Mail*, the *Toronto Daily News*, the *Toronto Daily Star*, the *Toronto Globe*, the *Toronto World*, the *Quebec Daily Telegraph*, and the *Halifax Morning Chronicle*. Closer to home, I am indebted to the columns of *The Times*, the *Daily Telegraph*, the *Morning Post*, the *Daily Express*, the *Daily Mail*, the *Daily News*, the *Morning Chronicle*, the *Daily Sketch*, the *Daily Graphic*, *Lloyds List*, the *Scotsman*, the *Glasgow Herald*, and the *Liverpool Daily Post*. Among the illustrated magazines of the time, the *Illustrated London News* contained much interesting and valuable material. The story of the Irvings is drawn largely from *the Stage*.

I have consulted very few books because there are very few to consult, and what few there are do not as a rule deal with the disaster at any great length. A most interesting exception is Carl Barslaag's admirable book *SOS to the rescue*, published

CONCLUSION

over 40 years ago, which not only contains an excellent account of the part that wireless played in the drama, but is to be recommended to anyone interested in the early history of radio at sea.

Since I believe the average reader shares my distaste for footnotes and is unlikely to be interested in detailed references, I have not provided any. Let me say simply that to the best of my knowledge I have not made or implied any statement of fact in this book that cannot be supported from one or more contemporary published accounts. Whether those accounts are wholly accurate is obviously more than anyone can say. But where it has seemed to me that there is any reasonable doubt about the matter, I have said so.

I make no apology for having used the terms left and right instead of the traditional port and starboard throughout this book. Apart from the fact that many of us find it difficult enough to tell left from right, let alone port from starboard, there is a peculiar reason for eschewing the time-honoured nautical terms. Until the 1930s, both the British and Norwegian merchant navies followed the archaic and confusing practice of giving helm orders, not rudder orders. These were precisely the opposite of modern orders, and the effect was that if the officer of the watch wished to turn his vessel to port he would order starboard helm, or vice-versa.

It was an illogical but time-honoured practice that seems to have been regarded as quite natural at the time, and there is no reason to suppose that it had any bearing on the events that led to the sinking of the *Empress*. But since the story turns to a degree upon the steering orders given aboard the two ships it seemed to me unreasonable to expect the lay reader to remember that in this context, port means starboard and starboard means port. At one point it even had the Court of Inquiry confused. Having deliberately resorted to left and right for the sake of clarity in describing steering orders, it also seemed illogical to revert to port and starboard for any other purposes.

In conclusion, it remains only to thank those many people

without whom this book would not have been written. They include the staffs of the British Library, and in particular of the Newspaper Library, Colindale, the London Library, the National Maritime Museum, the Strathclyde Regional Archives, Glasgow, and the Norwegian State Archives, Oslo. I am also particularly grateful to Mr Neils Jannasch, Curator of Marine History at the Nova Scotia Museum, Halifax, Canada, and to Mr Malcolm Mackay of that city, both of whom went to great trouble to assist with my inquiries.

I owe a particular debt of gratitude to Mr George Musk, the United Kingdom archivist of Canadian Pacific, who lent his unstinted and enthusiastic support, and produced some most interesting and valuable material. I owe another to my colleague Norman Lornie in New York, who enthusiastically researched the life story of Charles Haight on my behalf. I gratefully acknowledge the timely and generous advice of Mr Russell Braddon, without which this book might never have been launched at all. I am similarly indebted to Captain Andrew Codrington for reading and amending the chapter on the Rule of the Road, and for some very interesting comments on possible explanations of the tragedy that I have touched on in this conclusion. Any technical solecisms in this book, I hasten to add, are entirely my responsibility.

And finally and most essentially to Mrs Barbara Watson, Mrs Margaret Lumley and Mrs Veronica Lanza who between them not only typed this book from end to end, but also translated it from the original hieroglyphics, to them, above all, it owes its existence.

Graffham,
Sussex
February 1978

APR 0 4 1979
MAY 2 8 1979

APPROXIMATE COURSES:
EMPRESS ----------
STORSTAD -·-·-·-·-

20 FATHOM LINE

COCK POINT
FATHER POINT
RIMOUSKI WHARF
RIMOUSKI

SCALE: 1 INCH = 6.15 MILES

Collision took place here → **RIMOUSKI**

QUEBEC CITY

MONTREAL

ST. JOHN

HAL

UNITED STATES OF AMERICA